Copyright © 2019 by James R. Herron

All rights reserved, including the right to reproduce this book or any portion thereof in any form.

First Edition

JIM HERRON

Dedicated to these Grand Champions (in birth order):

Chibi Herron   24 May 1985 – 22 February 2002

Butch Herron 2 November 1987 – 30 August 2001

Chiro Herron   31 October 1993 – 7 May 2006

Peko Herron   31 October 1993 – 21 October 2008

Koro Herron   5 May 2004 – 17 April 2016

All are *survived by their nonfurry parents, Yoriko and Jim Herron, and their nonfurry siblings, Barb, Steve, and Brenda, of Orlando, Florida.*

Many a truism is summed up in Japanese proverbs. For example:
Neko wa sangatsu wo hitotose to suru [猫は三月を一年とする].
Literal English translation: "Three months is one year to a cat."
Figurative meaning: "Life is short for animals."

Foreword

In "The Dogs' Best Friend: A Cats Eye Vew," author Jim Herron merges his unique voice with magic realism on a tour through the years his family shared with a parade of pets.

You will meet Tommy, the feral cat who wouldn't deign to live in a house, but nonetheless loved the family. Their ministrations to him set the stage for many happy years as a pet-invested family.

Cleverly allowing the furry family members to "speak for themselves" gives us entry to the mind and musings of Chibi, the smart and sassy cat narrator who understands how superior her nature is. Although she recognizes the shortcomings of her canine housemates, she is quite tolerant of them and loves them in her own fierce fashion. Chibi and her four canine siblings are your companions over the next decades as the family moves between the United States and Japan.

Mom is shown to be the loving center of this family story. Grounded in Japanese traditions honoring all life, she takes every opportunity to enrich the relationships between her "furry" and "non-furry" children. Mom truly embodies the concept of family love.

The author has included references to many scientific studies aimed toward a better understanding of the unique symbiotic relationships we form with our pets. Additional background on Mom's early years in Japan, including some lovely beliefs and one special song, brings a heartwarming slant to the story.

Anyone who has shared even one day with a loving pet will find much to savor in this heartwarming tale, including the promise

JIM HERRON
of meeting again at the Rainbow Bridge!

Anne Harshman
Dedicated Reader

CONTENTS

Preface	1
Prologue	9
Chapter One—Me	32
Chapter Two—Mom and Dad	73
Chapter Three—Butch	110
Chapter Four—Chiro	146
CHAPTER FIVE—PEKO	184
Chapter Six—Koro	213
Epilogue	253
ENDNOTES	287
About the author	292

PREFACE

"I wish I could write as mysterious as a cat."
-Edgar Allan Poe

I was not a housecat in the ordinary sense, but a housecat nevertheless. Allow me to make something *purr*-fectly clear—there is no such thing as *ordinary* in the feline vernacular! Extraordinary is fairly common, but I was far beyond that. I was *the cat's meow* of all cats' meows, not quite su-*purr*-natural, but undeniably su-*purr* extraordinary. My giant ego derived from an ancestral lineage that made me a phenomenon, not a narcissist (much more on this distinction to come).

In view of my ethnicity, one might ask why a cat would serve as the storyteller for a series of anecdotes about dogs and humans. First and foremost, the compelling nature of these cumulative stories demands they be told. Granted, libraries contain a myriad of books centering on human and pet relationships, but nearly all have had a built-in human slant. Other books concentrated on bonding between humans and dogs, or on bonds formed between humans and cats, but these writings give equal attention to both. And that's not all—dog and cat interrelationships are also addressed.

Secondly—*no pussy footing around*—it was only fitting that this narration be done by the lone feline character involved. Other than yours truly, four canines and a single human being were the only ones knowledgeable enough to tell it. The human was the dogs' and my nonfurry mother, and since she is the center of attention, she's far too modest to write about herself. The dogs were too dumb to do it. Let's face facts—when compared to humans, a dog's mental capacity is equal to that of a 2 or 3-year-old toddler, while my intellect exceeds some adults.

That left me, who unequivocally had the smarts and the wherewithal to necessarily assemble all the highlights into dual literary genres. Although I was unable to vocally communicate with humans, I became confident that I could aptly bring home my point in written form.

Most of my life was spent as the only cat in a multi-pet household overpopulated by dogs. The more I observed canine behavior, the more I was able to confirm their feeblemindedness. Regardless of the fact that a brain is one of the biological commonalities shared by us, it did not take long for me to *paws*-itively determine that I had a distinct cerebral edge over them. No one —especially my canine housemates—can convincingly argue that I was not an intellectual among nincompoops. I intend to make the case that *nin-com-poop*—especially the last syllable— fits *Canis Familiaris* (aka: the dog) better than any other word in the human vocabulary.

Although, on average, a dog's brain is bigger than that of a cat, a cat's brain is larger as a *purr*-centage of overall body size. Small mammals have small brains, so a larger brain does not mean a more intelligent animal. It was not difficult for me to delve into the psyche of my slow-witted canine housemates. That aside for the time being, I must say I never suffered from boredom while constantly observing my acquaintances in the human and dog worlds, or I should say "their world" (singular) because, as you are about to find out, the boundaries were invisible.

***

When comparing the human race to the animal kingdom, one obvious conclusion becomes readily apparent—human beings are noticeably lacking in physical ability. Take me for example:

I could easily leap from the floor onto the kitchen countertop in a single bound—a distance equal to 5 times my standing height on all fours, and twice my stretched-out length standing up on both hind legs. Even though a countertop might only be one-half of an adult human's standing height, when's the last time you saw a human—not a su-*purr*-natural one like Spiderman, but a normal person—gracefully jump up onto the top of a counter in a single leap?

My point—the physicality of cats, dogs, and other animals is far superior to that of homo sapiens. Now, factor in the distinct advantage that humans have in mental ability, and try to imagine an intellectual human with the physical agility of a cat and the prescience of a dog (minus the death-dealing doggie breath), and you'd conclude an ordinary human could become a su-*purr* human comparable to a Spiderman *mew*-tation.

Even though I could jump very high and perform other astonishing feats, I was inclined to forget about my feline attributes, and gradually came to think of myself as just another being, albeit more human then feline. I experienced many of the same emotions as humans, and possessed the brainpower to match. I don't look down on my own cat race—I merely felt closer to humans than cats. I was never comfortable in the presence of other cats and never had a cat friend. Co-existence is the best way to describe my association with my canine housemates. I was fully at ease only around humans—certain humans, that is, whose attitudes molded my mindset.

Although my evolution from felinity to humanity was not biological, it surely was psychological as I no longer confined my interests to hairballs, rodents, and other cat things. I became engrossed in keeping a journal in my head. I believe my transformation qualifies me to comment about personal observations of the natures of the canine and human races, and provide examples of unique interaction between the two.

My reminiscence of firsthand events and conversations I overheard between my adoptive, nonfurry parents and their biological children, along with the many things I heard others say about them and their extended, furry family members, fascinated me to the extent that I felt obligated to put as much of it that I could into story form. I gave it my best effort, but, admittedly, fell short of being able to plumb the full depth of the human thought process. I trust my shortcoming did not preclude me from getting my message across in a focused and coherent manner.

***

Like cats and dogs is a phrase someone coined to describe friction among human beings. It's a catchy saying that's been around a long time. Many people think dogs and cats are incapable of living together peacefully. Granted, some cats do not make good housemates for dogs and vice versa. We are entirely different animals with distinctive *purr*-sonalities, so we cannot ever blend fully. However, under the right conditions, many cats and dogs can live together harmoniously. Every dog I met became my housemate, and I can genuinely say that, despite our minor differences, I never met a dog I didn't like.

Three purebred Akita dogs and one Spitz-mix mutt are the main canine characters you will read about. On second thought, in this age of political correctness, *purr*-haps I should use "mixed-breed" instead of "mutt." And, I have to wonder if some humans may be offended by "purebred." Sorry! I should not have gone off on that tangent, as upon short deliberation, it became clear that those passing thoughts were unworthy of further attention, so no changes were made.

Several outsider creatures that made a lasting impression on my nonfurry mother and her canine kids are mentioned in detail: a feral Tabby tomcat with a near miss at domesticity; a male Labrador Retriever with a soft spot for the opposite sex;

a female Chihuahua with a bite bigger than her bark; wild reptiles including a poisonous snake and an alligator, and a wide assortment of wild birds, including crows, vultures, hawks; and an itsy-bitsy sparrow. My nonfurry mother's later interactions with her four grandpuppies and a grandkitten are also given their due.

***

These writings represent the outcome of my efforts, all of which was aimed at documenting the remarkable relationship that my nonfurry mother established and cultivated with each of my canine associates (and me). To have been adopted into her home was serendipitous. She is a wondrous woman, not just a caretaker, but a hero, plain and simple. Copious data about the su-*purr* lady, who energized me to complete this work, is contained herein, but there's no need to ask forgiveness for the abundance of words I used to portray her. She deserves every bit of the attention she got.

My love for this woman goes beyond description, thus it was extremely difficult for me to adequately verbalize my true feelings in paying homage. I was so totally awe-inspired to generate the word about her out to the public that I wish I had the vocal cords of a pygmy tiger instead of a housecat, just so I could roar it out loud instead of merely having it written down in *mew*-ted silence. If only there was a way to make these words ear-popping, I would have done it. Hopefully, I bring eye-popping into play, and maybe that will suffice in achieving my objective.

***

Ashes to ashes, dust to dust applies to me. That's because I was cremated after my life on Earth ended years before this writing project became final. I felt driven to begin while still alive; however, procrastination was one of my few, unfortunate weaknesses; hence, this undertaking did not get very far off the ground until after I had passed. That's just as well because, although most of the events described took place while I was still alive, some of the content *purr*-tains to things that occurred after I was gone. Following my passing, I kept an eye on what was happening in and around my old homestead, and that enabled me to collect mountains of information, which I used to thicken the chapters that follow.

I give my feline word that I made an honest effort to be fair, objective, reasonable, and prudent throughout the entire process. My Egyptian heritage would not *purr*-mit me to do it any other way. However, since forgetfulness is also fairly common among humans, I trust that any memory lapse by this cat will be pardoned. I must add that although I was not opposed to realistically descriptive narration, a word-for-word record of every little action and interaction I observed is not only beyond the capability of even a su-*purr* extraordinary cat like me, but it would diminish the merit of my storytelling style. Therefore, no matter how much the paradoxical barks and bizarre behavior of my canine acquaintances may merit being told in exhaustive detail, I had not the talent, nor the energy or desire to write down every single oddity about them—maybe 99% of their peculiarities, but not all.

My nonfurry mother deserves to have volumes written about her; however, even this cat scholar has limitations. Although it's only a fraction of the totality, by combining many things I personally observed with countless things I overheard, I am confident this written account paints a pretty clear picture of how unlikely it would be for someone to transcend her gentle and caring nature. When all is said and done, I was not only an eyewitness and an ear witness, but a nose witness as well (more to come on this).

While proofreading, I cringed upon viewing all the egregiously hackneyed expressions that were built in. I trust the excessive usage of clichés does not make my handiwork appear banal. In all honesty, a large number of dog and cat phrases were inserted mainly to draw attention to the fact that so many of them exist. For example, *curiosity killed the cat* is commonly used by humans because cats are naturally curious, so the inference is that being overly curious can result in undesirable consequences.

When I first heard someone say the word *cathouse*, I thought it must be something similar to *doghouse*, so you can imagine how I felt when I found out its true meaning. Several cat clichés like these appear on subsequent pages, and believe me, most of them are by no means flattering. More derogatory clichés about cats than dogs are included just because that's the way it is in the real world, and in no way does that sit well with this thin-skinned narrator.

***

Visually, while hunkered-down on my hind legs into a thinking *paws*-ture, I could have been likened to the most exquisite, domestic cat imaginable, and that is how it all began. While imbedded in that position, a slew of actual events flooded my mind, and bright ideas to improve my storytelling capability came to me. An amazing number of illuminating memories flashed before my eyes. Despite being overwhelmed at times, unlike dogs, I have both short-term and long-term memory capabilities, and that enabled me to incorporate a long list of incidents worthy of attention into these writings.

A Prologue, containing information regarding important occurrences before I came along, is necessary to set the stage for the essence of my work. Next comes Chapter One that is graced with an explicit description and essential background information about me. Chapter Two was designed to list my nonfurry mother's many fine attributes, along with a word or two about her insignificant other, whose preference is dogs over cats. Please forgive me in advance for including more information than anyone could *paws*-ibly want to know about my individual canine housemates in Chapters Three, Four, Five, and Six. Finally, an Epilogue puts it all into *purr*-spective—and then some.

Besides quoting some of the human characters in my story, I've added a few relevant sayings here and there from other people—some famous and some not. Here's one I like from the great Austrian psychologist Sigmund Freud who said, "Time spent with cats is never wasted."

PROLOGUE

"One cat just leads to another."
-Ernest Hemingway

An average American guy meets an above average Japanese girl. Love at 1st sight—or 2nd depending on whether you talk to her or him. Wedding bells 1.4 years later. Three nonfurry kids—2 girls & 1 boy in the first five years of matrimony. Five furry kids—4 dogs & 1 cat, six nonfurry grandkids—3 girls & 3 boys, and five furry grandkids—4 more dogs & 1 more cat over the next 30 years. Happily evermore.

Serving in the United States Air Force at Misawa Air Base in Northern Japan was he—working on the base in a retail store called the Base Exchange was she. On the day they met, 21 April 1967, the headline of the local *Pacific Stars & Stripes Newspaper* read, "Massive Demonstrations Opposing Vietnam War Held All Over U.S."

Two years later, still in Japan, she gave birth to a tiny reproduction of herself they called *Barbara*. A son *Steve* was born the next year in Ohio, and a second daughter *Brenda* completed the brood three years later in North Dakota. Her name is Yoriko and he's Jim, aka: *Mom* and *Dad*.

Since Mom and Dad both grew up in families with canine pets and have fond memories of the dogs of their youth, they wanted the same for their children. There is no way they could have known that their luck with their first five pets—four dogs followed by one cat—would be all bad. Nor could they have known that their luck with the next five pets in reverse order—one cat followed by four dogs—would be all good. Lesson learned: get a cat first!

A separate chapter of this book is devoted to each of Mom and Dad's last five furry kids (four dogs and me). In advance, the misfortune surrounding their first five needs a brief description. A detailed explanation on how a homeless cat, who came along after the first five pets, directly impacted Mom and Dad's decision-making process regarding the next five is also in order.

***

Dad's brother Bob gave Mom and Dad a mixed-breed puppy while they were living in Central Ohio. Unfortunately, the pup had ringworms and died less than a week later. It was 1970—Barb was only 18 months old and Steve was a newborn. The gift puppy was a surprise. Mom and Dad had no intention of acquiring a pet while the kids were still babies, so they made no effort to find a replacement.

It wasn't until seven years later, after they had gone back to Mom's homeland of Japan on Dad's military assignment, that they tried to find a dog. Did they ever! In all, they received 3 puppies as gifts from friends in the same year (1977).

Pup #1 was a German Shepherd-mix male. He had roundworms. Deworming attempts didn't work, and the veterinarian couldn't save him. The poor thing died after only three days in their home.

Pup #2 was a Beagle-mix female. Within one week, she was diagnosed with terminal bladder cancer and was gone two weeks later.

Pup #3 was a Maltese-mix female puppy. She was healthy, but lasted only six weeks and was gone at the age of 3½ months. Four-year-old Brenda had taken her eyes off the cute pup in the front yard for less than five minutes, and that's all the time a dog-napper needed to snatch her up and disappear without a trace. The thief also took Brenda's baby doll, and that was a great sentimental loss as Brenda's maternal grandmother (Mom's mom) had sewn a handmade Japanese kimono for Brenda and a matching kimono for the doll. How anyone could demonstrate such cruelty by stealing a little girl's puppy was far beyond Mom's comprehension. Since the doll was also taken, Mom was convinced that the heartless culprit had stolen from one child to give to another child. Mom and Dad concurred that the twisted mind of the thief made it acceptable for him or her to deliberately cause great sorrow to a child they didn't know just to make their own child happy.

Mom cried for the little dog that was stolen knowing its destiny was in the hands of someone with a criminal mind. She still sheds tears every time she thinks about what happened on that terrible day decades ago, not only wondering about what her kids had missed by not growing up with that adorable pup, but also what the little dog had missed by not spending the rest of her life with them.

The misfortune of losing three puppies in one year was too great. Mom and Dad concluded the handwriting was on the wall and the message was loud and clear—no more pets! A very long time would pass before they'd change their minds and re-entertain the thought of bringing anything with four legs back into their home.

***

Six years after losing the three puppies in Japan, the family moved back to Central Ohio. Since it was Dad's final military assignment before retirement, they knew in advance that their stay at this location would last precisely 13½ months. They moved into a countryside home on Flint Ridge Road near the town of Newark in the first week of January 1983.

An encounter with a homeless cat they called *Tommy* made that time of their lives unforgettable. I cannot begin to count the number of times I heard Mom and the children talking about how Tommy's *purr*-sonality and antics had left everlasting impressions. He wasn't their pet, but he came close. They all talked fondly about him so often that I felt as if I knew him.

I never met Tommy, but I did see the only picture of him that was among Mom's prized possessions. I could unmistakably visualize his good looks after overhearing Mom and the kids' detailed descriptions at least 100 times. Based on what they said, he was a one-of-a-kind tomcat with a vagabond spirit. As a feline female, I truly regret not having had the chance to make his acquaintance (*wink wink*).

The family's relationship with Tommy was the reason they would later search for a pet, and end up adopting me. So, I owe him! That's why it was very important that I accurately account for every single bit of *purr*-tinent information I can recall having heard about Tommy. If it wasn't for him, my fate would have been up for grabs.

***

A few short minutes after waking up on Day 2 in their new home would bring more excitement than Day 1 in its entirety. It was a chilly January morning in Central Ohio with fresh snow on the ground. Barb, Steve, and Brenda (ages 13, 12, and 9, respectively) were heading to the shed out back to get their sleds. That's when Steve and Barb caught a glimpse of the feline silhouette. It was heavily overcast, but a glint of sunshine through the snow clouds provided sufficient light to make the big cat visible while he was sniffing and snooping around on the back porch.

"*Whoa!*" Steve shouted out as soon as he pushed open the screen door at the rear of the house. "Look at the size of that cat!" he added, his eyes opening extra wide. He hurriedly reversed direction without turning around pushing both sisters behind him backward into the house.

"Oh my God!" Barb screamed as Steve backed into her.

Brenda, still sleepy-eyed and too short to see anything since she was standing behind Barb and Steve, got a rude awakening upon tumbling to the floor after being shoved to the rear by the chain reaction, domino effect.

At the precise moment Steve retreated, the big cat bolted up and over the porch railing, and scooted out of sight into the gloomy semidarkness.

All three kids ran down the hallway yelling out in unison, "Mom! Dad!, Mom! Dad!" Dad was still asleep, but Mom was frying bacon in the kitchen. The kids excitedly began describing what they had seen to her.

"Biggest cat I ever saw!" exclaimed Steve who got the best view. "Big green eyes and scary looking!"

"Yeah, humongous!" Barb chimed in. "It was gray, black stripes on its back, and a white neck."

"It was so scary!" Brenda contributed, feeling obligated to add something even though she had not seen anything.

Mom ran to the back door and checked outside, but didn't see anything. Not knowing what to think, but concerned that the children may have seen a bobcat, Mom went next door and told the resident, a lady named Ginny, about what had happened. Ginny erased any fear Mom had by informing her that everyone in the neighborhood was aware of the big cat they all called *Tom* (derived from tomcat). She related he had been on his own for a long time. According to Ginny, Tom was a very young feral cat when she first saw him roaming on his own two years earlier.

As a warning to Mom to make sure the children were careful around the cat, Ginny felt the need to differentiate regarding the cat's status. She wanted to be sure that Mom would not wonder if he was a stray that had gotten lost or had been discarded by a human (indicating he may be receptive to interaction with humans), rather than a feral cat that had been born in the wild (meaning he would not likely be receptive to human contact). That's why Ginny made it absolutely clear that his origin was feral in nature.

The children didn't see the cat again that day. They did, however, see him again the next two mornings in the same place—not on the porch itself, but rather on top of the porch railing. A nosey, exploratory look on his face was unmistakable.

On the second day, he ran away like the day before, but he didn't go far. The kids readily spotted him crouched down in the snow next to the trunk of a small oak tree about 50 feet from the back porch. He stayed there for more than an hour watching them as they frolicked in the snow and made a snowman. The fun they were having, as evidenced by the free-spirited noises they made, had sparked his interest. The children knew he was there, but kept quiet and tried to avoid eye contact. That was Barb's idea so as to not scare him away. Plus, they were still leery of him.

The third day was different. That's when Brenda took some leftover canned tuna from the fridge and offered it to him while he was spying on them again from the same spot in the backyard. Brenda was neither cautious nor quiet as she stepped off the back porch and walked up to him calling out in her shrill, little girl voice, "Here kitty, kitty, kitty, kitty," while Barb and Steve yelled out to no avail for her to back off. Remembering what Mom had said about the neighbors calling him "Tom," she yelled out in her ultra-squeaky tone, "Here Tom, C'mere Tom." But that abruptly changed to, "Here Tommy. C'mere Tommy, Tommy," as she totally ignored the desperate calls to retreat from her sister and brother. The tuna was on a paper plate that she put down within five feet of his nose, after which she turned and walked slowly back to the porch.

It was as if he became a snow sculpture frozen to that spot as did not move even one millimeter. He didn't accept the offering right away, but as soon as Brenda was back on the porch, he couldn't resist. By scarfing it down as if he hadn't eaten for days, he sent a signal to the children that he might be starving. In actuality, he was a prolific hunter and wasn't hungry at all. Besides, tuna wasn't something he could catch in the wild, and the smell of it was tantalizing. It may even have come close to making him drool like a dog.

The neighbors knew him as Tom. Brenda started calling him Tommy, and Barb and Steve followed suit. *Tommy fits better*, Mom thought. For some reason, he seemed to like being called Tommy—maybe because the sound of it was more pleasant and cat-friendlier than plain old Tom.

Tommy became receptive to the children's daily handouts—not every day, but two or three times a week on the days of his choosing. Mom made assorted food items available for the kids to give him. She even bought canned cat food. He was too proud to accept every daily feeding they put out for him, so he picked whichever dishes and accompanying smelly odors struck his fancy. Since Mom and the children kept providing him with a wide variety of scrumptious edibles, Tommy probably thought they were great hunters like him.

Cow's milk in a saucer was something he took a liking to, as long as it was whole milk. He drew the line when it came to anything less than whole milk by refusing to accept the reduced fat variety. Mom caught on when Brenda once gave him 2% milkfat, after which he turned and walked away without drinking any of it. Mom replaced it right away with whole milk and he drank that to the last drop.

Two weeks after he began accepting food from the children, Tommy experienced something else for the very first time—

human hands touching his fur. Mom had instructed the kids to not get too close and followed up with constant reminders such as, "Do not try to touch him." She wanted to be sure there was no risk before trying to pet him. Mom was the first to touch his furry back right after he drank milk from a saucer she had placed in front of him. Barb was next, followed by Steve, and then Brenda, all just seconds apart. He thought about running away when their hands reached out to him, but thought twice every time. Each if them stroked his back separately, but only once or twice. He did not dislike it and elected to stay put.

After three days of back-petting, he became receptive to back rubs, and one week after that, he let Mom and the girls give him belly rubs. At first, he kicked their hands away. He didn't kick very hard knowing his sharp claws were capable of causing severe damage and he did not want to do that. It didn't take long for the kicks to subside as he gave in. That meant he had to lie on his back exposing his underside in a fully vulnerable and submissive position with hidden claws—a truly remarkable *paws*-ture for a feral tomcat.

While he was on his back, whoever rubbed his belly was susceptible to being on the receiving end of his finely sharpened claws, but they didn't have to worry since he never tried to scratch them. Eventually, he even gave himself up to chin rubs by allowing their fingers to get very close to his teeth. Not once did he ever try to bite them, and never even had the urge to hiss.

Upon observing the interplay between the big cat and the children, Ginny remarked to Mom, "I can't believe it! I wouldn't believe if I hadn't seen it with my own two eyes." Ginny, who had never heard Tommy meow until then, exclaimed to Mom, "When I saw him meowing at your kids, I did a double take, and then a triple take!"

Since feral cats are not known for socializing with humans, Tommy meowing like a kitten every time he got a belly rub from the children was a sight to behold, so Ginny's reaction was easy to understand. Ginny related that before Mom and family moved into the neighborhood, she had seen the cat roaming around nearly every day for at least two years. Ginny's husband Bud said Tommy seemed to hang around their house more than others in the neighborhood probably because they had a female cat named *Buffy* that stayed inside the house most of the time, but often stared out the window at Tommy.

Ginny added that although she had occasionally left food outside on her porch for him, he never accepted it, "Not once." Ginny reiterated she couldn't believe he was allowing the children to feed him and touch him because, under no circumstances, would he *purr*-mit her to get any closer than 30 feet. She said he kept his distance and so did she because he never gave her any indication that she could come close enough to touch him. His new name rubbed off as Ginny too began calling him Tommy instead of Tom.

Make no bones about it—Tommy was by no means a scrawny dumpster-diver. As indicated by his stout 20+-pound physique, he was a great hunter and never close to being malnourished. To put things into *purr*-spective, since some dog persons may not be aware, a 20-pound cat is equivalent to a 120-pound dog. Relatively speaking, he was a *huge* cat!

Tommy had two old injuries, both well healed. His right ear had been torn down the middle, and he walked with a slight limp caused by two partially missing toes on his right front paw. Since the wooded area behind their home was abundant with wildlife, everyone assumed his wounds were battle scars probably sustained during territorial disputes with another feral feline or a wild critter like a raccoon.

Mom only has one photo of Tommy, but it was a nice, full body shot. He was a rare, mixed-breed Tabby—one in a million since nearly all Tabbies are female. A gray fur base and dark brown overcoat with black swirls and patches of white made him a splendid specimen. He looked like a brute, not only because of his large physical frame, but also due to his bobcat-like head and face. His head was oversized and triangular, and his irregular facial features made some humans wonder if he was half cat and half something else—a raccoon maybe? A distinctive mark on his forehead resembled the letter "M," which prompted Dad to declare that it stood for "magnificent" (in actuality, all Tabbies have the distinctive "M" mark).

I must say it was out of character—to tell the truth remarkable! —for Dad to pay a compliment to a cat, but that's how impressive Tommy was. His contact with Tommy was quite limited because he was at work at least five days a week and often came home after dark when Tommy was long gone. He was able to see Tommy on weekends and became impressed by the connection the children and Mom had established with the likes of an undomesticated animal. Several points I want to make will become clear, and the fact that Dad is a dog person, and in no way a cat person is among them. (The terms *dog person* and *cat person* —how people self-identify based on their preference for either canine or feline companions—appear often in subsequent chapters)

Ironically, Tommy's voice did not match his stud appearance. His *meow* had a soft sounding effeminate tone, something Barb and Brenda thought was *cute*. Even though he heard them joking about it, he could not have comprehended that they found his voice unbecoming and amusing. I never heard his meow, but imagined it to have been somewhat charming (*wink wink*).

***

Tommy was allowing his *purr*-sona to evolve into a bonding relationship with Mom and the children. They didn't knowingly do anything to arouse his interest. After all, it was he who had initiated the contact by going to their home on his own free will out of curiosity. He was attracted to the children because they were playful and in no way intimidating like the other humans with whom he had previously crossed paths—all grown-ups. Although he had not become dependent upon Mom and the children, he somehow felt obliged to make himself available to them.

His keen sense of smell told him they did not have any pets. Technically, he did not become their pet since he never entered their house. More than once, the kids tried to *purr*-suade him to go inside; however, the closest he got was the rear doorway when his nose penetrated the interior airspace. He just couldn't force himself to take that one giant step needed to have the rest of his body follow his nose into the house.

It's just as well he stayed outside since he obviously wasn't neutered. "Look Mommy, why is he walking backward with his tail straight up in the air like that?" Brenda asked upon observing Tommy acting peculiarly on the back porch the day after she first gave him the canned tuna.

"That's how he marks his territory, honey," Mom replied. "He's putting his scent down to keep other cats away," she added as she watched him spray a perfectly aimed stream of urine into a corner of the porch.

It didn't take Tommy long to start offering tokens of appreciation to Mom and the children. Two weeks into their relationship, he left a headless mole at their front door. He followed that up the next day by dropping off a field mouse—sans its head—at the same location. It was the beginning of a string of countless small animals that he would leave decapitated at their doorstep.

He always waited serenely nearby to observe the reaction of whoever found each dead critter. He heard Barb and Brenda yell out, "*Eww!*" and "*Yucky!*," respectively, upon finding the first and second gifts. Based on the girls' shrieking tones, he couldn't help but deduce that their reaction seemed less than favorable. Mom explained to the children that it was his way of showing thanks to them. That did not stop the kids from feeling queasy upon viewing the *mew*-tilated tokens of affection that they unanimously referred to as "gross" and "disgusting."

Upon receipt of the third offering—a small, headless bird of unrecognizable species—Mom told the children, "The more presents he gives, the more he's showing how much he likes us." He must have liked them a lot because the gifts kept coming faithfully to the tune of 3 or 4 mutilated corpses *purr* week for the rest of the time they lived in that house—almost a whole year. A hunting machine was he! An old saying, *Look what the cat dragged in*, got a lot of usage by Dad in response to Tommy's gift-giving. He grossed-out Mom by telling her, "The head must be the tastiest part," since Tommy always saved that part for himself.

An expert on feline psyche, like me, would set the record straight by advising that Tommy's gifts didn't constitute payback to the family. Instead, they merely continued as part of a long-term, self-feeding, hunting pattern he was forced to begin in order to survive. He started to share portions of his kills to express gratitude to the family in expectation they would eat the dead animals and birds he presented to them. Some humans may consider his kills to have been trophies, but Mom believed they were tokens of appreciation, so let's leave it at that. Since he was receiving food from the family, it was no longer necessary for him to kill to eat. His reason for hunting had switched from survival to sport. He would still eat some of his kills—at least their heads!

Dad thought about buying a stuffed bird or a battery-operated mouse to serve as a surrogate for the dead critters that Tommy was leaving for them to possibly get him to stop. However, Mom, whose animal wisdom exceeded Dad's many times over, convinced him that it would be a waste of time and money. More than anyone, Mom grasped why Tommy did what he did, and she knew that giving him toys would not change his behavior.

***

Mom and the gang were seeing a lot of Tommy. He instinctively started coming to their home every afternoon at 3:00 p.m. sharp to wait for the children to get off the school bus in front of their house at 3:05. It was as if he had a built-in alarm clock that went off at precisely the same time every day to alert him of the approaching school bus. He seemed to enjoy showing off his proud, lion-like gait as he slowly paraded in the yard in full view of the driver and other children on the bus. He oozed confidence with every step, fully cognizant that all eyes were on him. It may have looked like he was showboating to the nth degree, however, that was not the case. Top-of-the-line cats like Tommy and me are by no means obsessed with our own good looks. There's just an air of dignity that naturally surrounds us and makes us strut or do whatever else is necessary to uphold the phenom image.

Without fail, at dusk every evening, Tommy headed up the hillside in the family's 2-acre backyard. Once on top, he disappeared into the tree line that extended across the horizon for as far as one could see. He was off into the woods on another hunting expedition, but would always reappear at their house to wait for the school bus the following afternoon.

Then one day it happened—Tommy failed to show up. Mom was quick to think the worst—hit by a car, or met his match in a head-to-head altercation with some wild beast. She was aware that like any feral, Tommy's life expectancy was about half that of an indoor, domesticated cat. She tried to calm the children's' anxiety by telling them, "Oh, he probably found himself a girlfriend." In an effort to comfort them, she added, "Don't worry, he'll come back soon." They all had a hard time falling asleep that night as Tommy was still missing at bedtime.

The next morning, the sound of distressed meowing aroused Barb from her sleep 30 minutes before the alarm clock was set to go off. Barb and Brenda shared a bedroom in the rear of the house and the noise was coming from outside their window. Barb opened the window slightly enabling her to hear and see better. Her eyes cautiously inspected the outside area, and despite the darkness, solar lights installed alongside the back porch emitted enough glow for her to notice the slightest movement of a cardboard box that Mom had left on the back porch for Tommy in hopes he would return. It appeared as if something was moving around inside the box. The movement was accompanied by whim-*purr*-ing meows loud enough for her to identify him as the origin.

"Tommy!" she yelled out again and again as she ran out to the porch. "Tommy! Oh Tommy! Are you okay?" Upon confirming with her own eyes that it was him, she gasped, "Aw, poor, poor Tommy."

His fur was covered in dried mud and blood. His left ear was severely damaged and barely still attached to his head. The deep, teeth-mark cuts were only slightly bleeding, but the significant loss of blood over time had obviously weakened him. He was lying motionless on his right side exposing the damaged ear to anyone who looked inside the box. At least one-fourth of the ear was missing. He was badly injured and had come back for help.

Mom came right away upon hearing Barb's hollers. Since it was obvious that Tommy had gotten into a fight for his life with some animal of equal or larger size, Mom was concerned about the *paws*-sibility of rabies. The chance of him being vaccinated was nil, and in all likelihood, whatever caused the nasty wounds was also unvaccinated. Raccoons were everywhere and she suspected he may have tangled with one of them. The day before, she had heard on a TV newscast that a rabid raccoon had been captured in the county where they lived.

"Don't touch him!" she shouted to Barb.

Mom knew that cats tend to self-heal by licking their own wounds to release a natural antiseptic contained in their saliva. But it was physically im-*paws*-sible for Tommy to lick his own ear. She had to do something in a hurry, and decided to use cotton balls lightly dipped in rubbing alcohol to disinfect the cuts. Tommy was too weak to resist the burning sensation, and merely softly meowed while she dabbed him with the moist cotton. Lying motionless, he *purr*-mitted her to cleanse his wounds.

Dad came out and, after taking one look at the mangled ear, had some discouraging words about taking Tommy to a veterinarian. He said because they didn't know what had bitten him, and would have to identify him as a feral cat, indicating it was unlikely he had ever received a rabies vaccination, the vet would probably suggest putting him down rather than quarantining him. With the kids anxiously waiting, Dad and Mom agreed the vet was not an option. It was decided that Mom would continue to nurse him while keeping an eye out for signs of the dreaded rabies disease.

One of Dad and Mom's favorite movies is *Old Yeller*, a story about a beloved pet dog infected with rabies. They both recalled some symptoms exhibited by the movie dog—drooling, convulsions, and attempts to bite its humans. Dad conducted some research at the local library and found out that, in addition to the three symptoms they remembered from the movie, there were at least 10 other signs indicative of rabies. He also learned that although the incubation period for animal-to-animal transmission could last up to 60 days, on average, symptoms usually appear in 10-14 days.

Dad and Mom decided Tommy would be allowed to stay inside the cardboard box on the back porch with one condition—immediate segregation in a crate if any of the 13 disease symptoms was noticed. Mom was the designated observer in charge.

With a lot of tender loving care from the entire family (even Dad), each of whom took turns handfeeding and watching over him, Tommy finally crawled out of the box after five days. He began to walk around gingerly on the porch as if it was a hot, tin roof even though it was cool to the touch. He wasn't back to normal, but was healing nicely day by day with no sign whatsoever of sickness. After getting out of the box, he started sleeping on the doormat outside the back door. He started roaming around the backyard at the beginning of the second week and, by the end of that week, he was running at half-speed. There was still no indication of any rabies symptoms or infection—on the contrary, he was looking quite healthy and gradually starting to act like his old self.

Remarkably, 2½ weeks after being hurt, a scarred Tommy resumed his nocturnal routine of heading into the woods at sunset. He also picked up where he had left off by coming back to the house at exactly 3:00 o'clock in the afternoon. The whole family was amazed not only at his quick recovery, but also at his desire to return to harm's way. He was hurting throughout the recovery process, but no one could detect it since cats, especially ones that aren't pets, instinctively hide pain, and they are very good at it.

"Hey Tommy Boy, tell them they should see the other guy!" Steve joked while stroking the top of the big cat's head.

Dad interjected "I'm gonna start calling you F-14!"—after the U.S. Navy's F-14 fighter aircraft nicknamed the *Tomcat*.

Tommy became closely attached to Mom and the children while he was on the receiving end of their medical care and companionship during recu-*purr*-ation from his injuries. It was a different story for Ginny and Bud next door and everyone else living nearby, as he continued to remain skittish around them after he was well enough to start moving about in the neighborhood again.

The 60-day anniversary of his injuries came with no sign of disease. To celebrate, Mom made a cake and they had a party for him on the back porch. He didn't eat any cake, but he did partake of canned tuna with whole milk in a saucer on the side. It would be the first and last party they held for him.

Although he recovered from the most recent wounds, his injury count was starting to take its toll. He wasn't able to move as quickly as before, making it no longer a sure thing for him to catch his own food. Mom and the children were making sure he had enough to eat. Regardless, he still enjoyed the thrill of the hunt and continued venturing into the woods every night.

**

Due to Dad's retirement from the military in February 1984, Tommy's contact with the family came to an end a little more than one year after it had begun. They discussed maybe trying to take him with them to their next home in nearby Pennsylvania, but reluctantly determined he would only be happy by continuing to run free on that Central Ohio ridge. Making the full transition from the wild to domestication just did not fit Tommy's free spirit. They unanimously agreed he was not meant to be a housecat, so they would leave and he would stay.

"You can take the cat out of the wild, but you can't take the wild out of the cat," was how Dad summed it up.

"Don't worry. I'll make sure he gets enough food to eat," Ginny assured them. Mom told Dad she wished they could have been neighbors with Ginny and Bud a lot longer because they were such nice people.

Goodbye day was extremely painful for Mom and the children, especially since Tommy had no idea what was happening. Dad wanted to get an early start, but that didn't happen. They waited for Tommy to show up.

Upon arriving precisely at 3:00 p.m., he took up his usual position seated near the front door where he always waited for the school bus. He sensed something was wrong because he normally had to wait five minutes for the children to get off the bus, but on this day, they were already there. All three kids sat next to him and waved at the bus as it passed by.

Each member of the family took their turn petting him. He remained seated looking at them with question-mark eyes. Mom and the children had a hard time going up to him to say goodbye, so Dad went first. After giving him a cursory pat on the head, Dad sat down in the driver's seat of the car. Brenda, Steve, Barb, and Mom, in that order, all stroked Tommy's furry back and sleek forehead one last time. Teardrops fell on fur. Muffled whim-*purrs* were met by soft meows.

Despite their already late departure, Dad made no effort to speed things up. It was as if everyone moved in slow motion. Once they were all finally inside the car, Mom and the children bawled in unison. Dad shed a few tears too.

"Can we take him with us Mommy?" Brenda pleaded. "Pleeeease," she persisted.

Wanting to say yes, but knowing there was no way, Mom attempted to be comforting. "He's better off staying here kids," she tried to say convincingly to reassure them. "Don't worry, he'll be all right." Choking back tears, Mom was unable to utter another word.

Tommy did not move from the spot where they had petted him. He just sat there quizzically overlooking the driveway as the family car backed out and slowly pulled away. Not knowing they were leaving for good, he would have been anticipating their return.

There was not one dry eye the whole way on the 3-hour drive to Pennsylvania. The children were accustomed to saying farewell to relatives and friends since they had been moving around from place to place every 2-4 years their entire lives. This time was different though, as they had never before said goodbye to a close animal friend. And, not knowing if they would ever see Tommy again was hard to bear.

One month after the family moved out, they received a letter from Ginny letting them know that Tommy had kept going to their old home every afternoon for one week after they left. She said after the school bus had come and gone, he waited on the back porch as if expecting someone to open the door before heading out on his nightly jaunts. She mentioned he had given up and stopped going to their old house after another family moved in. She added she still saw him in the neighborhood, but less often than before. She indicated he was occasionally accepting food from her and, in closing, added, "He looks as good as ever."

***

Six months after they had said their goodbyes to Tommy, Dad, Mom, and the children moved back to Ohio. They purchased a home in Reynoldsburg about 30 miles from their old home in Newark.

The house was brand new, so they were the first family to live in it. As it turned out though, they would stay there only two years. During that time, they made several trips back to Newark. They stopped by their old home on Flint Ridge Road and talked to Ginny occasionally, but Tommy was never there when they visited. Ginny said he didn't come around as often as he used to, but she still saw him about once a week when he'd stop by and eat some of the food she regularly left outside for him. They were highly disappointed by not seeing him on any of their half-dozen trips back there.

Primarily based on their cherished relationship with Tommy, Mom and the children decided that the time had come for a pet to join their household. Dad concurred. The four dogs brought into their home a few years earlier were there for such short times that no close relationship was formed with any of them.

They had been around a few pets at Dad's birthplace in Southwestern Pennsylvania. Dad's brother Bob and sister Becky had an Old English Sheepdog named *Fido*, who not only ate all the food given to him at barbeques and picnics, but devoured the paper plates on which the food was served as well. There was a gentle, mixed-breed dog called *Blackie* owned by Grandpap Russ and Grandma Nellie, who also had a cat named *Kitko*. Talk about fat cats! Kitko had layers of fat literally hanging down to the floor from her underbelly. She wasn't particularly fond of humans at whom she was quick to hiss, and she even left a scratch scar on Brenda's arm when Brenda tried to pick her up one time. The kids' contact with that cat and the two dogs in Pennsylvania had been limited to a dozen or so weekend visits over a one-year period, so after all was said and done, Tommy was still the closest thing to a pet they had known.

At 4-to-1, the voting on whether to adopt a dog or a cat wasn't even close. Mom, Barb, Steve, and Brenda did not cast their votes to add a cat due to an infringement of rodents upon their new home, or for some other obscure reason. On the contrary, they cast their votes for a cat solely because of the influence that Tommy had on them.

"What good is a cat?" Dad grumbled to himself after tabulating the votes. He wanted a dog; however, despite the disappointment, he understood how Tommy had impacted the voting.

On the day they went to the nearby county animal shelter, there were 18 cats and nearly twice as many dogs available for adoption. Those numbers really didn't matter because they had gone there to rescue a cat. However, seeing double the number of dogs as cats prompted Barb to ask Dad, "Why are there so many more dogs than cats?"

Aware that there were actually more cats than dogs in American households, Dad was hard-pressed to answer. He thought the shelter numbers should have been reversed. *How could more people give up dogs than cats?* he pondered to himself before replying to Barb with tongue in cheek, "Looks like more people give up dogs than cats." He couldn't believe he had just said that, as he was unable to comprehend why so many people had discarded their dogs.

He mumbled it one more time to himself, *More people give up dogs than cats.* As a diehard dog person, there was no way he could understand why fewer cat owners had given up on their cats, and that prompted him to disgustedly talk to himself the whole time they were at the rescue shelter. He reasoned that the numbers of cats and dogs available on any given day would vary, and the numbers on a certain day did not necessarily accurately portray the average numbers over a long period of time. If he had inquired, he would have found out that the numbers on the day they went to the pet shelter were, in fact, representative of the average numbers at that facility on any given day since it had opened many years earlier. The bottom line—more dog owners were giving up dogs than cat owners were giving up cats—at least that's the way it was in Central Ohio back then.

All the dogs and cats available for adoption were full grown, and they had previously lived in a human home for a long time. For any owner to give up a pet, with full knowledge that an animal not adopted within a relatively short period of time could be put down due to a lack of space at the shelter, was beyond Mom and Dad's comprehension. It was not easy for Mom to take the time to say *hello* and pet each and every dog and cat waiting for adoption, but that's precisely what she did. They all shared the look of despair and that increased her sadness level as she went from one to the next.

After taking a good look at each cat, Mom and the kids decided on a long-haired, silver-coated tomcat named *Socko*—a real beaut! At 20 pounds, he was about the same physical size as Tommy, and exhibited many of the same *purr*-sonality traits, including a mellow, laid-back demeanor and soft meow. However, he was a Persian breed and Tommy was a mixed-breed Tabby, so they did not look anything alike. They didn't pick Socko solely because of his good looks—they wanted a male because Tommy was a male, and Socko happened to be the only tomcat available on that day.

Socko's stay in Mom and Dad's household turned out to be short-lived. His total rejection of the litter box and absolute preference for peeing anywhere he felt like inside the house, and pooping on the bedspread in the master bedroom, not once but twice—on the first day and again the next day—did not go over well with Dad, in particular, or the rest of the family either. "You see!" Dad was quick to complain to Mom. "I told you we should have got a dog."

When Dad telephoned the rescue shelter, he was informed that not only the original owner, but another adoptive family had given up on Socko due to his potty problem. That was something someone at the rescue shelter had "forgot" to mention. Apparently at 3 years of age, there was no way to break his bad habits, so Mom and Dad had no choice but to return him to the shelter after only two days. Otherwise, an accumulation of urine stains on the wall-to-wall carpet would have gradually destroyed the flooring in their new house.

It wasn't as if they were signing Socko's death warrant because Dad was told the original owner had agreed to take him back if a new *purr*-manent home could not be found. Because they felt the shelter should have made them aware of Socko's behavioral problem before finalizing the adoption, Dad and Mom were dead set against adopting another cat from that place.

Up to that point in time, Mom and Dad's household had seen

4 dogs—and now 1 cat—come and go. Disease took 3 puppies after only a few days or a couple of weeks at most; 1 puppy was stolen; and the lone feline had an uncorrectable behavioral problem. Their luck was about to change.

CHAPTER ONE—ME

> *"A cat has nine lives.*
> *For three he plays,*
> *for three he strays,*
> *and for the last three he stays."*
> -English Proverb

Born in the Buckeye State was I. At eight weeks of age on July 19, 1985, Mom, Dad, and the children adopted me from a pet center in Columbus, Ohio. That was about 18 months after they had bid farewell to Tommy, and nine months after Socko had come and gone. I was very glad they didn't go back to the shelter where they got Socko even though it was located close to their new home. Fortunately, there is no way Dad or Mom would have considered going back to that place since they had been deceived when they got Socko there. So, they found me in another shelter.

I will never forget my first day in the Herron family's Reynoldsburg, Ohio house. I had previously observed many other human creatures, but none like my adoptive family. Mom, Barb, Steve, and Brenda would not leave me alone on that first day. I kept hearing over and over, "Nice little kitty" and "You're so cute." It's not surprising that I don't recall anything about Dad's presence during my first day in their home, and after getting to know him later on, I suspect he probably kept his distance on *purr*-pose.

I felt comfortable sitting in the kids' palms, but it went on far too long. No one put me down and my bladder couldn't hold it anymore. *Yikes!* I peed on Brenda's lap. Only a matter of minutes in my new home and I had made a mess. It didn't seem like a big deal to Brenda or anyone else; therefore, my anxiety was short-lived. That incident would be the only time I ever felt uneasy in the family's presence, and that feeling lasted a total of 10 seconds at most.

Mom and the children were lightning quick in making me feel welcome. Although I wasn't long gone from my birth mother's side, it seemed as if those days were long gone. I had a new family and all was well in the world. By the end of the first day, I already felt like a full-fledged member of my new family.

After I had cohabitated with them for two days, they started comparing me to Tommy, but the comparisons were limited. Aside from us both being Tabbies and our voices apparently sounding similar, Tommy and I were totally different—male vs. female, wild vs. domestic; scarred vs. unmarked; mouser vs. non-mouser (more on this to come); and the list goes on. I didn't make them forget about Tommy, and I didn't want to. They fell in love with him, and after he was gone, they fell in love with me. Over time, just as Tommy was influential in them bringing me into their home, my amiable character would become a factor for them to entertain the thought of bringing in more pets.

I couldn't help wondering what would have happened to me if the family had taken Tommy with them when they moved away from that Central Ohio countryside. I also wondered what it would have been like for me with Tommy as a housemate. He was four years my senior, but I'm sure the age gap would not have been a problem. However, I was neutered, he was not, and that would have presented a problem. If he and I were both sexually active or both sexually inactive, it might have worked out.

I realized that Mom and Dad would not have adopted me if

they had taken Tommy with them when they moved. I felt sad for Tommy because he was missing out on what I was enjoying. Mom, Dad, and the children had no way of knowing that my presence would forever change all their lives, as I was destined to become the first in a line of pets that would grow old in their household.

***

In the Japanese language, my name *Kimi* means *she who is without equal*. Okay, I lied. Wishfully thinking was I. My real name was *Chibi* [*tiny one*]. In view of my lion-like superiority, Kimi would have been more appropriate, but rest assured that Chibi is tolerable—I mean acceptable. Actually, I wasn't that small since my physical size as an adult was about average as far as domestic, female cats go. I must have been so little when the family brought me home from the animal shelter that Chibi seemed fitting. Anyhow, it stuck.

Taking into consideration that I was a lot smaller than all the dogs that would become my housemates tends to put the origin of my name into *purr*-spective. There were no sour grapes because I realized that an animal, just like a human, has no say in picking its own name. Even though I didn't have a powerful name, I was strong and healthy and lived a long life. Besides, I think everyone would be hard-pressed to argue against my thoughts on this topic—*powerful names are more appropriate for males than females*. I rest my case by asserting that my name Chibi may be cute for a female cat, but would not have been seriously considered for Tommy, or any tomcat for that matter.

While on the topic of names, if there was a way to go back in time, and I could have picked my own name, it would have been *Minerva*. An explanation is in order. Mom is a big fan of the *Harry Potter* wizardry series written by J.K. Rowling. One of the main characters is Professor Minerva McGonagall, who taught Transfiguration at the Hogwarts School of Witchcraft and Wizardry, and was among a few licensed Animagi—humans capable of changing themselves into animals at will. Ms. McGonagall transformed into a Tabby cat, which enabled her to spy on enemies and collect intelligence information.

The human-animal connection is why I can directly relate to Ms. McGonagall, and the reason I would have chosen her given name for myself if it were possible. Ms. McGonagall went on to become the head teacher at the school. Mom was impressed by her, and I admired her so much that *Minerva* became my pen name. Like all Tabbies, the letter "M" was clearly visible on my forehead—in my mind it stood for Minerva. By the way, that name goes all the way back to ancient times when the Roman goddess of wisdom was named Minerva.

Physically speaking in my prime, I was a well-proportioned Tabby and tipped the scale at a middle-of-the-pack 9 pounds. A lot of humans—many dog persons among them—believe Tabbies are a specific breed of cats, but they are not, as they are found in many breeds. They are distinguished by a color pattern and markings on their coats, including dark stripes and swirls. To have been associated with powerful wildcats like cheetahs and tigers, that also have the letter "M" on their foreheads, was a huge honor. A proud Tabby was I!

My facial features were quite sharp. A small pointy nose and piercing eyes made me appear clever and cunning—maybe even slightly bitchy (let's not forget that looks can be deceiving, and yes, the cover of this book is graced with a closeup of my face with a focus on my eyes). My eyes were, in fact, luminous. Like any other cat's eyes, they enabled me to see exceptionally well at night, but most of all, my eyes gave me the means to communicate with humans. Furthermore, unlike my fellow felines, my eyes provided me the uncat-like ability to read my canine housemates' feeble minds.

I won't dwell on my eye color—green—the same as Dad. Be assured that this is the only *doggone* thing that good ol' Dad and I had in common. At this point, in accordance with established procedures of the storytelling art, it would be customary to offer an explanation about the relationship between Dad and me. Instead, I would beg indulgence for a slight deviation from protocol. Please rest assured that, in due course, the relevance of the association between Dad and me will become crystal clear.

I was not a purebred per se (that was hard for me to say), but I closely resembled the Siberian breed. My veterinary records inadequately listed breed as "DLH," which stands for Domestic Long Hair—a catchall for mixed-breed felines. It was hard to believe that my vintage had been memorialized as merely DLH. That was an insult of the highest magnitude! Me, a Tabby of ancient Egyptian lineage, referred to with no respect. I would have appreciated it if they would have more accurately classified me as DCT (Domestic Calico Tabby). Anything would have been better than DLH.

Long, silky soft, calico fur with black streaks and shades of yellow, orange, cream, and white over a black and gray undercoating pretty much sums up my appearance. Like a box turtle with similar patterns, my hodgepodge of colors tended to fade with age; however, my heyday looks did make heads turn. I even made my own head turn every time I walked by the full-length mirror in the family dining room. I just couldn't resist admiring my own whole-body reflection. At the risk of sounding pompous and stuck-up, I must say that nothing incites a show-off, like me, more than a full-length mirror.

If I could have somehow transformed myself into human form, there's no doubt I would have been a top model strutting down a catwalk in fashion shows. Here's a picture of me in my prime—and yes, I am sitting inside a cardboard box—just wanted to find out what it was like inside a box not full of litter.

I not only adored my own physical appearance, but took pride in my brainpower too. Please know that I carefully selected my next statement in an effort to avoid sounding like I may have been on an ego trip. I was wise beyond my cat years. (I could have legitimately referred to myself as a feline Einstein, but modestly elected to play it down)

When I greeted humans, the shape my mouth made to say *hello* appeared to mimic a yawn. Since human-to-human and human-to-dog yawning appears contagious, it wasn't uncommon for someone to respond by yawning upon being greeted by me. I finally caught on one day when I looked in a mirror behind the *purr*-son I was greeting and noticed that it looked as if I was yawning. No sound came out, but my mouth was ajar and oddly shaped, and the lady I greeted started to yawn right after I did it. There's no explanation—it just happened naturally.

Like any other cat, my nocturnal vision was far superior to that of humans. A normal *purr*-son's standard vision is 20/20—mine was 20/100 enabling me to see objects very far away. However, beyond about 20 feet, I could not see details as clearly as humans. My advantages were the ability to detect movement in dim light up to 100 feet away, plus my field of vision was considerably wider than that of humans, meaning I saw a lot out of the corners of my eyes. Things up close appeared fuzzy, so I relied more on smell and touch to identify things directly beneath my nose. I favored using my feeler whiskers when trying to figure out what was right there directly in front of me. I was not color blind, but I didn't see colors well as even bright colors appeared like pastels to me.

Chasing a flickering light from a flashlight was my favorite pastime because the way my eyes could process speeding images was highly impressive, if I must say so myself. The children regularly brought out a flashlight to play because they seemed to enjoy watching me running around trying to catch streaks of light as much as I enjoyed doing it.

***

Dad and other dog persons *purr*-ceive all cats as being bitchy, and I had to spend my entire life on Earth trying to deal with that misguided, extremely dubious notion. There is no way I fit that stereotype—unless merely being assertive is the sole criterion. Instead of just reading this in my opening statement, I wish you could hear it come out of my mouth, as it would most certainly be the loudest yowl to ever stimulate your eardrums —*I WAS NOT A BITCH!* I just had to let that out due to my cognizance of one of the most overexposed phrases in the English language—*perception is reality*.

Since I was totally honest describing myself in detail on the following pages, and some things may seem self-flattering, I need to emphasize the fact that I did not possess any characteristic whatsoever that would, in any way, justify anyone using the B-word when referring to me. The B-word can be used—without prejudice—in reference to any canine female, and it can also be used—with prejudice—when referring to a human female filled with hate, spite, and ill-will. I did not fit either category. It's no wonder feline females, like me, get a bad reputation since, according to the English vernacular, the disparaging words *catty* and *bitchy* are synonymous. Not long ago, people often used the term *pussy* when referring to a cat, but in this age of political correctness and increased awareness of sexual harassment, we don't hear that word very much, and that's the way I like it!

Before going any further, I hope dog people will be open-minded while pawing through the lines in this chapter since they are all about me. I also hope that cat people will be tolerant and understanding while pawing through the next four chapters which pertain to each of my canine housemates.

In anticipation that someone might interpret my words and actions as slightly overbearing, or even mildly spiteful, I felt compelled to open up about my *purr*-sonality. I want to set the record straight: I admit to having been lofty, dogmatic, and egotistical, but not even borderline bitchy. I was known to cop an occasional attitude—"cattitude" as it is dotingly referred to by cat people—but only when someone *rattled my cage* and provoked an appropriate response.

I also admit to having possessed a twinge of arrogance. That's because I often felt quietly proud of myself. I was as philosophical as the Cheshire cat in *Alice in Wonderland* (minus the mischievous grin). I was also as dignified as *Morris*, the spokes-cat for Purina 9-Lives Cat Food on old TV commercials. I could have even been likened to the famous Japanese cartoon character known as *Hello Kitty* because I was great with children.

Despite what I just stated, I was not like certain other famous cats that humans laugh at in cartoons, movies, and books. There's just no way I would have demonstrated intellectual inferiority by trying to catch a mouse like the famous one called *Jerry*, or a canary like the one named *Tweety*, or any other bird or animal portrayed as mentally superior to their feline co-star. Something that still bothers me to no end is the portrayal of a certain rodent as a su-*purr* hero—*Mighty Mouse*—with flying capability, x-ray vision, and the ability to move objects by mental effort alone. How someone could have stretched their imagination of vermin so far is utterly baffling.

I don't understand why no one has yet created a feline anthropomorphic su-*purr* hero, or a comedy character that kids would love, like the mouse they call *Chuck E. Cheese*. The depiction of rodents, canines, and even birds as superior is unfair! Furthermore, far too many canines have been characterized as heroes on TV, in movies, and in books—*Lassie*, *Scooby-Doo*, and *Snoopy* to name a few—so the time for a hero cat to take center stage is long overdue. My hope is that someone who reads this will take the hint and use me as the model to create the ultimate animal character with human qualities. By all means, feel free to anthropomorphize me to the limit!

Mom and Dad's son Steve works for The Walt Disney Company. His employer is as much pro-rodent as any corporation could possibly be (please notice the respect I have shown—to Steve, not to Disney—as the term "pro-vermin" would have been apropos). I don't like Disney showing off *Mickey*, *Minnie*, and *Ratatouille* as models of the animal kingdom, while the cats in Disney movies are at best depicted as mischievous, if not downright villains, e.g. *Lucifer* who was hostile to Cinderella, and the *Cheshire Cat* who acted as a bully in Alice and Wonderland.

While on the topic of anthropomorphism, i.e. attributing humanlike characteristics to animals, the growing number of humans around the world who are part of the so-called "Furries" subculture deserve honorable mention. Since I had a natural fur coat, I would not have been eligible to join their ranks, but that didn't stop me from becoming part of their fanbase. I think it's great that Furries want to look and act like animals while walking around like the humans they are on two legs and wearing an animal suit. To me, the best part is that Furries even attempt to think like the animal they are mimicking to better understand its behavior. The fact that the number of websites and conventions for Furries are increasing is a clear indication that the Furries membership is on the rise. Those Furries that take on the personalities of dogs or cats could possibly give me some tips to broaden my literary horizon.

Anyone unfamiliar with Furries should not be quick to condemn or criticize them, but rather try to think of them in the same way they might view other people who are openly overzealous football addicts. Furries are in workplaces, schools, and living in neighborhoods everywhere. I doubt that Mom knows about the Furries phenomenon, but if she did, she'd likely become intrigued by it, and could be a great candidate for any of three anthropomorphic characters—dog, cat, or dragon. Yes, dragon! Mom was born in the Chinese Zodiac Year of the Dragon, and even though dragons are mythical, I trust that average Furries would accept someone imitating a dragon in their midst. (There's more to come on the Chinese Zodiac in later chapters)

***

Some humans—dog persons in particular—believe that no single cat can claim individuality, but that cannot be further from the truth. We do not look alike. We are all different from the color of our fur and the markings on our coats, to the way we hang our tails, and the length of our whiskers, and most importantly to the degree of our intellect.

Some humans think they know all there is to know about cats. The truth is only a cat can know everything there is to know about cats. Dad accused me of being capricious, something that couldn't be further from the truth since my behavior was constant and predictable 100 *purr*-cent of the time. It's not that he's an authority on cats—he just thinks he is! Acknowledging that there are numerous humans who know volumes about cats, my point is none of them knows all there is to know simply because their race is human, not feline. An old human saying applies perfectly—*It takes one to know one.*

An extensive, scientific research study identified only five reliable personality factors for domesticated cats—neuroticism, extraversion, dominance, impulsiveness, and agreeableness (Chiera, Kikillus, Litchfield, Quinton, Roetman, & Tindle, 2017). I happened to fit all the criteria for extraversion given by Chiera et al.—"smart, curious, inventive." I was also a match for agreeableness—"friendly... well-adjusted and happy, potentially serving as a source of enrichment for other cats" (Chiera et al.). So, I would have scored high on the two best personality factors identified by Chiera et al.

More than 2,800 cat owners responded to the survey used in the study conducted by Chiera et al., and it did not surprise me one bit that the majority were women. Based on my own socialization, I became totally convinced that the individual personalities of the humans in a home have a direct bearing on the behavior of their cat(s). I was most fortunate that the overwhelming majority of humans in my home loved dogs and cats equally. For cats, the difficulty in trying to understand human mentality is tremendous. Everything we do is out in the open. Sometimes, the only privacy available is inside a litter box. We can tell by instinct what is good and what is bad for us. Though I was undeniably a natural feline, since I spent my entire life in the company of decent human beings, I knew about kindness, affection, love, and a whole lot more niceties, all of which made me a better cat.

***

My ancestry can be traced far back to ancient Egyptian catdom —more than 5,000 human years ago! I felt obliged to provide a short history lesson to convey an important explanation regarding my roots of which I was very proud.

It is estimated that dogs may have been first domesticated about 15,000 human years ago—up to 3 times further back in time than cats, although some researchers believe it may have been more like 100,000 years ago. In any case, even though the ancient Egyptians had dogs as companions, they recognized cats as deserving preferential treatment over dogs and all the other domesticated animals at that time, including pigs, sheep, and cattle.

The ancient Egyptians not only loved cats, but also revered them as gods. Laws were established to protect and safeguard cats. Any human found guilty of killing a cat could be sentenced to death by stoning. When Egyptian royalty hunted birds, specially trained cats—not dogs—retrieved the birds. The Egyptian word for cat was *mau* (resembling *meow* in pronunciation), which meant "to see." People in Egypt revered *Bastet*, the goddess with the head of a cat and the body of a human female, who was linked to beauty, elegance, and fertility (National Museum of Natural History (Zax, 2007).

The Egyptians back then even afforded their cats mummification, an honorable postmortem treatment not bestowed upon any other animal, except for mice that were mummified along with a deceased cat to ensure the decedent had food to eat in the afterlife (Zax). My ancestors were embalmed like humans and then mummified as sacred. According to Zax, the underground cemetery in one ancient Egypt city contained nearly 300,000 cat mummies!

I have furnished sufficient facts to make sure there will be no doubt about my hallowed heritage. In that regard, the short history lesson ends right here, right now.

***

I inherited good manners from my Egyptian ancestors. For example, I always discretely retreated to privacy behind the sofa or another piece of furniture when I felt the need to upchuck a hairball. I didn't hack or gag much, and was fairly orderly in ridding my system of those nasty little balls of hair. I'm not proud of producing excessive hairballs. They just happened to be a natural byproduct of and tradeoff for my self-grooming obsession. I allowed Mom to brush my long hair regularly and that helped remove loose hairs, but it wasn't enough since I still inadvertently swallowed small amounts of hair while grooming myself. I licked my body countless times every day and some of the hair I accidentally swallowed got built up in my stomach, and eventually triggered a reflex action, which, in turn, would expel a hairball. Please forgive me for providing too much information regarding such a disgusting topic.

A human—or even a dog for that matter—watching me lick myself annoyed me to no end. It became my biggest pet peeve. Didn't they know I only did it to stay clean? I had a psychological preoccupation of wanting to be immaculate, so I cleaned a lot—I mean a lot! I self-cleaned by licking and licking and licking for an estimated one-third of the total time I was awake my entire life. That is a lot of licks, but it's not excessive when it comes to cat standards. I just made sure I was wellgroomed all the way down to the tip of every whisker. That doesn't mean I had Obsessive Compulsive *Purr*-sonality Disorder (OCPD), which is indicative of abnormal behavior. However, my licking was natural and, therefore, *purr*-fectly normal. It was not compulsive because I not only had full control over when to initiate the tongue-lick, but also when to terminate it.

When is the last time you saw a dog groom itself like cats do? It goes without saying that I was a whole lot cleaner than any dog. I was slobber-free. I did not smell as bad as a dog. At the risk of *paws*-sibly alienating myself, I would add that I believe I kept myself cleaner than some humans—not anyone living in my house, but one—make that two— who had come to visit there (*wink wink*).

In line with my efforts to keep myself as clean as *paws*-sible, I despised a dirty litter box. If no one scooped waste out of my box once a day, I would do my best to avoid eliminating there. I didn't expect to have the litter changed every day, but since I regularly pooped once a day, I wanted the poop particles removed on a daily basis. Regarding the frequency of having the old litter replaced with new, I considered once *purr* week to be reasonable, as long as the poop pieces were removed daily. Mom met all my expectations for the litter box, so I never went to potty anywhere else. I acknowledge that even though I was outnumbered 3-to-1 by canines for a long time, Mom bought more pounds of cat litter than dog food. That does not mean I emptied my bowels more than the average feline—proper perspective please!

No one ever tried to train me to use a toilet to relieve myself, but I learned to do it on my own. Once, after a moving company had packed my litter box and I had to poop, instead of making a mess on the floor, I went into a bathroom at home, climbed up on the commode seat, and took a dump. Mom saw me in the act and could not believe I had used the toilet like a human. C'mon—by then, I had been around Mom and her biological kids for more than a decade, and so much had rubbed off that I considered myself more human than feline. Granted, my little butt dangling over the edge of the toilet seat must have been a sight to behold, but in an amazing, not revolting, way. And no, I didn't flush!

My eating etiquette was unrivaled by any dog—or any cat as far as that goes. I never drooled. I always ate quietly. No one ever found leftovers in my food dish. I didn't spill any food so there were never crumbs on the floor by my dish. My display of good manners marveled Mom as she is a real stickler when it comes to etiquette.

Another example was the great care I took while weaving around human legs. I did everything I could to make sure I did not cause someone to trip. It was very easy to make them fall down, but I avoided it at all costs. Dad was the only one I ever tripped and that occurred just 6 times in 17 years. Please be assured it was purely accidental and only happened because he is such a slow-moving klutz (*wink wink*). As the saying goes—*Karma is a lady and she's a bitch*. And, since Dad and I are karma believers, we both give credence to another very popular adage —*It is what it is.*

***

A lapcat? Not me! By that, I mean I wasn't overly cuddly, with one exception—the depths of the nine long winters I spent in Northern Japan. That's when the howling wind outside sent chills up and down my back prompting me to cuddle in Mom's lap quite a bit in search of comfort and warmth. After leaving Japan and moving to Florida, I was not quick to jump onto Mom or anyone else's lap, and I wasn't fond of someone trying to pick me up, but that does not necessarily mean I wasn't touchy-feely.

Instead of cuddles, my preference was cheek-rubbing. No, not butt cheeks—face cheeks! That's when I would rub my cheeks on Mom or one of the children. I was the initiator of physical contact and that's how I liked it. Any other way was not an option. I marked them as loved ones by rubbing up against their hands or legs with my cheeks, at which time I would release my scent onto them. That was different than me rubbing against furniture or other objects, as, in the case of inanimate objects, I was leaving my scent merely to mark territory.

After cheek rubs, I sometimes enjoyed being petted—with emphasis on sometimes! I liked to be petted, but only on my terms. First of all, the time for petting was up to me and me alone—not only the start time, but the end time too. My threshold for touching maxed out at five minutes. Secondly, not just anyone could pet me. Mom, of course, was my preferred massage therapist, followed by Brenda, Barb, and Steve in that order. There's no inadvertent omission here 'cause it was obvious that good ol' Dad didn't want to pet me, and that was okay because I didn't want him to try. Thirdly, when it came to giving myself up to human touches, belly rubs were the most soothing followed by chin rubs.

When I was in the mood for petting (always after sunset since I didn't begin to wake up until the sun had gone down), I would position myself close to the *purr*-son I had picked for the next session. I'd nudge their leg to get their attention, then just wait until they got the message and began massaging my chin with no effort to pick me up. If I couldn't get their attention in a reasonable amount of time, I'd switch gears by making a sorry face, lower my ears, hold my neck back, and look up at them. There was no need for Plan C because Plan B always worked when Plan A failed.

I limited giving up my chin and belly to those rare occasions when I just couldn't wait any longer and needed to have one or both parts rubbed. I guess you could say I was manipulative, but that wouldn't have been a bad thing since the end-result was positive on both sides—*mew*-tual endearment between my humans and me.

I liked to head-butt Mom and the children. It's called bunting—no, not like in baseball! Bunting is nose-to-nose and that's how cats kiss. It was another way for me to show affection and, at the same time, release my scent onto them. Here's a photo of my favorite nonfurry kid Brenda and I engaging in bunting.

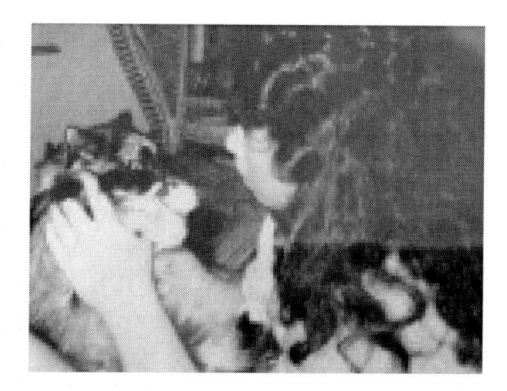

I didn't use my vocal cords to communicate with Mom. Instead, I silently sent her messages via my eyes. I couldn't verbally convey words to let her know how I felt, but when she looked into my eyes, she could readily tell if I was happy, sad, content, uneasy, hungry, or whatever. Dad accused me of having a "staring problem," but he's a dog person so what does he know? That was the main way I could transmit my feelings to Mom, and it worked quite well. For example, if I wanted to show affection, I would merely look at her for a few seconds (not stare, as there is a difference despite what Dad thinks). I'd slowly blink my eyes, and when Mom noticed me doing it, she would wink at me. I'd blink and she'd wink. We mostly did it in slow motion. For me, head-butt bunting was to kissing as blinking was to blowing a kiss.

I tried blinking with the children too, but only Barb and Brenda caught on. Steve wouldn't wink—he just gave me a smile—no wink, only a grin. He showed me affection in another way by giving the very best chin rubs imaginable. Those saturating interactions I had with Mom and the children can be attributed to each of us releasing the love oxytocin through eye-to-eye gazing. I felt love from Mom and the kids through the oxytocin they released to me and, in turn, that stimulated me to release oxytocin back to them.

Oxytocin is more complex and not as well-known as other hormones. When compared to adrenaline that provides an energy boost, oxytocin provides a bonding boost. Since the main focus of these writings is on deep bonding between humans and pets, the results of some scientific studies about the effects of oxytocin on humans and pets that are addressed in later chapters should be informative and interesting.

I consider the physical contact between Steve and me to be extra special because he is allergic to cat dander. His allergies were at their worst when he was a teenager, and that's when I first joined the family. Some humans believe cat fur causes allergies; however, that is not the case, as a protein in our saliva actually spawns it. When we self-groom by licking ourselves, the protein in the saliva combines with the same protein already in glands under our skin. The protein then rubs off as dander onto furniture and carpets, after which it can be passed on to humans.

Not all humans are aware that dander not only comes from cats, but also from dogs and birds, and it is similar to dandruff from head hair. There's also a saying—to get *one's dander up*—meaning something makes one angry. Presenting myself as a know-it-all is not my intent. I just felt compelled to make sure the important topic of dander is sufficiently addressed so it is not misunderstood.

My preference was more petting time and less playing time; however, playtime now and then made for welcomed stress relief. As was the case with petting, I preferred to initiate playing. I would spontaneously commence play in many ways—pouncing on someone's leg as they walked by, trying to grab a piece of string or thread that someone was holding, or chasing light streaks emitting from the sun shining through the skylights in the roof above our living room.

My point is I trained Mom and the kids to respond to my desires for rubbing, bunting, blinking, and playing. They responded every single time that I made known to them exactly what I wanted. I took the lead by training and conditioning them and got them to react accordingly—unlike the dogs who were basically trainees. Dad did not realize what I was doing, and that's too bad because he may have given me a little credit had he caught on.

Proficiency in giving massages was also among my many talents. It started one day at home while I was the only pet in the Herron household. I was just two years old, and it was a few months before Butch—my first furry housemate—came along. I was lying on the sofa in the living room, and Mom was sitting on the floor directly in front of me. Instinctively, I tapped her right shoulder with my right front paw, not once but repeatedly. She was taken aback, but seemed to welcome the liberties I was taking, so I sat up and used both front paws to massage both shoulders. Since I was declawed, it didn't hurt her. She grew to like it, so every chance I got upon observing her sitting or lying on the floor, I positioned myself behind and massaged her shoulders and back.

Mom especially liked my massages while she was lying down. I would stand on all fours on top of her back and massage her with both front paws. I loved this because it provided a means for me to show her how much she meant to me. It was a form of therapy for both of us. I became skilled at it upon discovering that the harder I patted, the more she seemed to enjoy it. When I began pushing harder with both paws, it apparently helped to relieve the arthritic pain she was experiencing. She wasn't the only recipient of my massaging as I occasionally did it to Barb and Brenda, and even Steve a few times as shown below.

My massages were not kneading—they were legitimate. Kneading is common among cats. It's when we lift our front paws up and down, one right after the other repeatedly, almost as if we're marching in place with eyes down on the spot where our front paws are touching. I did a lot of kneading, but not on Mom. I usually did it while standing on top of Mom and Dad's bed and kneaded Mom's blanket with my paws. It was just an instinctive way to relax myself—kind of like what a yoga workout does for humans.

***

I never bit anyone, but I did come close a few times upon becoming irritated. It only happened when Dad initiated rough play with me, something he did at least a dozen times. I hated the roughhouse style. To signal I did not want to engage in such play, I would raise and sharply retract my head, and then flick my tail briskly from side to side. Since Dad always refused to back off, he would end up on the receiving end of one of my infamous *hissy fits*. That's when I'd hunch my back and let out the sharpest sibilant sound I could muster while making myself as wide-eyed as I could get, and then some! That made him back-off and leave me alone.

Dad was the one and only human I ever targeted with those fits just because he was the only one that ever attempted to engage me in rough play. He mistakenly thought cats enjoy roughhousing as much as dogs, and that was one more reason for him to like me less. To him, I was a misunderstood creature.

There's a need for me to back-pedal here, as upon inserting the word *creature*, I suddenly realized that it was too close to another word—*critter*—that in no way fits me. I did not delete the word in order to make an important point—*creature* not only sounds more animal than human, it may also be interpreted as something from outer space. So, when referring to myself, since I believed I was philosophically aligned more with the human race than the feline race, my preference became *living being* instead of anything along the line of *creature* or *critter*.

Based on the tons of fun I had with Barb, Steve, and Brenda, I cannot understand why cats have gotten a bum rap for not doing well around kids. While playing with them, I didn't (couldn't) show my pleasure as openly as my canine mates did (could). Regardless, I had fun with them, and I'm sure they would all say they enjoyed their playtimes with me.

I would never refer to small children as vermin the way Dad and other humans sometimes do by jokingly using such a vulgar term as "rug rat." Maybe I shouldn't take it so seriously, but any reference to rodents, even in jest, is totally appalling to me. How rug rat originated is beyond my comprehension. Why not *rug-cat* or *rug-dog*, any animal other than rat? I think it may have been coined just for alliteration (the letter "r" at the beginning of both words—like Peter Piper picked a peck of pickled peppers). Whatever, likening a child to a disgusting rodent, even if whoever originally came up with it had a pet rat in mind, is a real slap in the face to kids everywhere.

***

I previously mentioned I'd get back to the relationship between Dad and me, so here's an example. Upon hearing me meow on one occasion when guests were in the home, Dad asked a visitor a dumb question—"What part of speech do you think meow is?"

When the guy shrugged his shoulders to indicate he didn't know the answer, Dad jumped out of his chair and stood up as if he had just remembered something important. "It's gotta be an interjection," he declared.

With all due respect, I think Dad's an interjection! According to the dictionary definition, the meaning of the noun meow is *the cry of a cat*. The word itself is an onomatopoeia with several human variations, including *miaow*, *myow*, and *mau*. To set the record straight, the pro-*purr* human pronunciation is the British variant miaow, so that is the way it will appear henceforth.

I miaowed for a number of reasons, but mostly when I wanted something, like feeding or petting. At an early age, I learned that miaowing inspired a favorable reaction from humans, so I did not hesitate to utter a few miaows from time to time to get what I wanted precisely when I wanted it. I usually reserved it for the times when I anticipated contentment. And I did not hesitate resorting to a soft *mew*—like a kitten in place of my grownup *miaow*—to get something I wanted very much.

Under certain stressful conditions, the sounds I uttered probably sounded more like wails than miaows. I did that for a day or two every time a new dog was added to our household. Since the dog was a stranger and I had no way of knowing if it may pose a threat, I was just trying to let Mom and Dad know that I was concerned.

My miaowing rate definitely peaked when I got off an airplane after flying from Japan back to the United States. Barb accused me of sounding more like a goat than a cat (imagine that). Separation anxiety had set in, plus being jammed inside a tiny pet carrier for 24 hours didn't make the ride any easier. Since I was nearly nine years older upon my return to the States than I was when I left to go to Japan, the trip back was much more nerve-racking. The sedation Mom gave me helped, but it was good for only 12 hours and our travel time was nearly double that due to a required early check-in and the need for a connecting flight.

Some airlines *purr*-mitted cats to travel in the passenger compartment, but none of the ones I flew on. The tem-*purr*-ature variation and assorted commotion in the baggage compartment of an aircraft's belly stretched my stress meter to the max. Being tossed around with the suitcases while changing from one aircraft to another made it an extra rough trip, but I survived and somehow made it in one piece.

Miaowing is intended for human ears, so I never miaowed at another cat. However, I didn't hold back on hissing at a cat I didn't know to show suspicion and express a genuine willingness to engage in a territorial fight if provoked. I had to hiss at other cats on a dozen or so occasions, each time upon spotting one trespassing on top of the fence in our backyard. It was my way of warning the intruder to retreat or suffer the consequences. It worked every time, so I never got the chance to find out if I could kick feline butt. That was a letdown, but I self-consoled with the realization that my hissing had made every single one of those cats back off in fear.

Like all domestic felids, besides miaowing, I vocalized by purring. My purring frequency range was exceptionally wide. I could slow down to 25 and speed up to 150 vibrations *purr* second, and at 150, my whole body vibrated. I made buzzing sounds loud enough to be heard by everyone in a large room. As a matter of fact, my purrs were many decibels louder than the average cat. Oh, what an esteemed purring machine was I!

When I purred, I was happy and content, and everything was right in the world. Mom became fully aware of this and made sure the children knew it too. She realized my purring had a calming effect not only on me, but on everyone around me. There's an old saying that goes, *It is for her own good that the cat purrs*. Nothing could be closer to the truth. Purring and miaowing were the two cat things I could effectively use to orally communicate with everyone in the family—even Dad. I only changed my purrs at mealtime when I added a slight whimper to signal Mom I was hungry.

***

I was declawed at a young age; however, that did not stop me from scratching things. I did not have a scratching post, so I'd substitute pieces of furniture, the carpet, or drapes. No one cared where I scratched since my declawed paws wouldn't do any damage. I couldn't help myself and had to scratch a lot. It was the way for me to refocus my energy.

When I stretched out and scratched as fast as I could, Butch looked at me as if I was crazy. When I stopped, I'd bop her on the nose with one of my dull claws to let her know I didn't appreciate the impolite staring. Even though I bopped her at least

5,045 times (once per day during the 13 years, 10 months, and 12 days we lived under the same roof), Butch responded every time by giving me her unforgettable dumb dog-look because she could not begin to comprehend why I had bopped her. She never figured it out.

Take away my excess cranial gray matter and I was no different than any other cat. My leisurely daytime activities did not make me tired enough to sleep at night. I was innately nocturnal and the nighttime was reserved for me. While everyone else was asleep, I would walk around the house. My paws made no noise even when I broke into a trot, so it was as if I could walk on air. Conversely, I spent most of the daylight hours snoozing—*catnapping* if you will. In all, I probably averaged a whopping 16 hours of sleep per day.

Quite often, while I nimbly treaded around the house at night, I heard many horrific catfights outside. There was always at least one colony of feral cats and usually a few strays in our neighborhood. The screaming and yowling were frightening. Sometimes, I wasn't sure if what I heard was the sounds of two cats fighting, or if a single cat might have gotten into a knock-down, drag-out altercation with a raccoon or some other wild animal. I was thankful to be domesticated and have a roof over my head, unlike the homeless cats that had to be constantly alert and ready to fight rivals in the wild, all the while marking their turf, and searching for something to eat just to survive.

Mom agonized over stray cats. Feral cats were one thing since they were born homeless, but not so for the strays. How any human could arbitrarily abandon a cat that had been living with them in their home is incomprehensible to Mom. The life expectancy of a stray is quite short because they do not know how to hunt, and they are unable to successfully defend themselves on the street or out in the wild. There was an apartment complex near our house, and it wasn't uncommon for someone moving out of an apartment to leave their cat behind because pets were not permitted at their next apartment, or some other inexcusable reason. Mom loathed these people for what they are—heartless, despicable nonfurry beings who do not deserve to breathe the same air as furry beings! (Second thoughts precluded the use of profanity here)

Although stray cats could always be seen hanging around our neighborhood, there were hardly any stray dogs—a clear indication that more people had been dumping cats than dogs. It seemed as if conditions had changed over time, as county government workers known as *dogcatchers* were around many years ago rounding up stray dogs. The term *dogcatcher* became obsolete in recent years and was replaced with *animal control officer*, whose job it is to not only catch stray dogs, but also stray cats and other animals. This change in terminology may indicate the number of stray dogs has declined while the number of stray cats has been on the rise.

My guess is that the title *dogcatcher* was created because stray dogs would have been more dangerous and threatening to human society than stray cats, plus cats tend to make themselves elusive and less visible in public than dogs. Hey cat people, be grateful you never had to put up with such a despicable word as *catcatcher*. Conversely, be repulsed knowing an endless number of homeless cats are wandering around out there in your neighborhoods at any given time.

***

A mouser? Not me as I never caught a mouse. Oh my, that was incredibly hard for me to admit. I am making this revelation because there is no point in trying to keep it a secret any longer. I decided the time was right for me to let the proverbial *cat out of the bag*.

Humans classify cats as carnivores, but there is always an exception to a rule. This cat can honestly state that I never ate a mouse, or rat, or any other kind of rodent, and that would

THE DOGS' BEST FRIEND: A CAT'S EYE VIEW

seem to make me a non-carnivore. However, I ate tuna, chicken, turkey, and lamb from a can. I often wondered why no one has yet produced mouse meat in a can since rodents are generally recognized as cats' favorite food. Don't get me wrong—I never wanted to eat mouse out of a can, and am *fur*-ever grateful that mouse meat has not made it into the marketplace. It will surely get my dander up should someone file an application to obtain a patent for canned mouse meat and it ends up on grocery store shelves in the cat food section.

For a long time in the days of my youth, catching a mouse was high up my on my *To Do List*. I quickly outgrew that notion however, and never delivered a headless rodent to Mom and the children like Tommy used to do. It's a given that female cats are generally better mousers than the males, but even though I was a female, I just wasn't sadistic by nature, so my mousing skills left a lot to be desired. The thought of *paws*-sibly ingesting parasites from eating a rodent sickened me. I did not consider myself an anomaly since it wasn't that I could not catch a mouse, rather that I merely chose not to give it a try.

Back around the time of my birth, the IBM Company came out with a video maze game called *Mouser*. It was similar to *Pac Man*, but never came close to gaining Pac Man popularity. The object of the Mouser game was to help a farmer get rid of mice by moving around the walls of a maze in an attempt to corner the mice and enable the farmer's cat to catch them. The cat in that game was called *Mouser* even though it did not actually "catch" any mice. I can certainly empathize with that cat. As a matter of fact, I would have been a great choice to play that role!

There's an old German proverb that applies to me—*The cat that frightens the mice away is as good as the cat that eats them*. I relentlessly miaowed loudly upon detecting a rodent nearby, and even though I never caught a single one, my vocal presence alone undoubtedly deterred all of them that came close to our house. I could sense a rodent a mile away, and they all fled a lot further than that upon hearing my defensive miaowing change to war-cry hissing. There was no way any of them could ever get close enough to stumble into my food dish (maybe the only way I could have caught one).

> Felineology 101: A domestic cat's sense of smell is much stronger than that of people—approximately 14 times stronger. This is because cats not only have twice as many smell receptors inside their nasal area as humans, but they also have a scent organ in the roof of their mouths that humans don't have. (Raiyan, 2017).

A cat's acute sense of hearing enables us to detect the presence of a mouse before we see it. My hearing that was as keen as—maybe even keener than—any other cat, and at least three times better than any dog, never once detected a rodent inside our house. I did hear countless mice and an occasional rat outside our house, and because they all knew I was inside, not one of them dared making an attempt to enter.

> Felineology 102: A cat can hear sounds from 45 to 60,000 hertz, as opposed to a human who can hear from 20 to 20,000 hertz. Dogs can out-smell cats, but a dog's sense of hearing, although much better than a human, doesn't come close to a cat's great hearing capability. (McCready, 2017).

Enough regarding my sense of hearing, and I will not elaborate any further about disgusting rodents. I just want to emphasize that although there were no vermin on my kill list, I did possess the killer instinct as evidenced by my significant number of lizard kills. The enclosed patio at the rear of our home in Florida was lizard-hunting heaven. Hunting small reptiles is only less bodacious than hunting rodents by the lesser degree of danger—a cornered rat will bite, but a lizard has no teeth. I wonder if Dad would have liked me more if I had hunted rodents instead of lizards, but that is something I'll never know.

Lizards are actually formidable prey because of their swiftness. Be mindful of the fact that they are merely quick and not lightning fast like me. If I must say so myself, my swishing tail would have been something to behold when I squatted down in position to pounce on one of those little reptiles. I never missed!

Upon making a catch, I always followed the same ritual. I would pat the little beast lightly on its soft head with the bottom of my right, front paw. It pleased me to see the expression on the tiny face that my love tap had caused—the look of simultaneously being frightened and puzzled. When I jumped around behind him, he was too scared to move and couldn't even show the long tongue he used to catch prey of his own. He would cock his head to one side in an attempt to see me. I'll spare the gory details about what happened next. Permit me to just say it wasn't pretty. A lizard's nightmare was I!

A zest for lizards was my ultimate hunting experience. However, I also scored a significant number of grasshopper and cricket catches, along with an occasional cicada. There is nothing in the world more pleasant than eating something delicious that one has never eaten before. I passed on cicadas until I was middle-aged and then, after discovering they were scrumptious, I kicked myself in the rear for all the years I had missed by not consuming them (*um-um good*). Their singing made it easy to zero-in on their location. There are two drawbacks that severely limit the time period cicadas make themselves available to predators like me—their lifespan is extremely short, and they only come out in the open at one certain time every year.

***

Playing with a ball of yarn was a relaxing activity for me. I got to do it a lot since Mom loves crocheting. She could count on me to interrupt her knitting projects, but it never upset her. She'd always dangle a piece of yarn for me to catch and appeared to enjoy this playtime activity as much as I did.

One day, I found a short piece of fishing line on the kitchen floor and had fun playing with it like I did with the yarn, that is until Dad tried to be funny by grabbing it away shouting, "Hey, cat-nut that's my catgut!" As always, his attempt at humor was nowhere close to being funny.

Seriously, terminology like *catgut* adds to the bum rap for cats. Why is it called catgut? Why not sheep-gut? Or horse-gut? After all, it's made of the dried, twisted intestines of sheep and horses, not cats. Woe is me! And, one living being (Dad) insulting another living being (me) in a joking manner was downright unacceptable. Woe to me once more!

Pouncing on carpet interlopers—or I should say trying to pounce on them—was another source of enjoyment for me. They are not visible to the naked human eye, so people would laugh when they saw me leap in an attempt to catch one. I was good at sensing the presence of an interloper, and wanted very much to nab one to prove they do, in fact, exist. However, I have to admit that their lightning speed was too much for me to match and I was never able to grab one. Chasing them and always coming up empty-handed was a constant source of frustration, and that was compounded by my inability to provide evidence of their existence to humans.

I couldn't blame people for thinking I was crazy by running around, often in circles, trying to pounce on something they could not see. The reality is I was able to stop an invasion of interlopers by chasing every one of them away, just as I did with all the rodents that had visions of coming into our house. A layperson may not figure out why I seemingly acted quirky at times, but a cat behavioral expert would fully understand my unorthodox ways.

Mischievous? Not me! I did eat the leaves of potted plants. And, I climbed up the branches of live Christmas trees, but that is about the extent of my mischief. Oh yeah, I almost forgot about peeing on Mom's house plant one time. That was certainly out of character for me and, to this day, I cannot provide a reasonable explanation as to why I did it. It's the type of behavior expected of dogs, not cats. That incident was a constant source of embarrassment to me. It didn't matter that no one saw me do it. And it doesn't matter that no one else remembers it. I did it; I know I did it; I am sorry I did it; I never did it again; and I still regret doing it.

***

I could be described as serene and playful, but as far as sociability goes, I was more often than not content to be left alone. In short, I was self-contained and felt most comfortable when by myself. I habitually went to hide in the den to recharge my morale, or if I just needed a break when the children became rowdy.

The kids didn't get boisterous very often, but when they did so in my presence, I felt intimidated. It wasn't so much the activity they were involved in that bothered me, but rather the loud noises that their combined voices generated. Even though the intense volume was not directed at me, the back and forth shouting, with occasional yelling by the three young audiophiles, scared the bejesus out of me. I tried miaowing my discontent at them when they got loud. I really did try, but no miaow would emerge. Second and third tries only produced soft *mewing*—not anything close to miaowing. And yes, the kids may have been wondering, "*Cat got your tongue?*" Here we go again with another preposterous idiom that insults the feline race by implying that a cat has taken control of someone's tongue. Really!

"Conceited" was one of the descriptive words that Dad and some of his cronies expressed when referring to cats, in general, and me, in particular. They also used "anti-social" quite a bit, and an unflattering, profusion of words was common including, "spitefully looks down on humans" and "dumber than dogs." If only they could have gotten to know me like Mom and the children did, they may have said I was a special kind of feline worth getting to know, which was totally unlike what Dad and some other humans had been led to believe.

I knew Dad and other dog persons looked down on me by stereotyping. I became accustomed to their rudeness by telling myself, *My nature is what it is and I can't change it.* Dad was quick to notice that one of the ways I showed affection to Mom and the kids was by approaching them with my tail straight up in the air slightly twitching. He must have caught on after repeatedly seeing my tail in the down position with no twitch whatsoever when he came close to me.

A social butterfly? Not me. My preference was a calm environment. Solitary by nature was I. Due to my shyness, I found pleasure in doing things alone. Most intellectuals fit in this category. I was still highly companionable, not only with nearly all the humans in our house, but also with all my canine housemates too. I never fetched a ball or caught a frisbee like a dog, so no one could label me a *copy-cat*. Me stooping so low to copy the actions of dogs would never happen. The dogs copied each other, but not once did any of them copy me—too bad as they surely would have benefitted by imitating my style.

Because I was not trained to do the things that dogs can do, Dad was inclined to think of me as less intelligent and not as social as the dogs. No wiser words were ever uttered than that by a leading animal behaviorist in the United Kingdom, Dr. John Bradshaw, who declared, "Cats suffer from stress because their owners expect them to behave like dogs" (Singh, 2014). If only the Russian scientist and Nobel Peace Prize winner Ivan Pavlov had used cats instead of dogs in his early 20th century experiments to develop the renowned conditional reflex theory, feline socialization and interaction with humans could have been entirely different.

I often wondered why Pavlov chose dogs instead of cats or other animals. In his experiments, he taught dogs to associate a certain sound with the presence of food. I heard one idea that seemed as if it might have merit—Pavlov picked dogs to complement the food used in his experiments because they do not merely drool, but rather salivate to extremes at the mere thought of food. Since such disgusting behavior was obviously acceptable in Pavlov's studies, if cats had been considered, they may have been later disqualified for being too sophisticated.

I would be remiss for not mentioning that dogs can self-train. I noticed this a lot with Butch, who worked herself into a frenzy at the sound of Dad jingling car keys in his pocket because it generated the expectation of going on a car ride. Not long after Chiro joined Butch and me in the Herron home, she began lowering her head in anticipation of heading outdoors for a walk as soon as Mom or Dad picked up her leash. The list goes on and on. Reverse self-training by the dogs was in response to training that had been initiated by Mom, Dad, and the kids.

By doing certain things, dogs actually train their humans to react. For example, Dad jingled the car keys on purpose to solicit Butch's response and, in turn, her frenzied reaction made him grin every time. Mom and Dad could not help but chuckle when Chiro lowered her head and glanced up at them smiling while waiting for the leash. So, it was a two-way learning street. And yes, dogs really do smile! Chiro smiled more than my other canine housemates. The others each had their own version of smiling, but the way they did it was slight and nowhere near the beaming face that Chiro showed.

***

The family brought one dog into my life (Butch), then a second and a third (Chiro and her sister Peko). Those canines and I were able to coexist without serious incident making us exceptions to the dog and cat natural enemy theory. We had a few skirmishes, but all minor in nature with no bloodletting. My life span of nearly 17 human years was longer than any of my canine housemates, hence I spent more time around humans than them. The dogs interacted a lot among themselves, and since I was left out, I had lots of time on my paws, and that was a blessing since it enabled me to take note of what was happening around me in explicit detail.

As opposed to the dogs who were totally dependent on human support, I was basically self-sustaining. If the family wanted to go away overnight or for a weekend, I could take care of myself as long as they left food and water. The dogs, on the other hand, were not accustomed to using a litter box and needed human assistance several times a day. The only time I needed help was for a 6-day period when Mom, Dad, Steve, and Brenda went to Japan to attend Barb's wedding. During that time, our good friends Taeko and Atsushi, who had a dog and cat of their own, graciously came to our house 2-3 times a day to feed, water, and play with Butch, Peko, Chiro, and me.

My independence led to me being misunderstood by Dad. Cats give space to humans by sensing when they need it; however, some humans, like Dad, mistakenly interpret this to represent antisocial behavior. Conversely, dogs don't give space, they take it! And, that's okay since it's their nature, as long as they do it in a non-hostile manner.

I was never at a loss for something to say, and neither were the dogs, albeit we expressed ourselves differently. The dogs would bark, howl, growl, or whine; I would miaow, purr, hiss, or yowl. All of us quickly learned to communicate with humans by adjusting the sound of our barks and miaows, the tone of our howls and purrs, the intensity of our growls and hisses, and the pitch of our whines and yowls. Unlike Butch (the only non-Akita canine in the house), none of the Akitas barked very much, but they would often mumble and grumble. It was their way of *talking* to each other and to the humans in our house.

It may seem complicated but, honestly, pidgin language worked quite well for us furry kids and our human companions since we did not have a specific language in common. Mom would miaow and purr at me and Dad would bark and howl at the dogs, and even though there was no *talk* per se, those cat and dog-like vocalizations were effective ways of communicating. The dogs and I enjoyed this type of positive interaction as much as Mom and Dad did. Mom's miaow was cute and mimicked mine perfectly; however, Dad's barks were ludicrous as they sounded more Poodlese than the Spitzese that came out of the mouths of all my canine housemates.

For the record, since I spent a number of years in Japan and three of my canine housemates were born over there, the Japanese people say *wan-wan* instead of *woof-woof* for dog barks, and they say *nya-nya* in place of *miaow-miaow* for cats. Mom preferred the English onomatopoeic expressions woof-woof and miaow-miaow, but she often made it known to Dad and the children that she wished the dogs and I could speak—I mean literally *speak* as in people-talk. She was quick to bring this up every time one of us appeared to be feeling under the weather, or got hurt, or was diagnosed with an illness or disease. Not being able to hear directly from us when, what, and where it hurt caused her emotional pain.

Butch and I had recurring ear infections—her condition was chronic while mine were due to ear mites. After I was diagnosed by a veterinarian who said something like, "The inside of her ear is raw and bright red," and then allowed Mom to look into the ear canal to see for herself, Mom felt bad each time. She would always tearfully say something like, "Oh my Chibi, it must hurt so bad. I wish you could tell me when it hurts so I can help you." My wishes to have a human voice matched Mom's wishes for me to not be voiceless. If only I could have been able to speak English or Japanese, I would have provided her more than just nonverbal emotional support.

JIM HERRON

***

Brenda was in middle school when she began reading children's storybooks to me not long after I was adopted. She read to me several times. I sat attentively within paw reach of her, but didn't comprehend anything she was saying. Regardless, not only did that give Brenda and me the chance to bond, but it also got me interested in learning English at a very young age, and the rest is history. She later read to Butch as a means to tighten the bond between them.

From early childhood, mainly through repetition, humans learn their native language. Having spent 9½ years of my life in Japan and 7¼ years in the United States, my dual citizenship enabled me to become familiar with the vast difficulties associated with learning the native tongues of both homelands. We cats have our own ways of communicating—some are verbal, some nonverbal; however, they are not nearly as complex as the multitude of communication methods used by humans.

Should someone, who may be seeking to catch me in an inconsistency, inquire if I comprehended everything I heard spoken by humans in American English and Japanese, and also vocalized by my canine housemates in dogese, if I were able to speak, my unwavering reply would be, *How else do you think I could purr-form the necessary research to put this narrative together*? Despite the two vernaculars—American English and Japanese speech on the human side, and peculiarities (for lack of a better word) on the dogese side—I was able to stay focused and finish this—my first storytelling project—with more satisfying results than I anticipated going in.

The Southwestern Pennsylvania dialect—known as Pittsburghese—was particularly difficult for an Ohio native like me. Since Dad was born and raised in that part of the world, he took Mom and the children to that area umpteen times to visit relatives. In that locale, the inhabitants say *yinz* for the plural you, *crick* for creek, and *serp* for syrup, among many other twisted nouns and pronouns. And, they are notorious for substituting their own words for standard English, such as *pop* for a soda soft drink, *icebox* for refrigerator, and *gum band* for *rubber band*, among many others.

The small town of Bentleyville, where Dad's parents settled while Dad and his 6 siblings were still together, is part of a region dubbed "Mon Valley," short for Monongahela River Valley (the Monongahela River flows from West Virginia northward through Southwest Pennsylvania into Pittsburgh). The drawl of the Mon Valley residents varies slightly—albeit noticeably—from basic Pittsburghese. The best example is them stretching *yinz* into *yew-unz*. Something heard a lot during football season is, "Are yew-unz goin' to watch da Stillers game? [*Are you guys going to watch the Steelers game?*]" (The Pittsburgh Steelers are a professional team in the National Football League). "Annem" is common for "and them" meaning someone's family—for example, "Rich anem are comin" [*Rich and them (his family) are coming*].

It took a while for an outsider like me to become familiar with the Mon Valley manner of speech and the accent associated with it. I heard it spoken so much by so many different humans that it eventually sunk in. I feel I have more than adequately addressed this odd dialect to which I was subjected. Here's the bottom line: I became fluent in Mon Valley Pittsburghese, so there is no need to wonder if I may have misinterpreted something that was said in that lingo.

Furthermore, since I spent more than half my life in Japan with a Japanese Mom, my Japanese-to-English and English-to-Japanese translating abilities are equal, if not superior, to my skills in translating Mon Valley Pittsburghese. That is saying a mouthful, as besides regular talk, the Japanese language is loaded with what are known as *Engrish* and *Japlish*—recreations of English words—a topic far too complicated to explain here.

These anomalous speech mannerisms in Japanese are comparable to the Mon Valley Pittsburghese version of American English, making both languages equally difficult to master, but not impossible, for a non-native speaker like me.

Culturally speaking, in view of my Japan connection, I was proud to have been likened to what the Japanese call Maneki-Neko [*Beckoning Cat*]. The Maneki Neko is a popular ceramic sculpture believed to bring good luck to business owners in Japan. Traditionally, it's a calico cat like me positioned near the entrance of a business—standing up on its hind legs with one paw raised in a hello gesture—to welcome customers. It is widely displayed in front of or just inside the door of shops, restaurants, and other commercial establishments. The Japanese choice of a cat to symbolize prosperity—instead of a dog or other animal—was, without question, a wise decision.

Among the many idioms and proverbs with canine and feline references included herein, one proverb, in particular, is consummately offensive—*There is more than one way to skin a cat*. I know humans do not mean this literally, and it is just their way of saying there are different ways of achieving the same results. It still sends a chill down my spine every time I hear it. If you were to visualize how horrendous the removal of skin from a cat must be, you'd understand why it makes me shudder. The fact that there are far more unfavorable sayings about cats than dogs not only in English, but also in other languages—Egyptian excluded—is no surprise, but that doesn't make it any less disturbing.

***

I spent the first year of my life in Central Ohio. In May 1986, just two days after my first birthday, Dad went back to work for the Air Force as a civilian, and the family and I accompanied him on a road trip. In actuality, it was a major journey—all the way from Ohio to Japan!

Upon our arrival in the Land of the Rising Sun, Dad's police connections enabled him to get me through inspection at Tokyo's Narita Airport without the required quarantine. Later that first day, we were on a U.S. Air Force base and Mom sneaked me into billeting—military jargon for hotel—where pets were prohibited. To succeed in both endeavors, I had to remain quietly hidden in a shoulder bag that Mom carried past a multitude of humans whose job it was to catch us. Since I was precocious in my young age and able to go with the flow, it all went smoothly without a hitch.

After we went to Japan, Mom and Dad heard from their ex-neighbor Ginny only once a year—a card at Christmas time. She wrote a note in the first two cards letting them know Tommy was okay. They all wished they had not gotten the 3rd-year card, as Ginny disclosed she hadn't seen him for six months. Regrettably, she would not see him again and never had a clue regarding his fate. Just as mysteriously as that majestic tomcat had first appeared on that Central Ohio ridge six years earlier, he disappeared there without a trace. To this day, Mom and the children often wonder what happened to him. They can only presume the worst-case scenario. (As an enticement to keep you reading on, more information about Tommy's status will surface in a later chapter of this book where it was deemed both appropriate and timely)

More than one-half of my life was spent in the cold and snowy climate of Northern Japan, where my natural fur coat kept me warm. Butch liked playing in the snow, but not me as I was perfectly content staying inside. The only times I went outside were for once-a-year checkups at the veterinarian's office. No big deal as Mom carried me so I didn't have to walk in the snow. I only stepped on snow once and it was so cold to my sensitive paws that I never wanted to do it again.

Not going outdoors in Japan wasn't really a drawback because

I was perfectly content to stay indoors. And I earned my keep because although Japan wasn't overrun by rodents, they were pretty much everywhere. My presence scared away mice and rats every place I lived, but there's no doubt I deterred at least 10 times as many in Japan as anywhere else.

***

Upon leaving Japan, we moved to Orlando, Florida, and that's where I spent my last 6+ human years on Earth. I had to incisively adapt by wearing my fur in the hot and humid *Dog Days* of Florida summers. Fortunately, central air conditioning was a lifesaver so I did not have to swelter in those could-be unbearable summers. Unlike Japan, I got to go outside and spent a lot of time in the back patio of our home in Orlando. That's where I was able to indulge in my favorite sport—lizard hunting—to my heart's content, and it turned out to be the last place where I lived.

Near the end of my time on Planet Earth—sometime during my last 30 days—Dad mentioned to Mom that he had seen me wandering around as if I was lost, implying I might have Alzheimer's disease. I would not have admitted it back then, but now I have to say that Dad may have gotten it right. I won't go into great detail, but looking back, I did show some symptoms of senility —my acuity of vision and hearing had started to fail, and I began to occasionally catch myself walking into a room and stopping right away while trying to remember why I had gone there.

Rest assured that my memory lapses were brief and temporary and, in no way, adversely affected my ability to accurately compile all the parts necessary to make these writings complete. Suffice it to say that during my last two or three months of earthly life, I experienced what I can best refer to as my fair share of senior moments.

I was very well cared for and proud to say I experienced a total of zero sick days my entire life that ended just three months shy of my 17th B-day. I was not ill at the end. On the day I passed, I was actually feeling pretty good. I was walking around the house in the early evening and felt the urge to pee. I started heading from the living room to my litter box in the den. I made it to the den, but stopped short of the litter box, as all of a sudden, I felt the need to lie down. Lethargy had abruptly made itself known and I became listless.

Mom was alarmed when she found me lying there about 30 minutes later. She immediately called Brenda—my favorite nonfurry kid—who came over and spent precious time with me. I was too weak to even miaow and didn't get back up. I just slowly fell asleep an hour or so after Brenda arrived. There would be no awakening. It was the mother of all catnaps, and turned out to be a fitting way of final departure for someone of my aloofness. There was no pain at all. I could not have scripted it any better.

It wouldn't have mattered if I could speak to tell Brenda and Mom that the end was near, as I did not sense that I was going to die. I learned about death a few months earlier when Butch passed, but I had no warning that it was my turn to go. It happened so quickly, and my instincts did not give me any clue about my impending passing. Brenda and Mom grieved heavily for me. Mom kept telling Brenda and Dad that she should have been able to detect that I was in pain. I wished I could have somehow let her know that I did not experience any pain, but that will have to wait.

Upon detecting that I was no longer breathing, Mom used her fingers to perform CPR to no avail. When Mom realized my spirit was gone from my earthly form, she held my lifeless body in her arms and gently rubbed my chin. She and Brenda dropped a flood of tears on my fur. While weeping, Mom said, "My dear baby Chibi. I am so sorry I couldn't take better care of you. Say hi to Butch for me at the Rainbow Bridge. I love you guys so much." (I outlived Butch by only 6 months—her passing is documented in Chapter Three)

Mom kept on rubbing my chin saying, "Tap Butch with your paw again. I know she won't mind." As the number and size of the teardrops increased, she started running sentences together—"You were such a cute little baby… love your beautiful calico coat… miss your head-butts and playing with my yarn… you gave such good massages…" She ended by saying, "I wish I could hear you buzzing again… I wonder how many lizards you caught," and best of all, "Thank you for keeping the mice away."

***

When I reached the spacious meadow by the Rainbow Bridge, Butch came running up out of nowhere. She literally tackled me! She was so happy that her tears dripped all over my fur. I teared-up big-time too. Oh, my gosh—talk about a tearful reunion! We have not been separated since then. We're just waiting for the time when we'll be reunited with that special someone so we can cross the bridge alongside her. Oh, what a great day that will be!

I furnished this glimpse into the afterlife for one reason: for the most part, both dog people and cat people believe, or want to believe, or at least are familiar with the infamous Rainbow Bridge. That's where pets, who pass from earthly life before their humans, wait for their humans to join them. This extraordinarily special place is further described on pages to come.

CHAPTER TWO— MOM AND DAD

> *"In order to really enjoy a dog, one doesn't merely try to train him to be semi-human. The point of it is to open oneself to the possibility of becoming partly a dog."*
> -Edward Hoagland

Dad blurted it out in front of Mom and me—"Cat piss sure is potent! Smells a lot worse than dog pee."

He just had to throw in that insult while complaining about my litter box odor. It was quite telling that he would use the more vulgar word "piss" for cats since he always used "pee" for the dogs. No ifs, ands, or buts about it—an equal opportunity pet *purr*-son would not have worded it the way he did. Besides, my box only stunk when no one emptied dirty litter for a long time. Let it be known that I always immediately covered up my body waste, but he never expressed appreciation to me for doing it, and the dogs never learned about humility from me in that regard.

Not much about Dad in these writings is flattering or *paws*-itive. That's mainly because he is a devoted dog person with little respect for cats. He never physically abused or neglected me, but he pretty much ignored me in favor of my canine housemates. I don't think he disliked me, but he wasn't fond of me either. He made it known that he thought I was "sneaky." He also indicated that, in his mind, I was selfish and only "pretended" to like people to get what I wanted.

My idiosyncrasies and independence probably contributed to Dad viewing me as weird and asocial. In addition to being a die-hard dog person, he's also an admirer of the former great leader of the United Kingdom Winston Churchill who, by the way, had several pets, mostly dogs and cats. More than once, I heard Dad quote something that Churchill had said—"Dogs look up to us. Cats look down on us." I wonder if that may have some bearing on how Dad feels about the pets in his life.

Dad often tells his friends some hair-raising tales about his encounters with what he called, "the biggest rats I ever saw," while living in mainland Japan, and especially during business trips he took to the Japanese island of Iwo Jima. Without going into detail because the rat stories he told were beyond disgusting, I heard him express how much he not only despises, but outright hates rodents. There is reason to suspect he probably doesn't think much higher of cats. In all honestly, even though he tried to make it sound as if he was joking, it wasn't surprising to hear him once tell a visiting dog freak, "The only thing worse than cats might be rats!" I don't think he meant it, but the unseemly nature of that remark abhorred me to no end.

Since I was nocturnal, I saw Dad crawl home countless times after a night out on the town partying with his Japanese counterparts. He looked *like something the cat dragged in* (a little feline quip to prove this cat does have a sense of humor). He always had the same lame excuse—"It's part of the job"—in reference to the excessive number of social functions "he had to attend" with business associates.

***

Way, way back in time, dogs were somehow labeled *man's best friend*. Take note that the part of speech of the keyword in that catchphrase is a masculine noun. Cats do not expect all men to condone us, but we do presume that most of them will make allowances for us. On the other hand, we expect the overwhelming majority of women to like us. I am in favor of canning a new phrase for cats—*woman's best friend*.

Generally speaking, it seems as if it's more masculine for a man to have a dog and more feminine for a woman to have a cat. While holding that thought, try to visualize a 6'6", 265-pound human male brute walking a little Yorkie dog around town. Each to his own, as I have witnessed that very sight once, and similar sights a few other times. Because most women—along with some men—love cats, we obviously have something lovable to offer. We mustn't forget that cats are the best friends of not only millions of women, but millions of men too. With this in mind, since "man" has been commonly used to include everyone in the human race regardless of gender, perhaps the old saying *man's best friend* should be modified to *man's best friends*—plural to include both dogs and cats.

Dad doesn't realize cats understand a lot of what humans say to them. More than once, he has made unkind remarks about my race. He even went so far as to state in general terms, "Cats have feminine traits and dogs are more masculine." His biggest problem is that he's dog-biased and unversed in cat matters. There were times when his hard looks made me feel as if I had the plague. He seemed to find me repellent, something I did not take personally because I was not singled out knowing that's how he views all cats period!

Too bad Dad isn't equal opportunity-driven like his son Steve. As the only other human male in our household, Steve made it *purr*-fectly clear that he is equally pro-dog and pro-cat. The dogs in our home would say the same thing about him. He's the one and only human male to ever pet me the way I liked it and, at the same time, send *paws*-itive signals to show affection. He's quite a guy!

I was in the household for more than two years before the first dog arrived on the scene. Furthermore, my time in Mom and Dad's home was longer than any of their dogs. Regardless, Dad was usually oblivious of my presence. He didn't like it because, unlike the dogs, I wasn't eager to please him. He and I never really shared any quality time. He stroked my fur a few times, albeit in the wrong direction—I preferred north and south, but he always did it east and west.

I once had a fleeting thought that Dad was actually trying to become my friend, but realization sunk in—*You can't teach an old dog new tricks*! His goodwill gestures were merely intended to appease Mom. I never felt at ease when he touched me, and I could sense he really wasn't comfortable either. I was not any different than other domestic cats that make humans work for it to develop an interactional relationship, and in Dad's case, he was not willing to do that.

After allowing Dad to stroke me for one minute at most, I would always turn my back and strut away. I didn't want him to think he was making progress by not alienating me. From the start, he sent clear signals leaving no doubt he did not want a close association between us, and the situation never changed. Just between you, me, and the gatepost, let it suffice to say he is what his own children refer to as, "An *RC Cola, Moon Pie* kind of guy"—a roundabout way of saying he's a dog person. I just cannot imagine a cat person drinking RC Cola and eating Moon Pies.

On occasion, I was known to purposely sit on a cushion next to Dad, and, with unamicable eyes, coldly gaze up at him as if to convey, *Who the hell do you think you are*? That always ruffled his feathers. He would stare back at me while silently conveying an identical intolerable thought. More than once, I heard him mutter words including "stealth-like," "uncanny," and "weirdly intelligent," while describing me to other humans. Based on the insincere tone in his voice, he wasn't paying compliments—he was making me the brunt of his criticism, and that stressed me out.

Even though, to my knowledge, Dad called me "butt-licker" only one time, it's something I never forgot hearing him say. Admittedly, I did engage in that specific activity as part of my self-grooming routine; however, I always did it in private out of everyone's line of sight. There's no way he ever saw me do it, so he had no proof. He was just being his usual self by stereotyping the feline race in a derogatory manner. Fastidious was I! Indiscriminate was he!

One way that I got even with Dad for discrediting me was to lie down in the kitchen doorway and play *dead cat* just to inconvenience him and make him step around me while he was carrying in groceries. I'd also occasionally lie down on the floor on his side of the bed so he would have to step over me when getting up in the night to use the bathroom. I admit to deriving enjoyment upon hearing him mumble a few expletives when he had to navigate around me. I don't think it ever crossed his mind that I might have just been testing his coordination. In all, as already mentioned, he tripped and fell over me only a half-dozen times.

At least a dozen other times, I pretended Dad had stepped on me, and the extra loud, extended screech I faked on those occasions nearly scared the you-know-what out of him. (Don't forget what I said before about karma. Uh-huh)

In my opinion there is nothing more unbecoming of a human than to sleep with the mouth open like Dad does. Not only is it unsightly, but the noises produced when the human mouth assumes the respiratory function of the nose are downright nasty. I don't know which was worse—that grotesque look or the repulsive sounds that accompanied it. A few dogs—even some cats—may snore, but they would never exhibit such a despicable appearance.

I never understood why Dad shaves his face nearly every day. I often watched him with a razor in his hand and tried to imagine what it must feel like to remove facial hair. I just couldn't make heads or tails of it. Shaving is something no sensible cat would ever want to have done. I guess if I had my face shaved, I wouldn't look much different than him. What a ghastly thought! I can only surmise he must think—mistakenly I would add—that shaving improves his appearance.

Human beings have some bad habits unique to their race—smoking cigarettes, drinking alcoholic beverages to excess, and eating too many sweets, to name the most common ones. Mom has been guilty of only one of those three and her lone vice was in moderation. Dad, on the other hand, has been guilty of all three and none in moderation. No cat could ever begin to rationalize why humans would *purr*-sist in such unhealthy behavior. To their credit, it's been a very long time since Mom and Dad indulged in any of those undesirable tendencies.

***

I once heard Dad say to a group of visitors in our home, "Dog spelled backward is God," which pretty much sums up how he feels about the canines in his life. He went on to express his belief that dogs are God's gift to humans explaining they were chosen over all the other animals on Earth to be the favorite human companions. He put a lot of feeling into what he was saying, so it obviously came from the heart. To my delight, he added, "God made cats a close second behind dogs," and that was the end of it. That made up for some of the unfavorable things he had previously said about my race; however, there was no doubt in my mind that more unpleasant statements about cats would come out of his mouth.

Dad sometimes talks about his strong Christian upbringing, but by no means is he a religious zealot. He's never attempted to push the notion about dogs and cats being gifts from God, or any other aspect of Christianity. Just as abruptly as he stopped talking about the so-called gifts from God on that one occasion, my thoughts on religion will come to a halt here and now.

I doubt Dad is aware that the ancient Egyptians favored cats over dogs so much that they treated us like gods. His preference for dogs bothered me at first. It troubled me so much that I once wished he would be reincarnated as a mouse. That was right after he held up a dog snack in front of me and teasingly said, "C'mon smarty cat, speak!" He did that a lot with the dogs —minus the "smarty cat" part—and, of course, they'd respond with a quick bark to get the treat. He knew I wouldn't react the same way. When I predictably failed to orally respond, he went off chastising me for being "dumb" and praising the dogs for being "smart."

Dad also belittled me for not being playful like the dogs. He failed to take into account that it's not that cats do not like to play, but they naturally prefer fewer and shorter play periods than dogs, and that, perhaps more than anything else, prevented him from becoming a dual dog-cat person. Since he tolerated my presence—in the sense of live and let live—he cannot be labeled a cat hater. I wish he would read about recent, empirical research performed by Japanese scientists with findings based on the results of a variety of episodic memory tests that proved cat intelligence is equal to that of dogs. His biggest problem was trying to apply what he knew about canines to me, without taking into consideration that dogs and cats are totally different species with significantly different capabilities.

I gradually learned to accept the way Dad felt after realizing some humans are cat persons who dislike dogs, and some are dog persons who do not like cats. He is the sole breadwinner and the master of the house. A considerable amount of the money he earned was spent on the dogs—and me—for veterinary care and food, so I cannot begrudge him. He did it mostly for Mom and the children. Fortunately, many humans outside my home are fond of both dogs and cats, so they are just like most of the humans inside my home. I am elated to report that members of humankind who dislike both dogs and cats are in the overwhelming minority—only about 5%.

***

The distinction between dog persons and cat persons has been around ever since canines and felines have shared domestication. Two Australian scientists completed a study regarding personality differences between dog people and cat people that I found interesting. They conducted two online surveys with more than 500 people, most of whom were from the United States, participating each time. They concluded that the participants who scored high on a social dominance trait preferred dogs as pets because dogs are submissive and can be trained to obey commands, while those scoring low on that trait had a preference for cats since cats are more independent and not as easily controlled as dogs (Alba & Haslam, 2015). They also found that those humans who scored high on competitiveness —having a desire to be superior by out-performing others— were dog persons, again because dogs are submissive and cats are not. In a nutshell, dog persons seem to be assertive so they would likely lock horns with cats, while the compliant nature of cat persons would avoid bad blood to make them perfect companions for cats.

My first thought about Alba & Haslam's findings was they made sense because they were consistent with the pack mentality of dogs. My second thought was that their findings fit Dad as a dog person since he possesses both social dominance and competitive traits. Then, along came my third thought—what about those humans who love both dogs and cats—like 4 out of the 5 in my household, none of whom are weak-willed or unassertive.

The study done by Alba & Haslam also suggested that the human participants who had both dogs and cats as pets scored higher on the social dominance and competitiveness traits than those who had just cats. I believe there are other factors involved, such as the independence of cats—needing far less time for care than dogs, less expensive to feed, and they can be left alone for long periods of time, etc. The to-do over the personalities of dog people and cat people is perplexing. I wonder if the relationship between Mom and Dad would have lasted as long as it has if she and he were opposites, i.e. what if she were a cat person with a disliking for dogs. Enough said, as there is no doubt that the comparison of personalities between dog people and cat people may never end because most humans consider themselves to be one or the other and sometimes both. It's one of those discussions that will likely continue till the end of time.

***

Just like human beings, dogs and cats have good days and bad days, and we need emotional support on the bad days. The crux of my message—*some humans are more or less sensitive than other humans, and some pets are more or less sensitive than other pets*. The main thing humans need to remember is that we do not grow mentally the same way they do. We develop like human babies in a number of ways, such as toilet training, playing with toys, and learning early social skills, but we do it at a lightning pace. For example, puppies and kittens can walk in a day or two after being born, not 10-12 months old like human babies, and it only takes us a matter of days for toilet training, not months like the human tots.

When it comes to mentality, we also tend to max out quickly at the human equivalent of a toddler—a 3-year-old at best. I was a rare exception to this rule, and although my canine colleagues' mental capacity was stymied, I will say this about them—their curiosity knew no bounds and they never stopped exploring the world around them. Like all cats, I was naturally curious too, but, unlike the dogs, my nosiness had limits.

Getting back to the toddler mentality of adult dogs, there is nothing wrong with this. It is actually a good thing. Healthy human toddlers are in a state of happiness. Being alive is all it takes to make them excited. They have no baggage at this stage of life, so there's no reason for them to experience hate, anger, depression, or other negative emotions. And this is precisely what dogs experience their entire lives. It is all positive. So, humans should envy them and not view them as low intelligent beings.

When compared to dogs, part of the problem for cats is that dogs show feelings not only by vocalizing (barking), but also by exhibiting facial expressions, and cats do not. It's not that we don't want to show how we feel through our faces, it's just nearly physically impossible. I could smile, but it was barely noticeable—Mom was the only one who ever detected it.

Granted, a dog's ability to show facial expressions similar to humans makes them appear more human-like, and dog persons love that. Humans frown and otherwise exhibit surprise, show fear, and grin through expressive faces, and so do dogs, but cats do not. Don't blame us for the inability to change facial expressions, blame Mother Nature. Mom fully understands, as she used to look into my eyes all the time and intimately comprehend what I was feeling, so there was no need for me to make a facial expression too.

***

To be fair and objective, I must say Dad does have one or two good traits. He is a humble and understated man. He regularly shows self-control and self-composure. In addition to his native American English and Mon Valley Pittsburghese, he became an accomplished, certified, government linguist by learning other languages, including Russian and Mom's native tongue Japanese. He can accurately be described as not only self-sacrificing, but also self-effacing. He is articulate and a proficient wordsmith.

Okay, I got carried away—far more than enough in the way of pleasantries to describe him. Adding the good to the bad and the ugly should provide a sufficient representation to enable everyone to reach their own impression.

I remember hearing Dad use a couple of unflattering Japanese expressions containing *neko*, the word for cat. For example, he often says, "Neko no te mo karitai [*I'd even borrow a cat's paw*]"—a saying used to indicate one is so busy and shorthanded at work that they would even be willing to borrow a *useless* cat's paw. He also likes to say, "nekojita," meaning "a cat's tongue"—an expression said to indicate a certain drink or food item is so hot it will burn the tongue. My point is that I do not recall hearing him use any such defamatory Japanese expression containing *inu*, the word for dog.

Dad spent most of his career as a federal law enforcement officer. During the time period when the family received 3 of their first 5 pets—all doomed puppies—he was working on a narcotics interdiction team and spent a lot of time interacting with Military Working Dogs (MWDs) trained to detect illegal drugs. There's no doubt that the work MWDs *purr*-formed in his presence made him even more of a dog person than before. Maybe I should be thankful he looked the other way and did not bust me for having a catnip addiction (*wink wink*).

"Well, hello Miss Kitty." That's how Dad acknowledged me sometimes. He got that from his favorite TV program *Gunsmoke*, in which one of the main characters, a pretty lady named Kitty, was called *Miss Kitty* by everyone who knew her. So, I have to believe Dad was complementing me when he addressed me in that way. How's that for impartiality? Not by him, by me!

Dad found it difficult to discipline Barb, Steve, and Brenda when they misbehaved as children and teenagers, which, I must say, was a rare occurrence. Mom was stricter than him, but like him, she was able to keep her tem-*purr* under control. Corporal punishment was a no-no; however, that doesn't mean Mom and Dad were *purr*-missive and had a non-intervention policy regarding their kids. On the contrary, they interceded on a regular basis and were successful in controlling the children's behavior because they knew how far they could go and, more importantly, when it was time to back-off. Their parental techniques obviously worked since their three offspring all displayed exemplary behavior as kids, and grew up to be successful and respectable, law-abiding adults. I know because I was in our home while all the children were living there. and long after they had all left to go their separate ways.

I was in a position to observe the vast amounts of oxytocin that flowed between Mom and Dad. If each loving moment, during which I saw affectionate interaction between them, were represented by a grain of cat litter, there would be enough to fill a gazillion litter boxes. Their oxytocin levels are constantly sky-high because no one else shares the same amount of love for both their two-legged and four-legged kids. They realize the dogs enriched their lives and their marriage, and that is something they are genuinely thankful for. And, deep down, there's no doubt Dad appreciates Tommy and me for favorably impacting the lives of Mom and the children.

Like Mom, Dad does everything possible to ensure domestic harmony, and that has surely contributed to their peaceful coexistence as life partners for 50+ years and counting. Except for one time when Mom expressed displeasure with him for bringing home something totally disgusting (more on that incident in the next paragraph), I never heard either of them raise their voice toward each other or their children.

***

"Eek!" shrieked Mom.

If a chair had been within leaping distance, she would have been on top of it, feet first, in a flash. "*Eww!*" she moaned in both grief and disgust.

She and I were the only ones at home when this happened. She was standing in the laundry room doorway and I was sitting at her feet when she made the repulsive discovery.

Moments earlier, an unusual odor emitting from the laundry room that I detected aroused my interest. It was unlike anything I had smelled before. After narrowing down the origin to a lump in a sock on the floor, I tried to use my paws to remove it. When the thing got stuck, my paw speed increased while I furiously attempted to dislodge whatever was inside the sock. As soon as she noticed what I was doing, she snatched the sock from my grasp. Upon turning it inside out, she let out a terrifying scream. A small, brown object dropped to the floor and landed a few inches in front of me. I leaned forward to get a closer sniff and discovered it reeked of soy sauce. It appeared to be a corpse about the size of a mouse, but there was no fur. It had a head and wing-shaped appendages hung down on each side. It could have been a bird, but there were no feathers. A stick protruded from its rear end, and half its butt was missing.

After closing the laundry room door to keep me from further analyzing what it was, Mom backed away with a puzzled look on her face. Since it was Dad's sock, she would await his return from work.

When Dad finally arrived an hour later, Mom met him at the front door. She had been fuming. Her wrinkled brow and evil eye left no doubt she was displeased about something. She did not speak a word and merely signaled him with a head nod to follow her. She went directly to the laundry room, opened the door, and with her head turned away, pointed down at the tiny carcass on the floor. Upon viewing the object of her ire, Dad let out a long gasp. "I… I just… I thought…" he stuttered.

"What's the matter? Mom inquired in an unmistakable sarcastic tone—"Cat got your tongue?"

Dad's dejected response was a single Japanese word—"Gomen nasai [*I'm sorry*]."

He explained to Mom that while at a local drinking establishment with three buddies the night before, the mama-san (proprietress) gave each of them a grilled sparrow-on-a-stick to eat. Since he knew it was an expensive delicacy and didn't want to offend the mama-san by declining the gift, he said he took a bite out of the hind end. According to Dad, he did not want to eat anymore because he thought he might throw up. He related he waited till no one was looking, and then stuffed the rest of the bird inside his sock. He said he was then able to convince everyone present that he had eaten the whole thing. He continued by telling Mom he had forgotten about the bird and left it inside his sock, after which it was destined to end up in the dirty laundry hamper.

After finishing his explanation, Dad let out a controlled laugh in an attempt to make light of the situation. Mom, however, was not humored by his account of what happened. He was about to learn that one sure way to exacerbate her feeling of irritation was to trivialize the situation. She started to lose her composure as soon as he began to delineate how "that thing" ended up in his sock. The silence was deafening while he waited with bated breath for her to say something.

"Are you crazy? What if I put that thing in the washing machine?" she inquired in a restrained, soft voice. "Why are you eating stuff like this?" she continued by questioning his judgment. Her facial skin tone reddened to match her rising voice intonation. "I touched that thing!" she yelled out. Teardrops formed on the inside corner of each glowering eye while she waited for him to respond.

That's it! Dad thought. She wasn't mad because he had placed the remnants of a dead sparrow in his sock. She wasn't mad because he had eaten part of it. She wasn't mad because she had found it.

She was mad solely because she had touched it.

Without delivering a lengthy diatribe, Mom scowled at Dad leaving no doubt she was highly *purr*-turbed. Cleverly, he did not utter another word. Maybe like me, that's the only time he ever saw Mom fit to be tied. He just let her rant and rave for a few minutes until she ran out of things to say. Dad's extreme antipathy to quarrelling enables him to avoid getting into arguments with Mom. His philosophy on married life is simple—*A happy wife is a happy life. Or is it, A happy life is a happy wife?* (I'm not sure since either way seems to fit). He realized that all he could do to mitigate her anger was to remain silent while letting time pass.

Mom showed her reprobation for Dad's act by refusing to speak to him for two days. His offer to take her to dine at her favorite eatery helped to placate her. After he finally coaxed her to go out to eat and order her favorite dish—the proverbial *doghouse special*—all was well and back to normal on the home front.

Dad's decision to *let sleeping dogs lie* in this case was a sound one. He still occasionally tells the sparrow-in-the-sock-story to friends and acquaintances because he thinks it is funny. So far, he's made sure Mom is not within earshot, so she has yet to overhear him recounting the incident, but if he keeps it up, he's bound to get caught. And there's no way Mom will be the least bit understanding because what happened is something she has tried to completely forget.

Getting back to something Mom said to Dad while he was at a loss for words upon observing the sparrow carcass on the laundry room floor—"Cat got your tongue?"—I'd explain the meaning of that old idiom if I could; however, I have no clue as to how such a dumb saying developed. It makes no sense. It's just one in a long line of human expressions detrimental to the feline race. I have to believe that cats get more respect from humans today than they did way back when all such idiotic idioms started gaining popularity. Why humans at some point in time long ago started picking on us is baffling.

By the way, sparrows (*suzume* in Japanese) are served and consumed in certain Japanese restaurants. The only thing missing is the feathers. The birds are dipped in a thick soy sauce-mix, grilled, and served whole, individually skewered on a stick protruding from the rear end up through the beak. According to Dad, the meat and skin are "a bit bitter," while the bones and beak are "really crunchy." Dad cautions that this particular dish must be washed down with an alcoholic beverage to bring one's taste buds back to normal.

I've had reason to question some things Dad expressed in the past; however, since humans have far more taste buds than dogs and cats (approximately 9,000 for a human to 1,700 for a dog and less than 500 for a cat), there is no way I can even begin to question the veracity of his sparrow-eating experience. It makes no difference since neither dogs nor cats would take the time to season and cook anything to eat before putting it in their mouths.

Mom would never ever consider eating a sparrow. For the record, she regularly interacts with these tiny birds. Her neverending routine at the end of a meal in a restaurant is to discreetly break apart a piece of bread, wrap the crumbs in a napkin, and then scatter them outside on the ground for sparrows to find. This expression of kindness to birds is yet another example of her gentle nature.

***

Like mine, Mom's bloodline demands respect. Her father was born into a highly regarded and honorable Japanese family. His family's stature was a factor in him being appointed to serve in an esteemed position as a bodyguard for Japanese Emperor Hirohito during World War II. Mom was raised in the strict code of ethics existent in a typical, rural family at a time in history when family ties were the bedrock of society in Japan. Cardinal virtues back then were many: oya koko [*love of family*], kodomo no tame [*for the sake of the children*], giri and on [*duty and responsibility*], gaman [*withholding emotion on the surface*], gambatte [*strength and resourcefulness*], and haji no kakete [*not bringing shame on the family*]. Her six siblings and she were rightfully proud of their heritage and its accompanying gentility.

It became readily apparent to me that Dad is totally in awe of Mom's sublime naivete' and how it combines intriguingly with her suavity and sophistication (wow, that was a mouthful!). As a sagacious judge of character—am I on a roll or what?—Mom can spot a phony human upon sight or sound. Conversely, Barb, Steve, and Brenda share a winsome manner that, to varying degrees, attracts new friends. Although Mom does not know very many humans whom she has called "friends," her upbringing and manners enable her to interact nicely with Dad's friends and associates, most of whom he became acquainted with at work.

Mom is by no means unsocial. She's been great with Barb, Steve, and Brenda's pals, many of whom still affectionately call her "*Mom*" after more than three decades. One thing is clear—Mom truly feels that Butch, Peko, Chiro, and their fourth dog Koro were not only some of the most loyal friends she ever had, but they were also among the most trustworthy. Unlike some humans she knows, the dogs never pretended to be something they were not. She has yet to find a human who excitedly runs to the door to greet a loved one every time they return home. Dad likened her hardline attitude toward friendship to a line he once heard in a movie—"A good friend will help you move, but a great friend will help you move a body"—in other words, *great* friends are hard to come by.

Mom has expressed intense loathing of the title of *housewife*. Instead, she finds *homemaker* to be *purr*-fectly acceptable. She always lists "homemaker" as her job title on income tax returns and other forms requesting occupation. Although they are interchanged at times, upon looking closely, one will notice there is a difference when defining housewife and homemaker—the more profound impact goes to homemaker. Mom's job description is lengthy and included the role of catalyst to bridge the gap between her nonfurry, biological children and her furry, adopted kids.

Even though Mom and Dad's nonfurry kids are half-Japanese, they grew up in a mostly American culture. That didn't stop Mom from making sure they celebrated unique Japanese child events, such as the Doll Festival [*Hina Matsuri*]. That's when every year on Girl's Day (March 3rd), while Barb and Brenda were little girls, she painstakingly assembled seven layers of platforms in the shape of a stairwell, and then covered the entire contraption with a red carpet on which she displayed a set of ornamental dolls representing the Japanese Emperor, Empress, and their Court.

Mom also had Dad fly a carp streamer [*koinobori*]—a large, colorful windsock displaying a carp fish—on a flagpole outside our house for Steve when he was a boy (another popular Japanese custom for kids). In addition, her family enjoys a feast of special Japanese cuisine every New Year's Eve that makes the big American meals on Thanksgiving and Christmas look like glorified snacks. She Japanized Dad who, at times, according to Mom, acts more like a Japanese than an American.

When it comes to expecting others to exhibit good manners regardless of age, Mom can best be described as not merely old-fashioned but downright obstinate. It is difficult for her to accept any breach of etiquette by a human, especially her own brood. Her penchant for mannerliness makes her meticulous when it comes to displaying pro-*purr* behavior. She fusses each and every time anyone slips up, especially if it's someone near and dear to her. She has the propensity to continuously teach etiquette to her children and grandchildren so they may behave with due propriety in any social situation and not embarrass themselves. She never fails to softly scold any family member who displays poor table manners or otherwise acts below her expectations in or outside the home.

***

Being on the receiving end of food is important, but that was not the main reason the dogs and I felt a special attachment to Mom. Her manner of speech when talking to us blurred the boundary between human and animal. Her calm voice was truly soothing. She was also able to directly communicate with us mentally by making eye-to-eye connections. The body language she used to indicate impatience—hands on hips—let us know when we came close to getting on her wrong side. Even though we were 100% animal physically, intellectually, she made us feel like human-animal hybrids—*mew*-tations. Because she imprinted each of us at a very young age, we were as close to being chimeras as the animal kingdom would allow.

The quality of Mom's connection to each of us and our individual ties to her were nothing short of the ultimate in bonding. None of us ever felt the call of the wild and we were totally thankful for being domesticated. Each of us gradually became humanlike in our mannerisms. Of course, my powerful intellect propelled me toward human characteristics far ahead of my canine housemates. (The preceding sentence was carefully reworded to avoid sounding condescending or possibly indicative of something a b _ _ _ _ would say)

Mom was a lover of dogs and cats before she became our advocate. She is highly vocal for animal rights. When Dad broke the news to her that, by law, dogs and cats are considered *purr*-sonal property rather than living beings, she could not believe it. When he let her know that a veterinarian can only be held responsible for a pet's market value as compensation if found guilty of negligence for causing a pet's death, her blood pressure started to rise. She feels it is unfair for the courts to not recognize the strong emotional bonds known to form between animals and humans. She knows firsthand that worrying over the physical well-being of her biological kids and that of her furry kids has affected her own well-being.

Although she has not lost a biological child, Mom has experienced the feeling of devastation many times due to the loss of a furry kid. She doesn't care about the market value of any of her pets. She feels it is hypocritical for a veterinarian to charge thousands of dollars to treat a sick pet since they know full well they will only have to pay a fraction of what they charge if found guilty of malpractice. It troubles her to no end that the law enables vets to shirk their responsibility, if they so desire, with no fear of being held anywhere near fully accountable for their actions.

To Mom, *property* implies inanimate objects, and there is absolutely no way it should include dogs and cats. She balks at using the word *owner* for someone who has a pet because the implication is ownership of property. Having said all that, I must add that Mom still talks about Dr. Donald Mickey, the very first veterinarian that Dad and she dealt with in Reynoldsburg, Ohio. She still tells others how fantabulous he was with me, and how sorry she was to move away and have to find new pet doctors, none of whom could hold a candle to Dr. Mickey. I can vouch for that because I went to four other veterinarians after Dr. Mickey, and not one of them came close to matching his skills in preventing, treating, and curing animal diseases and injuries.

Mom discovered that every dog and cat has a distinctive *purr*-sonality with a unique way of acting and reacting. She came to realize that, like humans, we possess strengths and weaknesses, and our tem-*purr*-aments vary. We can express a wide variety of feelings, and can be remarkably patient without making a fuss while waiting for something. In short, we can display greater patience than most humans. Of course, there are exceptions and they involve many more dogs than cats. The renowned British scientist Charles Darwin conducted a series of experiments that were addressed in his book *The Expression of the Emotions in Man and Animals*. Darwin drew the conclusion that animals definitely have emotions, albeit with a lesser degree of feelings than humans, but feelings nonetheless.

I would like to take credit for all the words of wisdom contained in this book, but honesty precludes me from doing so; therefore, I have done my best give credit where credit is due. Since my passing, insightful research regarding pet emotions —like that performed by Darwin—and studies about bonding between humans and dogs has been conducted by several renowned scientists. The findings of some of that research are addressed, in detail, on subsequent pages.

***

The more humans Mom met, the more she loved her pets. She never met an animal she didn't like, but she cannot say the same for humans. She isn't particularly fond of snakes, rodents, and spiders; however, she's *purr*-fectly ready, willing, and able to coexist with them, unlike a few inconsiderate humans who have drawn her ire and, in her mind, whose numbers seem to be on the rise.

Mom was quick to let first-time guests in her home know that if they did not at least condone her dogs, they would not be welcomed back. To merely say she was passionate about her furry kids is understated. The *dog eat dog world* mentality that many humans seem to embrace is troubling to her because she cannot understand why anyone would deliberately try to hurt someone else just to get a material thing they want. Upon becoming aware of a human trying to take advantage of another person, she's been known to mumble, *Dogs would never do anything like that.*

The litmus test that Mom uses to identify nice people is

whether or not they like dogs. To her, it's un-American and un-Japanese to dislike dogs. Her impression of human acquaintances is always influenced by their individual feelings about pets. She is quick to inform everyone she meets about her dogs even after they had passed, then she closely evaluates their reaction and response. If a *purr*-son shrugs off the topic and does not ask at least one question (like "What kind of dogs?"), she will scratch them off her potential friends' list for appearing wishy-washy. Anyone that shows some interest in dogs will remain on her list for further evaluation. Everyone who somehow indicates a dislike for dogs will be immediately eliminated from consideration. And all those who have a dog—along with those who say they don't have a dog but they do have a cat—become an instant friend.

Mom takes into consideration that some people who do not have a dog or cat may have a legitimate reason other than disliking them—frequent travels, excessive work hours, or renting a place that does not allow pets—and that's copacetic with her. By *purr*-sonal choice, she has very few human friends, and each of them either likes dogs or cats or both. She wouldn't have it any other way. Just like us (dogs and cats), she has a sixth sense that enables her to quickly ascertain if another human has a liking or disliking for pets, and she always relies on her gut feeling to pass final judgment.

Mom has also relied on the reaction of her own dogs when they would meet a certain human for the first time, as there is no doubt in her mind that dogs are an excellent judge of human character. She believes that any dog who shows dislike for a certain human is aboveboard. I found some research findings that support her belief. Scientists at Japan's Kyoto University found that dogs "are extremely sensitive to social signals from humans," and it does not take them long to not trust people who "behave negatively" toward their human companion (Anderson, Chijiwa, Fujita, Hori, & Kuroshima, 2015). Here is a summary of the study done by Anderson et al.:

> A total of 54 dogs were divided into three groups of 18 dogs with each group participating in a slightly different variation of the same interactive activity. Each dog's owner pretended to have a difficult time trying to remove the lid of a transparent jar containing an object of no value to the dogs. In each situation, actors portraying bystanders, who were all strangers to the dogs, would do 1 of 3 things: either help, refuse to help when asked, or just turn away before being asked for help. After each experiment, the dogs "were significantly biased against the non-helper actors demonstrating they were able to identify inconsiderate people and then steer clear of them. It was noted that such "negativity bias" had also been demonstrated by 3-year-old human children and certain capuchin (so-called "organ grinder") monkeys.

Because Mom treated her furry canine kids like honorary humans, they, in turn, accepted her as an honorary dog. She has never referred to, or thought of, herself as a pet owner or a master, but rather a companion and trustee. She considered herself the primary caregiver for her furry kids—precisely the way she feels about her biological children. In her mind, when it comes to pets, the words ownership and relationship are a mismatch because the association is reciprocal, not one-sided. To her, ownership implies property; therefore, the possibility of an owner having a healthy relationship with another living being considered property is zilch.

"I have two legs and they have four," is something Mom has repeatedly told Dad and her children about what she considers the most distinct difference between her and her furry kids. She has also been known to say something apropos like, "*Purr*-fect companions have twice as many feet as people."

Barb, Steve, and Brenda will never forget Mom's teachings, particularly the one about animals having the inborn ability to sense what is in a *purr*-son's heart, and whether their motives are pure or not. She brings up this topic quite often because she believes it is why pets immediately shy away from certain humans—the ones who either show a black heart or tip an evil hand. Her nonfurry kids were in no hurry to leave the nest; hence their school friends often visited our home even after they had graduated from high school or college. Every one of them was accepted by the dogs, which meant her nonfurry kids had good taste in selecting their own friends.

The *purr*-vasive odor of pets was immediately evident to any visitor upon entering our house—mostly canine smells since what I emitted was minimal. Mom could care less. Her altruistic attitude regarding her furry kids became readily apparent to anyone who didn't know her well. Her motto: *Love me, love my dogs*! She has an aversion to euphemism, preferring to speak directly and not pull any punches. Pithy is she!

At first it bothered me that Mom didn't mention to her new acquaintances that a cat was among her furry kids. Eventually, I realized she would only say she had dogs for a couple of reasons —the dogs outnumbered me as much as 3-to-1, and she understood I was standoffish. She knew I would hide and not make a fool of myself when someone came to our home, while the idiotic dogs would greet visitors with despicable treatment, such as jumping up on them and licking their faces. She was forced to make first-timers aware of the dogs before they first visited our home, but she didn't feel the need to let them know about me beforehand, and I was fine with that.

I usually hid when our doorbell rang, but that didn't stop me from keeping an eye on what was happening in the house at all times. I would stay within range to be able to see and hear the interaction between the dogs and visitors. I just preferred to stay in the shadows and go unnoticed. Sometimes, I wouldn't hide, but pretended to be asleep while keeping my eyes open the slimmest of slits (1/16th of an inch). I hoped that no visitor would come near me, but if they should approach, I knew it was in my best interest to start purring. Fortunately, the need for me to purr at a stranger was limited to a handful of occasions, and it always involved a nice lady like Mom, so it went smoothly. Since all male humans remind me of Dad, I was very thankful for having no encounters with strange men.

***

There's a special place in Mom's heart for dogs in the company of homeless *purr*-sons. She feels compassion for the human and the dog, albeit 90-to-10 in favor of the dog. She's glad each has the other for companionship, but cannot help wondering if the dog might not be getting a fair share of the food that becomes available. She doesn't usually give money to homeless people, but she has been known to give them something to eat when a dog is present.

Mom took the phrase *doggie bag* literally. When eating out, without fail, she used to save meat pieces from her entrée to take home to her canine kids. One day, she walked out of a restaurant with a doggie bag and saw a homeless man and his dog sitting on the sidewalk adjacent to the parking lot. She went straight up to the man, handed him the bag containing leftover steak strips, and instructed him to, "Give half the meat to the dog." The guy immediately stood up, and, without saying a word, walked away followed by the dog.

"Wait just a minute," Mom shouted as she scurried after them.

When the guy refused to acknowledge her and kept on going, she quickened her pace and got in front of him and the dog. She blocked their path and made him stop, while she sternly repeated her request, "I said I want you to share with your dog."

Dad had come out of the restaurant shortly after Mom and saw her chasing after the guy. He was outside hearing range, but realized something wasn't right, so he ran after them. By the time he caught up, the guy was sitting on the sidewalk feeding meat pieces to the dog. Because Mom had become convinced that the guy had no intention of sharing with the dog, she forced him to feed the dog in her presence. She refused to leave until the dog had consumed at least one-half the meat.

While walking back to the car, Dad scolded her for confronting the strange man without seeking his assistance, "Don't you know that guy could have hurt you?"

Displaying an obviously fake sheepish grin, Mom promised, "I will never do anything like that again." I wouldn't bet on it though, and neither would Dad who realized it was not in his best interest to push the issue, so he didn't say another word.

***

The way Mom sees it, all animals, including humans, belong to the same species of God-created beings with varying classes. She is quick to remark about some humans having physical features that strongly resemble their dog's looks. She enjoys determining which canine breed each of her family and friends resemble. It doesn't bother her if someone thinks she looks like a certain dog, but she knows others might be offended should she indicate they bear a canine resemblance. This causes her to self-chuckle.

While out in public, Mom has often jokingly commented about how much a human looked like his or her dog as they passed by. She intended it as a compliment to the human—not the dog—but there's no doubt some humans would not have felt flattered. She is of the opinion that some people choose a particular dog to become their companion because they subconsciously think some part(s) of the animal's physical features resembles his or her looks—usually the face, not the rear-end! What struck me most about this was that only dogs have been discussed.

Hearing someone say a cat, or a pig, or a hamster, or any other domestic animal looks like a certain human would not be unprecedented, but nowhere near as much as dogs are mentioned.

According to Dr. Sadahiko Nakajima, Ph.D., a psychologist at Kwansei Gakuin University in Nishinomiya, Japan, upon viewing a photographic lineup of individual owners and their dogs, other humans, who participated in a research study, consistently matched 73-80% of the humans with their dogs (Nakajima, 2013). Since 50% can be considered equal to chance, Dr. Nakajima's findings were significant numbers. It should be noted that among the actual pairs not matched, there were some dogs having very little or no resemblance to their owners.

Another experiment conducted by Nakajima involved a total of 502 Japanese undergraduate students, who each viewed two sets of 20 dog and human photograph pairs. One set contained 20 actual dog and human pairs, while the other set contained 20 fake dog and human pairs. Assorted dog breeds were represented, and the humans were both male and female ranging in age from 20's to 60's. All photos were in color and consisted of head shots only. Eighty percent of the more than 500 judges selected photos that matched dogs with their owners basically equaling the results of the previously mentioned study.

Nakajima found that when black bars covered the mouth region of the owners' faces, the results were 73% of the judges picking the actual dogs and owners; however, when the eyes of the owners and the dogs were blacked out, the results dropped to 50%. Nakajima's studies concluded that dogs and owners most closely resembled each other in the eye region. These studies did not rule out the possibility that other human physical features, such as hairdos, thin or full faces, facial hair, or eye color, might be used in determining dog and owner resemblance; however, they made an especially strong case for the eyes. Per Nakajima, the main reason for the dog-owner resemblance phenomenon was the so-called *mere exposure effect*—humans selecting a dog that somehow looks similar to themselves due to a preference for familiarity.

Nakajima's conclusion about the eyes being the focus of dog and owner's resemblance did not surprise Mom. She had reached the same opinion when matching Steve to Butch, Barb to Peko, and Brenda to Chiro. She knew it was mostly about the eyes.

"*Naa*. I think dogs and owners morph into look-alikes over time," Dad jokingly once said in disagreement with Mom while they were out for a walk in the park with Peko and Chiro. When Dad inquired, "What kind of dog do you think I look like?"

Mom blew him off by replying, "You look like the next dog we're gonna get."

"What do you mean by that?" he asked with a discombobulated look on his face. He got no response, so he went on, "We haven't talked about getting another dog, have we?" Still nothing out of the mouth of Mom. "Do you know something I don't?"

Finally, a controlled reply, "Just a joke," and she left it at that.

And that was the end of it. Dad let it go with no way of knowing that their next dog would be named *Koro*, or that he could rightfully be proud if anyone were to think of Koro and him as look-alikes since Koro would be best described in a single word —*stud*! (More on this to come in Chapter Six)

Unlike dogs, cat faces do not resemble people. A long-running Broadway musical called *Cats* had human performers who looked like felines. The resemblances were made possible by the application of excessive makeup. That was unnatural and totally unlike the natural canine-human lookalikes who do not alter their appearances.

Not having human lookalike faces is only one of many differences between cats and dogs. We do not sniff out narcotics or explosives, and we don't guard homes or bark out warnings. We don't chase and catch criminals, nor do we lead the blind and other handicapped people around. However, fortunately for humans, a cat's *purr*-sonality is much closer to that of a human than a dog. Humans with a dog-like disposition can be annoying —a loud, overly excited *purr*-son constantly in your face, trying to get your attention because they want something. I'm glad most people are not like that and act more like cats than dogs— *dignified* rather than *dognified*!

***

Let's face it (pardon pun please)—the basic components of the human face are fixed by Mother Nature—two ears, two eyes, one nose, one mouth—the same as a dog and a cat, and nearly all other animals. And the dimensions of these constituents are nearly the same for all humans, give or take a few millimeters, or centimeters in larger animals. Regardless, even though the myriad of human faces contains the same parts, each one differs from all others, which is unlike animals that look remarkably like all others of the same species.

Humans obviously pay close attention to their individuality of appearance. Some of them admire their own looks, or how other people look, or both, while some look down upon themselves or others for their homely appearance. Rest assured that cats and dogs generally view the appearance of other animals only with indifference. Most of us could care less how other animals look, and we only take notice to ascertain whether they appear to be the same or another species, along with whether or not they may be hostile. There are exceptions, of which I was one because my visualization of Tommy's earthly looks made me feel infatuated with a member of the opposite sex—yet another example of the human characteristics I had acquired.

Even though I had two eyes like humans, my field of vision was not the same as theirs. I could simultaneously see objects to my left and on my right side without moving my head. It goes without saying that a human's vision is limited to one side or the other, depending on which way their head is turned.

Another striking difference between cats and humans is leg usage. I put all four of my legs to use while walking, so I wondered why humans use only two of the four they have. Sure, they call two of their appendages arms instead of legs, but while playing on all fours with me, they demonstrated the ability to move around on all four appendages. Their way seemed like a waste of natural body parts. I guess when you take into consideration that they use their arm appendages for things their legs cannot do, and vice versa, they might have an edge by not walking on all fours. I just could not relate because it was physically impossible for me to stand up on two legs and walk around.

Dogs and cats do not understand why many humans—females in particular—are obsessed with hair styles. Some women appear to try every conceivable type of hairdo. They should just let their hair grow naturally and not ever cut it—like me! I cannot count the number of times Barb and Brenda changed their hair styles, and even their hair color. Steve, on the other hand, could care less since the top of his head is common among scholars—it's bald!

Human obsession with clothing is something else dogs and cats fail to comprehend. Humans must feel that items of apparel make them superior to animals because they wear clothes and we do not. I think it's important to establish the importance that clothing is to human beings because neither my canine associates nor I had the need or the desire to wear any kind of garment. Graciously, Mom did not dress us in clothing, although the same cannot be said for Barb and Brenda since they put costumes on us a few times at Halloween. I was grateful they did not dress me up as much as they did Butch. This brings to mind a common phrase—*to each his own*—as I did not like wearing clothing one bit, but Butch seemingly grew to enjoy it.

THE DOGS' BEST FRIEND: A CAT'S EYE VIEW

To human eyes, the canine and feline ways of life may appear quite simple. That's because they are! We do not worry about changing our physical appearance so we look the same year-round. We wear the same old suit throughout all four seasons. We feel the heat and the cold, but we're naturally able to adapt by shedding fur when it gets uncomfortably hot, and growing an extra layer when the temperatures drop to near freezing.

Feline body-cleansing is totally different than the human way. There were times when I thought I wouldn't mind soaking myself in bathwater just once, but I knew if my fur ever got soaked, it would take *fur*-ever to dry out. That is why I grinned to myself and bore the mild stink of my own sweat without ever stepping into a bathtub. Anyhow, baths are for humans and dogs, not cats!

The internal battle over bathing went on and on in our house because the humans showed no inclination to lick themselves clean as an alternative to the bathtub and shower. They gave the dogs a bath on a regular basis. After three or four unsuccessful attempts to coax me into the bathtub in my younger days, they eventually gave up and allowed me to do it my way. Humans will never be able to comprehend why licking is the ultimate in self-body cleansing. How could they if they never tried it?

***

When Dad, or one of the kids, or a friend tells a kind story or an amusing tale about any of her furry kids, a warm glow quickly kindles Mom's face. The love she has for us is transparent. It's something no one can miss upon seeing her beam with pride while talking about any of us herself, or hearing someone else fondly mention us. She does the same thing for her biological kids and grandkids, and her grandpets too. She is God's gift to us all.

There I go again glorifying Mom with no mention of Dad. By

now, it should be obvious that these writings contain very little favorable information about him. C'mon, no one would expect a cat to write nice things about a dog person. However, since my conscience will not *purr*-mit me to purposely omit anything of relevance, I will hereby set the record straight from here to the end of this chapter.

One dark and stormy, summer evening in 2014, Mom heard *miaowing* cries outside her bedroom window. Upon looking out the window, she saw two very small kittens lying on their sides on the ground in a pool of water in a 6-inch space between the backyard fence and a storage shed. She described what she was seeing to Dad and then blurted out, "We have to do something or they'll drown!"

The rain was pounding down amid streaks of lightning and booms of thunder every 30 seconds or so. A tornado warning had been issued for their neighborhood. Dad was faced with two options—take action to rescue the kittens, or do nothing and let them drown in a pool of water that was becoming deeper. Surprisingly, there was no indecision on his part, as he ran outside in the torrential downpour just as a lightning strike crashed down along a tree line only 100 feet behind the house. He climbed up a ladder that was leaning against the shed and looked down behind the shed. He saw a total of 5 newborn kittens—3 crying while trying to hold their heads above water, and the other 2 noiseless and lying motionless on their sides with their heads partially submerged in water. There was no sign of their mother.

The only way Dad could reach the kittens in time was to tear down a portion of the fence or take apart the shed. Neither option was good because he took great pride in the wooden fence that he had recently repaired, and also in the storage shed that he had assembled himself. That did not slow him down though as he elected to dismantle the shed and did so immediately by pulling it apart with his bare hands. After turning into a one-man wrecking crew, he scooped up the babies one by one and handed them to Mom who had followed him outside. She had fashioned a makeshift carrier by folding a bath towel in which she placed each kitten. While Dad was trying to rescue the last kitten, a bolt of lightning struck the highest tree in the woods behind the house slicing the wide trunk in two. The deafening bang nearly caused Dad to fall down on top of the sole remaining kitty. Miraculously, he was able to balance himself by grabbing onto a fence post with his left hand while bending over and scooping up the baby in a single flowing motion with the other hand.

The kittens were caked in mud and shivering. Dad and Mom didn't have time to put on raincoats and holding an umbrella was not an option, so they were both water-soaked head to toe, but that did not stop them from caring for the kittens. Mom hurriedly took them into the bathroom through the rear patio door, placed them into the bathtub, and rinsed them in warm water. Until the mud was removed, they had no way of knowing there was one yellow male, one brown female, two tiger-striped females, and a scrawny, black and brown female that was only about half the size of the others. The miaowing cries of all 5 babies in unison was music to Mom's ears as she removed them from the tub separately, and placed them inside a cardboard box that Dad had brought from the garage.

Now, all of a sudden, Mom and Dad faced two more options— either call animal services to pick up the kittens, or nurse them until an adoptive human could be found. Mom was all for the second choice, and, surprisingly for the second time that night, Dad agreed. On his own volition, he quickly drove in the lingering rainstorm to a nearby pet store. He bought newborn kitten formula to feed the kittens, along with pads to keep them dry inside the box. Barb and her two children, Ricky and Erika, along with Brenda and her 3 children, Jack, Nia, and Lily, came over to play with the kittens while Mom and Dad cared for them.

They were concerned about the runt of the litter, a little female, who was weak from Day 1, but gradually showed signs of gaining strength. On Day 3, the runt, who was usually beneath her 4 siblings as they climbed on top of her to sleep, appeared at her strongest when she began copying the others by attempting to climb up on the inside of the box. That's why everyone was so sad and disappointed after Mom found her lifeless body inside the box the next morning. The damage done by the storm had been too much for the littlest one to bear. Dad buried her in the backyard.

On Day 5, Mom and Dad, accompanied by Barb, Ricky, and Erika, took the remaining 4 kittens to a local pet store. A volunteer supervisor estimated the kittens to be about one week old. The supervisor agreed to take them saying a nursing mother cat with her own litter of older kittens was available at the facility, and she had enough milk to feed them and her own kittens too. Mom was pleased after meeting the lady supervisor because she seemed to be a genuine animal lover who would likely see to it that the kittens were well cared for prior to placing them up for adoption. When Mom and Dad returned to the store 6 weeks later, they found out there was a happy ending to what had started out as a potential tragedy—all 4 kittens had been adopted!

Only 5 months after finding the 5 kittens in the backyard, Dad found 2 more kittens back there. He heard their miaowing cries while cleaning the patio. Like before, they were newborns and the mother cat was not around. Unlike the prior incident, this time was a bright, sunny morning. These kittens were lying on their bellies in the yard near a corner of the fence adjacent to where the other kittens had been found. After taking one baby inside for Mom to clean, Dad headed back outside to get the other one.

Upon opening the patio screen door, he found himself eyeball-to-eyeball with a large Cooper's Hawk perched on top of the fence 6 feet directly above the crying kitten. The big bird immediately took its eyes off the kitten and stared at him. Thinking to himself, *It may have already eaten other kittens in the litter and came back to get more,* he believed the hawk probably viewed him as a competitor who wanted to eat the only kitten remaining in the yard. Standing only 25 feet from each other, they were locked in a stare-down situation with the hawk's yellow eyes glaring.

Despite recognizing the hawk as a formidable foe, Dad was determined to maintain eye-to-eye contact, and although it wasn't easy, somehow he was able to do so. Perhaps because it had already filled its belly with other kittens from the litter, or for another unknown reason, after approximately one minute of having their eyes fixed on each other, the hawk suddenly turned away and flew up over the tree line behind the house. Dad breathed a heavy sigh of relief, and then ran over to the kitten lying on the ground up against the fence and quickly picked it up in both hands. He didn't waste any time carrying it into the house just in case the hawk might change its mind and return to do battle. Go Daddy go!

Mom cared for these two kittens for three days, after which Dad and she took them to the same pet store that had accepted the previous four kittens. A few weeks later, both of them were adopted.

So, Dad's quick actions to save baby cats—not once but *twice*—swayed my opinion of him in his favor. I was sufficiently moved to change my overall assessment of him from *not good* to *not bad* —if you catch my drift (*wink wink*).

Some insight regarding the Cooper's Hawk species is in order since Dad had gotten up close and personal with one. There's a need to distinguish it from a Red-shouldered Hawk that Mom had encountered a few years earlier (an incident that's detailed in Chapter 5). Both species are considered medium-size birds of prey, but the Cooper's Hawk is slightly larger. Both have very keen vision, and rely on the element of surprise to swoop down on their prey, seize it with their feet, and then break its neck with their sharp talons. They both hunt smaller birds and little mammals. (Regarding Dad's run-in with the Cooper's Hawk, since the kitten was lying up against the fence, the hawk would not have been able to swoop down and seize it, so instead it perched on top of the fence instead where Dad disrupted whatever it had in mind)

***

Dad's main profession was criminal investigations. He was a special agent for a federal government agency—the Air Force's Office of Special Investigations (AFOSI). His job included *purr*-forming the duties of Crime Scene Investigator (CSI). As a result, he had a lot of experience collecting items of evidence in plastic bags. He once told Mom, "I wish I had a penny for every bag I placed evidence in at crimes scenes, and for every bag I used to pick up dog poop." He added, "We could've retired 10 years earlier."

Actually, 99 times out of 100, Mom was the one who would place a plastic bag over their dogs' poop in the grass, pick it up, carefully turn the bag inside out, tie it closed, and dispose of it in a designated trash container. Dad wasn't as careful as Mom, so it wasn't uncommon for him to get poop particles on his hands and sometimes under his fingernails. When that occurred, without fail, Mom half-jokingly and half-disgustedly would simply utter, "Otousan!" [polite Japanese for *father*—the father of her children in this case].

One time, she told the children what Dad had done shortly after it happened, and threw in, "I hope he wasn't this messy while picking up stuff at the crime scenes."

He came back with, "Why don't we teach them [the dogs] to pick up their own poop?" As is usually the case, Mom failed to see any humor in his intended funny remark. He wouldn't admit it, but she always got the best of him when they had this type of exchange.

Since thousands of humans exercised their dogs in the park that Mom and Dad frequented, they had to be constantly on the lookout for dog poop because many humans ignored the county ordinance to pick up after their dogs. Mom never stepped in it, but the same cannot be said for Dad. At least a dozen times, I heard Mom mention to her nonfurry kids that Dad had to hose down his tennis shoes after making a *waffle* by stepping on poop.

Of all Dad's antics, this particular one always drew the twisted-face look of disgust from Mom, which made me wonder, *Was she disgusted at the purr-son who didn't pick it up, or at Dad for stepping on it?* Permit me to expand on that thought. Not picking up the poop was a conscious decision, but stepping on it was a misfortune. My conclusion—Mom's yuck factor was evenly directed at Dad as the waffle-maker, and also at whomever left the poop on the ground thereby presenting him with the opportunity to make a waffle. For the record, I recognized that poop and waffle do not complement each other, but they aren't my words— they're Mom's—and the activity described actually happened. All one has to do is visualize the imprint that the typical pattern on the sole of a tennis shoe would make on a pile of dog poop.

This chapter devoted to Mom and Dad ends here. That does not mean you won't read more about them, as tons of additional information regarding Mom can be found in the remaining chapters, and you may also find another snippet or two about Dad.

CHAPTER THREE —BUTCH

"The more I learn about people, the more I like my dog."
-Mark Twain

Mom and Dad had been thinking for some time about getting a puppy to become my companion, but someone beat them to it. It was December 1987, and Barb's boyfriend at the time decided on a puppy as a surprise Christmas gift for Barb, who had just graduated from high school and was still living with Mom and Dad. So, after several years in a dog-less home, Mom and Dad had become pup parents again; however, unlike more than 10 years earlier when they had lost four puppies through no fault of their own, this time was destined to be long-term.

We were living in Japan at the time and that's where this bitch was born (it sure felt good to use the B-word for a dog and not me for a change, and it is correct usage in this context). Like Mom, Barb is a big-time animal lover. Here she is holding the little pup on the same day she received her as a gift.

Mom is a Japanese citizen, the children are all bilingual Japanese and English, Dad is a Japanese linguist, and I was given a Japanese name, so it would not have been unusual to select a Japanese name for this dog. Barb originally picked the name *Mimi* —the Japanese word for *ear*—in reference to the dog's ears that were quite small in relation to the size of her head. Mom wasn't fond of that name because it sounded like the redundant *me-me* in English. That was her reason for nicknaming the dog *Butch* one month later. From then on, for the rest of her life, she was known only as Butch.

In the argot of Mon Valley Pittsburghese, Dad deliberately paused for emphasis prior to vocalizing each syllable, "Jeez-o-man! [*Jesus C _ _ _ _ _!*]." Displeasure was clearly evident in the tone of his voice. He had come close a few times, but always managed to stay out of the doghouse by refraining from the use of profanity around Mom, who, in line with her social etiquette protocol, is a devout proponent of non-vulgar speech.

"Why in the heck would you call her Butch?" Dad's blunt query was accompanied by the most puzzled look I'd ever seen on his face.

As indicated by Chibi (the name she gave me), Mom had previously indicated partiality to Japanese names. This time, she picked an English name, and a masculine one to boot for a female dog, rather than any one of a multitude of other common, feminine, canine names. One thing is certain—it had nothing to do with a female of the human species exhibiting male characteristics, as her limited command of the English language at that point in time would not have enabled her to associate the name Butch with that particular meaning. She indicated she had heard someone say the name, probably in a movie or on TV and liked it, forgot it, subsequently remembered it, and ultimately decided to substitute it for Mimi.

In the veterinarian's office, at first, they called her Mimi—the official name in her records—to which she never responded. She answered only to Butch. The veterinary staff gradually learned to address her as Butch; however, without fail, a new staff member would call out the name Mimi in the waiting room and get totally ignored by both Mom and Butch. She never knew her own *legal* name, but so what—in her mind, she was Butch and nothing else mattered.

When someone asked what breed Butch was, Dad replied *Heinz 57*—a label given to mixed-breed, mongrel mutts in Southwestern Pennsylvania where he grew up (Heinz 57 is the marketing label for the many varieties of products sold by the H.J. Heinz Company that is headquartered in Pittsburgh). She closely resembled a full-blooded German Spitz, but was actually a Spitz-mix. Her body and head shapes looked a lot like the Japanese Spitz, except, unlike the pure white Japanese breed, her double fur coat was mostly shiny black like the German breed. She did have a patch of white on her tail, a lot of white fur on her belly, along with her four trademark white shins, indicating she was *paws*-sibly a Japanese and German Spitz hybrid. She was six weeks old when she arrived, an age that some would have considered too young for weaning. Maybe that's why she came hungry and seemingly remained in a constant hunger state for the rest of her relatively long life.

Her head appeared somewhat foxlike, but it was round, not thin as a fox. She had triangular ears and her tail curled back like a fox. An extra toe on one foot made her slightly deformed, but she had no other physical im-*purr*-fections—21 toes instead of 20 was barely noticeable. My pithy description of her upon arrival in the Herron household was a tiny bundle of black and white fur with extra-large, dark brown eyes, and unbridled, face-licking energy.

***

As mentioned earlier, shortly before Butch came along, Mom and Dad had started thinking about bringing another pet into their home. The decision as to a dog or cat would have been a no-brainer. Why would they get a second cat that would end up spending its whole life competing in an effort to equal me with absolutely no chance of success? There is no doubt they decided on a canine to eliminate any chance of feline-on-feline competition—or I should say opposition. I wasn't exactly thrilled over getting a dog for a housemate, but that was better than the feline alternative.

The statistics for the year in which Butch came into our home (1987) were not readily available; however, more recently, 69.9 million dogs and 74.1 million cats were living in human households in the United States (American Veterinary Medical Association (AVMA), 2012). Putting 2 and 2 together, one would deduce that more homes had cats than dogs. Not so fast! According to the AVMA, even though cats outnumbered dogs, a larger number of households had dogs—43.3 million or 36.5%--compared to 36.1 million or 30.4% with cats. That's because dog houses averaged 1.6 dogs and cat houses averaged 2.1 cats. This meant that even though cats outnumbered dogs, there were more dog people than cat people in the United States.

Since I preferred living in a one-cat home, learning that the average household had at least two cats caught me off guard. My first thought was that the numbers should be reversed, but upon reviewing the statistics again, it was confirmed they were correct. Perhaps, the most surprising stat would be that 2 out of 3 households in the United States (66.9%) had either dogs or cats (AVMA). Throw in birds, fish, horses, exotics, and other companion animals, and the total number of households exceeded 75% (AMVA). The numbers could be higher because there are many people who would like to have a pet, but do not either because they live alone and work long hours, or travel a lot for business or pleasure, or have severe dander allergies, which means they could not or would be unable to properly care for a furry kid.

Here is a mental stimulus for intellectual nourishment (aka: *food for thought*): when it comes to the total number of pets in American households, fish and birds were 3rd and 4th behind cats (1st) and dogs (2nd). That being said, since Mom, Dad, and the children all felt that a dog or a cat was far more compatible with humans than a goldfish or a parakeet, the only way they would consider taking in something with fins or feathers would be if they already had a cat or a dog.

There may be *paws*-itive aspects of having two cats in a single household (I can't imagine what they are); however, any favorability would be negated by the likelihood of cohabitation anxiety. After living with no furry housemates more than two years, I needed my space and could not imagine sharing a litter box, not to mention food and water bowls. It is also important to note that cats take much longer than most other animals to become acquainted with members of the same species. It is not uncommon for cats, at a minimum, to squabble (or worse) upon being introduced to each other, and they may never become friends, while a dog will decide within a few short minutes if it can be friends with another dog. This also holds true for a dog's introduction to a cat, as it didn't take long for Butch and I to nicely complement each other, and we went on to become *purr*-fect examples of how dogs and cats can harmonize while occupying the same living space.

Despite their inherent differences, dogs and cats do not have to live together antagonistically. Put yourself in our paws for a moment. Imagine going out on a blind date and the other *purr*-son announces, out of the blue, that they are going to live with you *fur*-ever. You'd likely be hard-pressed to feel the same way. Well, that's exactly the way I felt when Butch first stepped onto my turf. I was senior, had joined Mom and Dad's household two and one-half years earlier, and, until then, had been enjoying myself as the only furry kid in the Herron home. I had my doubts in the beginning, and it took a while, but I was able to adjust and amicably co-exist with Butch as a housemate.

It goes without saying that a freshly weaned puppy is far less threatening than a full-grown dog. I still needed to let Butch know from the get-go, and in no uncertain terms, that she would have to respect me before I'd *purr*-mit her an easy integration into the household. I stayed out of sight on Day 1, but surfaced on Day 2. As soon as she saw me the first time, she approached and came within paw range, so I smacked her on the nose. I knew she just wanted to play since she was so young. Please understand that it is not a bad thing for a cat to bop a dog. Since I had been declawed, my punch didn't hurt her, but it sure got the attention I desired. She gave me a startled look, and then just turned around and ran off, a scenario that would repeat itself thousands of times during the 14 years and 8 months that we spent as housemates.

I bopped Butch at least once a day while we lived together, and right after I bopped her each time, she always gave me the same surprised look obviously thinking, *I can't believe you did that*—as if she never saw it coming. Canids and felids are scent-oriented, meaning any strange new scent on what used to be their turf could cause one or more of a multitude of instinctive reactions. My response toward Butch's scent was natural aggression because, to me, she smelled like a dog. To keep her in check and preserve *my space*, I regularly swatted her on the snout with a quick right jab—more than 5,000 times total by my conservative estimate!

***

My meals came from a can, so I was a bit jealous over Mom always cooking from scratch for Butch. The quality of my food left nothing to be desired, but I just didn't like her spending more time on Butch than me. To be honest, I actually enjoyed eating my canned foods that were premium brands, highly nutritious, and low in calories, so I never had to worry about being a *fat cat*. In one sense—not the literal one—I was a fat cat because I had all the necessities and comforts I could ever want without having to stalk and kill a living thing in order to eat. I enjoyed a cozy life that enabled me to sleep rather than hunt. Pam-*purr*-ed was I!

Sometimes, I'd try to get Mom's attention while she was preparing Butch's dinner. I didn't want to eat the same food as Butch—yuck! I just wanted to show Butch that there wasn't a *Dogs Only* sign hanging in the kitchen. The assorted odors every single day whetted Butch's appetite and made her ravenous by the time each meal was served. While she was lying on the floor waiting for Mom to finish cutting up her meaty meal into bite-size pieces, I made it a point to go into the kitchen. I'd repeatedly walk by and twitch my tail across Butch's face just to irritate her. The only other time I would twitch my tail was when I felt threatened, but it was different with Butch, as my twitches toward her were a form of mild aggression rather than a defensive measure. Please do not consider my action as being bitchy in nature, but rather put it into context—cats naturally do this sort of thing to dogs.

THE DOGS' BEST FRIEND: A CAT'S EYE VIEW

Right after twitching Butch, I would rub against Mom's legs, one by one, to distract her. Then, I'd stare at her until I got her undivided attention, after which I'd blink at her and she would wink back at me. As previously mentioned, this was our way of *mew*-tually expressing the love bond between us. Many times after exchanging blinks and winks, Mom gave me a prized treat—a saucer filled with milk that I lapped down to the last drop.

Okay, I admit I was a bad cat for purposely diverting Mom's attention away from Butch. That having been said, I believe all cats need to make a point at times and, if that necessitates *bad* behavior, so be it.

***

Butch and I were the only furry kids in the household for six whole years. During that entire time, we lived in Japan, and Mom and Butch went for a walk nearly every day. They were not only inseparable—they were BFFs.

The big sparkling eyes and the manner in which Butch jumped up and down and spun around as soon as Mom popped the question—"Wanna go?"—left no doubt in any observer's mind that she was overly joyed about going outside with Mom. The walk with Mom was Butch's favorite time of day. They went outside in the morning while Dad was on the job and the kids were either in school or working, so it was just the two of them most of the time. Early on, Mom offered to take me along, but I politely declined and elected to stay behind to stand watch for any rodent that might dare think about trying to invade our homestead.

Mom occasionally tells a story about the contempt that Butch had for a certain feathered species they frequently encountered on their walks. The first of many side stories about Butch and the other Herron dogs' run-ins with a variety of birds follows.

One day in Japan, while on their routine morning walk, 10 crows appeared overhead out of nowhere and swooped down onto the middle of a football field 25 yards away from where Mom and Butch were walking along the sidelines. Butch let out a war-bark and lunged in the flock's direction. She got only as far as the 12-foot leash would allow—no closer than 20 yards of the birds. The nearest crow slowly turned its head toward Butch and appeared to be grinning like a half-wit. Within a matter of seconds, the other crows all displayed the same mocking grin. In unison, they suddenly broke the silence with a combined, loud and raucous cackling, *CAAAW-CAAAW-CAAAW*!

Butch glared at them with an evil eye for a full minute until they quieted down, after which they all turned their backs as if to ignore and insult her. It should be noted that Japanese crows are twice the physical size, 10 times more aggressive, and 100 times more irritating than American crows. Intimidating were they!

Despite their size and haughty manner, Butch was not about to allow the lowly black birds get away with such offensive behavior. She couldn't stand their *fowl* language, and refused to be outsmarted by birdbrains. Becoming impatient and wanting to confront the flock in a showdown, Butch's eyes begged Mom to unfasten the leash and *purr*-mit her to take offensive action against the winged tormenters. With little delay, Mom gave in and set her free.

Although outnumbered 10-to-1, Butch took baby steps inching toward the big black birds while they were standing around. When she got within 15 yards, the nearest crow tentatively stirred its wings as if maybe considering retreat; however, the mocking bird merely shifted its position so as to present its arse in Butch's direction, thereby sending a clear signal of outright insolence! Then all the crows, oblivious to Butch's slow advancement, began talking—or squawking, whatever crows do—amongst themselves.

The birds took no evasive action until Butch got within 10 yards. That's when Butch paused for a moment before suddenly taking off like an airplane accelerating down the runway for takeoff. At the last second as if on cue, with Butch less than 5 yards away, the birds all flapped their wings and lumbered up 8-10 feet off the ground where they hovered like remote-controlled, toy helicopters while letting out more loud screeches, *CAAAW-CAAAW-CAAAW*! The air over the entire football field resonated with that god-awful sound.

Butch went berserk, barked uncontrollably at the airborne marauders, spun around in a circle, and repeatedly jumped higher off the ground than she had ever gone before, but came nowhere close to latching onto her target—the closest bird's tailfeathers. Mom was able to pull her back to a safe distance approximately 10 yards away, after which just as fast as they had gone up, the demonic birds dropped back down to the turf. They resumed their total disrespect for Butch by glaring back eyeball-to-eyeball, while bobbing their heads and tails up and down. Their piercing eyes, which matched the color of their feathers, were meant to taunt.

Wondering why the crows were refusing to fly away, and puzzled by their lack of fear, Butch reacted by continuing to bark hysterically. As soon as she made the slightest movement in their direction, the crows switched to a hideous cawing—much hoarser and more raucous than before—which enabled them to show their sharp beaks as weapons.

It was a standoff until Butch endured all the humiliation she could take. Dogs are thought to be dichromate and thus, by human standards, color blind, but in this situation, Butch saw red. She must have been self-declaring, *I'm a bad-ass dog up against mere birds*. She shook her booty and then stood erect in a near *purr*-fect pointer position, as if asserting, *Guess who's going to win this battle!*

There was no more barking, only death-defying yelps, as Butch lunged toward the middle of the flock, dragging the leash that she had ripped from Mom's hands. The birds were caught by total surprise and barely got away bumping into each other while flying up. Butch jumped again, this time with all fours off the ground, and landed with a single black tailfeather in her mouth. Go Butch Go!

She had to be thinking to herself, *That'll teach 'em*! She proudly strutted slowly back to where Mom was waiting with outstretched arms while watching the airborne crows hastily retreat and disappear over the horizon. Mom couldn't help but notice that Butch's face was beaming, prompting her to exclaim, "Oh my Butch, you're smiling!" Then, she hugged and caressed the victor.

Butch's facial features and routine expression, with her teeth slightly showing, made it often appear as if she was smiling, but, no doubt, in that moment of victory, there was an extra curve in the corners of her mouth. The curve got even wider when Mom cried out, "You are my hero Butch! I love you so much."

Mom pulled the feather from Butch's mouth with the intention of keeping it as a trophy. Upon returning home that evening and hearing from Mom what had transpired, Dad hung the feather on the patio wall for others to observe. Numerous visitors got to see that trophy, which prompted all of them to compliment

THE DOGS' BEST FRIEND: A CAT'S EYE VIEW

Butch on her crow-bashing skills.

A few weeks after the crow incident, Mom's girlfriend Takako and her Shetland Sheepdog *Chappie*, who were our neighbors, began accompanying Mom and Butch on their morning strolls. Without fail, they came across either the same bunch or another flock of roving crows. That's because Butch would always steer them to where the birds were located.

Butch was quick to show Chappie how to handle the feathered nuisances by taking the initiative. She had learned that the element of surprise gave her a definite advantage because it forced the crows to immediately go into a defensive mode. During football season, Dad could be heard declaring, "The best defense is a good offense," a phrase that Butch may not have understood. but it was something she sure knew how to put into practice. Never again would she give any crow the chance to be an aggressor.

Butch's intentions became clear to Mom, so when they got close to the football field or wherever else the crows could be found, Butch's leash came off, and Mom told Takako to set Chappie free too. Upon sighting their very first flock together, with Chappie to her rear, Butch slowly crept toward the birds, and when she got within 10 yards shifted into high gear and ran straight at them with Chappie on her heels. The startled crows took off like bats out of H_ _ _. Chappie seemed impressed and was soon running side by side with Butch on the bullrush attacks for many days to come.

Although they never took down a crow, Butch and Chappie were each able to assemble a collection of tail feathers as souvenirs during the two-year period they paired-up. The constant yapping that went on between them as they romped after the big, black birds was unmistakable canine crow-bashing at its best. Dad designated them "Crow Busters." Dad made a big deal out of Butch outsmarting the crows because he knew they had been nicknamed "feathered apes" after scientists determined that they were highly intelligent and comparable to chimpanzees (Clayton, 2015). By the way, as can be seen in the photo below, Chappie wasn't bad-looking—for a dog, that is.

At one of our family barbeques, I overheard Dad telling a guest about something that had gone terribly wrong at work, after which he "had to eat crow." I couldn't hear everything he said, but from what I could gather, it made me wonder how crow might taste. I bet there's no white meat! Since Dad has a history of being a *fowl* connoisseur dating back to the sparrow-on-a-stick episode, it was not surprising to hear him talk about eating crow. Hmm, first sparrows, then crows. What could possibly be next?

***

Butch enjoyed winter more than any other season. Diving, nose-first, deep into a snow drift was her idea of outdoor fun. She had plenty of fur to keep her warm despite the chilling winds common during the long winters in Northern Japan, where she spent the first eight years of her life. She came to the United States in 1995. It was a long trip and riding in the belly of an aircraft amidst the suitcases and other baggage was highly stressful. I know firsthand because Butch and my pet carriers were side by side during that trip.

It doesn't snow in Central Florida where Mom and Dad made their new home after leaving Japan, so Butch never got to enjoy winter weather again. Unlike Butch, I didn't miss the cold climate since my paw-bottoms were highly sensitive to snow and ice.

Barb and Brenda, along with Peko and Chiro, had left Japan for Florida to attend college 18 months before the rest of us, so it was great to be reunited with them (at least the humans) after such a long time. Butch and I made sure we got more than our fair share of human attention from Barb and Brenda even though we had to compete with the Akita sisters, who Barb and Brenda had added to the family six months before they left Japan to return to the States.

Upon rejoining Peko and Chiro, Butch didn't waste any time by reasserting herself as the alpha dog. On their first ride to a nearby park in the family SUV, Butch insisted on sitting in the front passenger seat. Until then, Peko had ridden shotgun, but after Butch arrived, Peko was *purr*-manently delegated to the back seat where Mom and Chiro sat. Mom sat in the middle between the two Akitas. Peko wasn't happy at first, but didn't resist and readily became used to sitting in the rear by accepting it as a matter of *age before beauty* (Butch was 6 years older than her). Afterall, that's the way the seating arrangement was in Japan before Peko and Chiro left.

One day, after a walk in the park, Dad stopped at a supermarket. He went inside to buy something leaving Mom and the dogs in the car. As usual, Butch sat in the front and Mom was sandwiched by Peko and Chiro in the back. A woman and a toddler girl walked by, at which time the little girl yelled, "Look Mommy, four dogs in there," as she pointed toward the car. Mom didn't think it was funny, nor was she embarrassed by being mistaken for the 4th *dog*. After all, her head was at chest level with Peko and Chiro when they sat on either side of her, plus it was at sunset and getting dark, so she wouldn't have been clearly visible to anyone walking by the car. Dad, however, thought it was hilarious when Mom told him what had happened. To Mom's chagrin, he often brings up this story to family and friends, making her wish she had kept it to herself.

***

Butch was a bit pudgy, but it wasn't a problem since the excess poundage did not present a health risk. According to the veterinarian, her weight that leveled off at 55 pounds in her prime was 13% above her "ideal" weight (48 pounds). "So what!" Mom blurted out to the vet. Butch was destined to live a long, healthy life despite a few extra pounds. Mom took it *purr*-sonal when the vet hinted that she should consider altering Butch's diet by giving her commercial, low calorie dog food instead of the meals she was preparing by hand.

Granted, she was chubby, but by no means obese, so there was no way anyone could convince Mom to change the type or quantity of food to prepare for her. Butch's chubbiness was a frequent source of enjoyment for Steve, who cracked up while watching her slide her rather large posterior to one side while slightly straining to push herself up from a sitting position. It wasn't a single, quick motion, but rather a series of twists, turns, and grunts to get up onto her feet.

Skinny legs in relation to her body size made for a top heaviness that caused Butch to waddle slightly when she walked, and that made her appear heavier than she actually was. The extra pounds resulted not from the meals Mom cooked for her, but rather from the treats and snacks that Barb, Steve, Brenda, and Dad gave her. Butch loved American junk food like pizza, cookies, and hotdogs. Her favorite snack, however, was a healthy one—raw broccoli, which Mom made sure she got plenty of.

She also enjoyed many Japanese dishes, including soba (buckwheat noodles) and sukiyaki (meat, tofu, and veggies slowly cooked in a pot), but her all-time *ichi-ban* (number one) food was yakitori (pieces of grilled chicken skewered on a wooden stick). Having become a pro at removing the chicken meat with her teeth without damaging the stick or getting a splinter in her tongue, she especially loved it when skin was left on the meat. The only time she got her fill of yakitori was during the summers in Japan when the family went to one local festival after another where endless yakitori was available from hordes of street vendors.

After going to the United States, Steve made sure she still got occasional yakitori to eat even though it was a major chore and highly time-consuming to prepare. He would painstakingly cut up the meat into tiny pieces, skewer it, and then cook it on the grill. The whole family likes yakitori, but Steve did it mostly for Butch.

Before moving to Florida, Butch participated in scores of backyard barbeque parties in Japan. The cookouts continued in Florida with Steve taking over as Top Chef, and every time he fired-up the grill, Butch was first in line to sample the steak, ribs, salmon, or whatever kind of meat he was cooking. It always worked when she begged with her eyes, as everyone in attendance would go out of their way at some point to give her food items. She'd move around from Ruthie to Les, then over to Goh, Koh, Atsushi, Taeko, Toshi, Takako, Yoji, and whoever else happened to be there. She didn't miss anyone in attendance, but saved the family members for last knowing full well that visitors would be the most generous.

Acting as if each bite might be her last, Butch wolfed down food with little or no chewing motion. While watching her enthusiastically chow down, a visitor remarked, "Now there's a dog that eats like a horse." Someone else said, "She sure relishes dinnertime," and there were many other assorted remarks to that effect.

Butch didn't miss picking up any crumb dropped on the floor prompting Dad to nickname her *Hoover* after an American vacuum cleaner manufacturer. The kitchen odors generated by Mom never failed to stimulate Butch's appetite every single day and made her appear famished by the time dinner was served. She never found any kind of food (canine or human) to be unpalatable. A true food lover was she! In summation, a picture of Butch would fit *purr*-fectly in a dictionary next to the word *chowhound*.

By transferring the basic idea of digestion from the stomach to the brain, food for thought (pardon pun please) came to mind. That prompted me to bring up the topic of communication between pets and their human companions. Since humans are recognized as the cream of the intelligence crop among all living beings, why can't they find a way to more effectively communicate with domestic animals? I don't mean simple, one-word commands like *sit, shake*, and *speak* common with canines, but rather complete sentences. Further, why can't they learn how pets exchange thoughts and feelings with each other through sound, touch, smell, body language, and other non-verbal means, and then develop a way to exchange ideas with them by doing it the same way?

***

Butch never felt confined by being kept inside the house. She believed she could go outside on her own with no interference any time she wanted. When she was permitted to go outside by herself, usually in the backyard to potty, she never tried to go beyond the fence even when someone forgot to close a gate. Smart dog! It's not that she wasn't adventuresome—she just preferred to go outside the fence in the company of Mom, in particular, or with Dad or one of the children on those rare occasions when Mom was unavailable.

First-time visitors to our house aroused Butch's suspicion. She would loudly bark at them until Mom calmed her down. As soon as Mom showed a sign of friendliness toward a *purr*-son, Butch stopped barking and instantly became their friend too. Her protective nature, along with a loud and forceful bark, made her an outstanding watchdog. Sometimes, she would excitedly bark to excess, even upon hearing a doorbell on the TV, but she was quick to quiet down upon Mom's command. She was like a burglar alarm and it did not take much to set her off. Fortunately, she was just as fast calming down and returning to normalcy.

Mom's all-time greatest companion was Butch. She shadowed Mom's every move. Some other dogs may match Butch's devotion to a single human, but there is no way any other dog could top her—maybe equal, but no way surpass! She took food and accepted affection from others, but would tag along only after Mom to the exclusion of all others. Everywhere Mom went, Butch followed. Mom didn't even have privacy in the bathroom. Butch and Mom not only clicked, they clicked more than any two humans, or any two canines could possibly click. A guest in our home once asked Mom, "Do you have Butch on an invisible leash?" Mom smiled and amusingly nodded in the affirmative.

Mom understood Butch to a T. She knew some dogs never think about wanting to have time alone, and due to their total devotion to a single human, they always want to be by their human's side. She was glad Butch fit this personality type--and was even gladder that she wound up the object of Butch's affection.

Mom anthropomorphized Butch after Butch had totally mesmerized her with those dreamy eyes. If my usage of such big words was impressive, how about this—Butch was cynomorphizing Mom at the same time Mom was anthropomorphizing Butch. Whew! I really must ease up on using 5 *and* 6-syllable words to preclude any misconception and eliminate the possibility of being defamed by the B-word. It may have become apparent by now that I view myself as charismatic and captivating; however, I do realize it's more important for others to see me in that light.

Among Butch's many great physical qualities, her big, brown, doe-like eyes pleased Mom the most. That was because Mom and Butch engaged in *mew*-tual staring, face-to-face, at least a dozen times per day. It was sort of like the way Mom and I did, but with a slight variance—their glances weren't quick, but rather gazes into each other's eyes for minutes at a time. Drowning in the love hormone oxytocin were they!

Researchers in Japan from Azabu University in Kanagawa and the University of Tokyo teamed up to conduct research to determine if oxytocin promotes social bonding in dogs. The results of their experimental study appeared in a 2004 article on the Internet webpage of the Proceedings of the National Academy of Sciences of the United States of America (Romero, Nagasawa, Mogi, Hasegawa, & Kikusui, 2014).

A total of 16 domesticated dogs were involved in the experiments—8 females and 8 males, all older than one year (Romero, et al.). Each dog was nasal sprayed with either oxytocin or a saline solution away from their owners, after which they were permitted to interact with their owners. The findings by Romero et al. disclosed that the dogs sprayed with oxytocin showed much more affection to their owners—licking or pawing or staring at them—than the dogs sprayed with the saline solution. Furthermore, the dogs sprayed with oxytocin spent more time socializing with other dogs involved in the experiment than the dogs sprayed with the saline solution.

Later, some of the Japanese scientists, who had conducted the aforementioned oxytocin research, asked 30 of their friends and neighbors to bring their dogs to a laboratory for a follow-up study. They also got a few people with wolves as pets to participate. Urine samples were collected from all the pets (males and females) and their humans (males and females), after which the humans spent 30 minutes in a room petting and talking to their pets. Per instruction, one-half of the humans gazed into their pet's eyes for brief periods, while the other half did not. Afterward, second urine samples were obtained from the humans and pets. It was found that the dogs, who had spent time exchanging gazes with their owners, had experienced, on average, a 130% rise in oxytocin levels, and the owners' oxytocin levels had risen an average of 300%.

There was no increase in oxytocin levels for the dogs and owners who had spent no time gazing at each other. It was interesting to note that there was no change in the oxytocin levels for any of the wolves and their humans, 50% of whom participated in the gazing group and the other half in the non-gazing portion of the experiment.

The aforementioned experiments suggested that human-dog bonding is comparable to parent-infant bonding through simple eye contact. Another conclusion was that since the wolf pets were not affected, *mew*-tual gaze-bonding between humans and dogs likely coevolved over a long period of time—after dogs had diverged from their wolf ancestors and became pets.

Other recent research studies conducted by Japanese and American scientists have left no doubt that dogs are capable of several mental activities, including thinking, understanding, learning, and remembering. This means that dogs have the undeniable capabilities to communicate and comprehend, not only with other canines, but also with humans—with limitations of course.

CatDog was an animated television series about anthropomorphic animals produced by Nickelodeon. First airing in the late 1990s, it depicted the life of conjoined brothers with a single body and two heads, one a cat and the other a dog. They were best friends, but as different as cats and dogs—Dog loved rock n' roll, Cat did not; *Dog* liked to chase garbage trucks, Cat did not. CatDog reminded me of the relationship between Butch and me. We were not at all alike, but we were friends. She and I could have been the models for CatDog.

***

Although Barb started out as Butch's main companion, it didn't take long for Mom to take over that role. Besides me, Mom and Butch were the only ones in our home much of the time, as Dad went off to work and the children were at school or had part-time jobs. Butch was empathetic by recognizing when Mom didn't feel well and constantly watched over her until she got back to normal. She had Mom's back all the time.

Butch was quick to let out a low growl and display teeth to anyone who showed a sign of affection toward Mom, especially when it involved physical contact. Her line of thinking, *No one touches my Mom!* Dad and the children were constantly aware of this, and that was a good thing because it enabled them to avoid getting bit.

Like me, Butch had an aversion to roughhousing by the kids. Even though they were merely playing around, she took all types of physical contact seriously, and did not hesitate to voice her disapproval by getting in the middle and showing teeth in what appeared to be a threatening manner. In short, she didn't mind being on the receiving end of good-natured physical contact by roughhousing with Dad a lot, but she did not like to see anyone engaged physically with someone else. Butch never bit anyone, so her action in trying to stop physical play by

THE DOGS' BEST FRIEND: A CAT'S EYE VIEW

the children and protecting Mom may have been just for show. Whatever—it worked!

Throughout her life on Earth, Butch tagged along behind Mom, sometimes so close that she tripped Mom by getting under her feet. Other times, Mom stepped on Butch's feet. The *mew*-tual tripping was a sign of their intensely close-knit relationship. She was lucky to be Mommy's little girl and showed it by constantly getting as close to Mom as possible. In view of the countless times they tripped each other, how both of them were always able to avoid falling was a miracle.

Speaking of tripping, Dad stumbled over Butch more times than he could count. There's no question that Butch was not doing it on purpose since she was just lying down on the floor when Dad happened to come along and accidentally stepped on her tail or foot. Unlike Mom who never fell, Dad toppled with Butch under his feet a few times, and it was his fault for being such a klutz.

Butch slept in the master bedroom with Mom and Dad every night—on their bed. Since dogs have a higher body temperature than humans—somewhere around 101 degrees Fahrenheit—and Mom's body temperature was naturally a little bit low at 97.9 degrees, it was always comforting for her to snuggle up next to Butch. This meant Dad was left to snuggle up with himself—if you know what I mean (*wink wink*).

Butch snored, but it didn't keep Mom awake as she offset Butch's snores with her own. Their combined snoring did not bother Dad as his own deafening sounds—like sawing wood—drowned out both of them. Every time Dad got up in the middle of the night to pee, he got a chuckle out of the snorting noises emitting in broken unison from Butch and Mom's nasal passages. He couldn't tell which sounds came from Butch and which ones belonged to Mom. I can attest to that since I heard them too—it was as if they snored in sync.

When it came to oral communication, Butch was the most versatile of all my canine housemates. Mom could quickly differentiate between her beggar whining when she wanted to eat, and her back-to-back *ruff-ruff* barks when she wanted to go outside. And her sudden, rapid, non-stop barking was a clear signal that a strange human or animal was outside in close proximity to our house.

***

What I liked most about Butch was she did not have a strong doggy odor. Of course, my fine sense of smell readily detected her nauseating canine scent, but it was so comparatively minor that human nose buds didn't readily detect it. Due to the fine texture of her shiny coat, Mom was able to easily brush out dirt, mud, bugs, and whatever else clung to her fur, and that made her nice and clean by keeping shedding to a minimum.

The bathroom was Butch's least favorite place simply because a bathtub was in there. To resist bath time, she used what Mom called "butt power" by hunkering down as hard as she could on her hind end and rear legs. Mom or Dad had to drag her dead weight to the tub and then pick her up to get her into the water. This scene repeated itself each time Butch was bathed every three months or so.

Butch taught the butt-power maneuver to Peko, who went on to use it more effectively than Butch since she weighed 30 pounds heavier. I got a lot of laughs watching Mom or Dad trying to catch and then carry Butch and Peko, one right after the other, to the tub. This went on for those two dog's entire lives.

The bath aftermaths were funny too because Butch and Peko shook their booties as hard as they could spraying water all over Mom and Dad. The dogs all hated being washed outside with a garden hose rinse, so Mom insisted on bathing them inside. Although Chiro wasn't particularly grateful for baths, unlike Butch and Peko, she always climbed into the tub on her own willpower with no resistance.

Butch did have one nasty habit. After pooping outside, she would drag her butt along the grass to wipe. In all fairness, she was only trying to clean herself. Sometimes, upon going into the house, she'd do dog-wheelies by dragging her butt on the carpeted floor in an effort to rid herself of a piece of fecal material that had not wiped off on the grass and was hanging from her butt. Dad and the children thought it was disgusting, but Mom didn't seem to mind because, like I said, she was just trying to keep herself clean.

The noise the vacuum cleaner made terrified Butch. She must have thought it was an electric monster on a mission to chase her down. She stayed in the same room while Mom vacuumed because she didn't want to leave Mom alone with *that thing*. She always backed into the corner of the room furthest away from it. Each time Mom slightly turned the vacuum in Butch's direction, she would take off running to another corner of the room. I got away by exiting to another room, but Butch stayed to protect Mom.

It was scary for Butch to watch the vacuum start up with a dreadful purr-like sound, move forward, stop, start moving again, bump into walls and furniture, stop, turn, and stop again. Partly due to observing Butch's reaction, and partly because of the machine's terrifying presence, Peko and Chiro were instantly scared stiff when Mom started up the vacuum cleaner the first time in their presence, and they, in turn, passed that fear on to Koro. The dogs' evasion of the invading vacuum cleaner was started by Butch and became a commonplace occurrence in the Herron home.

What Butch hated the most was loud noises. At 8 months of age, she first heard fireworks exploding above our house. Since I had been through it the previous 4th of July, it wasn't new to me, but I understood why Butch freaked-out and ran around in circles inside the master bedroom. She must have thought we were the target of an artillery attack! The family was in the backyard watching the display and could not hear Butch's petrified yelping. Halfway through the fireworks show, Mom went upstairs to check and found her curled up and shaking inside the bedroom closet, so she stayed and comforted her until the noises subsided.

The fireworks that scared Butch were being launched from a high school football field across the street no more than 100 yards away, so the noise level was deafening. The community program lasted for almost an hour and included detonation of the largest firework explosives available in 1988. That was the last time a fireworks show was so close to our house, but it didn't matter, as every 4th of July thereafter, even though the big fireworks were launched far away in the distance and sometimes barely audible, Butch still quivered and sought refuge by snuggling up close on Mom's lap.

***

Butch's delightful *purr*-sonality was lively and entertaining. The more attention she got from humans, the more she craved. For a dog, she was very bright. The primary objective of her lifelong mission was to ensure the condition of well-being for everyone in our house, albeit Mom in particular.

Like me, Butch believed she was more human than dog. In many ways, she acted like a person, and gave visitors the impression that she was a human trapped inside a dog's physical frame. For instance, she was never able to hide guilt just like some people cannot do. Without fail, upon being accused of something bad, if she was guilty, she would do whatever it took to avoid eye contact while slowly crawling toward her accuser. The problem was she reacted the same way when innocent that she did when rightfully accused, so she always appeared guilty. Peko was the wrongdoer countless times, but it wasn't unusual for Butch to take the blame for Peko because she looked and acted like the guilty party, while Peko was efficient at disguising guilt.

Although she always appeared happy, when aroused to a state of extra happiness, Butch wagged her tail so vigorously she had to cling hard with her front paws to keep from falling over. She often laughed, not only with a smiley face, but also with her tail, and that made her whole-body wag. It was more than a simple wag—she literally shook! Her flowing black hair was a sight to behold.

She wagged a lot when Dad came home from work by greeting him exuberantly every single time he walked through the door as if she hadn't seen him for days even though it may have been only a few hours. She acted the same way when Barb, Steve, and Brenda came home.

Something else that led to a whole-body wag by Butch was Steve coaxing her to join him in a sing-along duet. The soprano tone of Steve's voice set her off every time. Her howling must have been a shared trait with her wild ancestor wolves, notwithstanding that her sing-along version was not directed at the moon. (Not to get too far off the subject, but I must say that wolves howling at the moon has to be a bunch of malarkey, as there's no doubt they also howled on moonless nights)

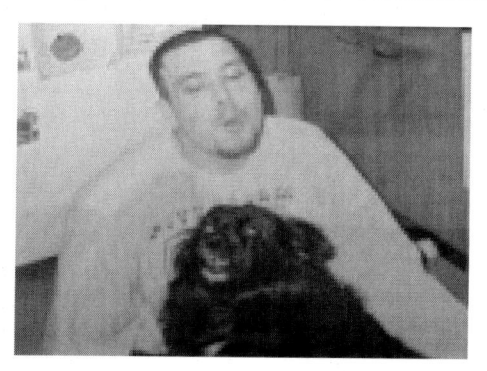

Butch wagged the most in response to Steve's high-pitched squealing "Boo-bay-san," a nickname he had given her that had a distinct Japanese flair. In view of the way she acted by not only squirming, twisting, and shaking her entire body, but also by imitating Steve with her own shrill howl, she seemed to simultaneously love and hate his oral presentation of that nickname. A song dog was she!

***

Even a cat of my dignified stature derives amusement from teasing dogs. So what, since it's not uncommon for humans to engage in teasing other humans. I saw enough of it to realize that teasing comes naturally, and the only ones who object to it are those on the receiving end.

For amusement, I would swat Butch's head with my paw as she walked by. Even though I did it on average at least twice a day, as has already been mentioned, the expression on Butch's face was the same every time—total disbelief that I would do such a thing for no apparent reason. Much of the time, I had no reason to swat her. Provocation was not my intent. It was all in fun with nil ill will. Frankly, I did it just because I could! Eventually, Butch came to expect it, and it became a way for us to intermingle.

By the way, I was right-pawed, but able to occasionally throw a left-paw punch with equal surprise and accuracy. That was the full extent of playful interaction I had with Butch. Okay, I admit my action could be construed as minor bullying—a role reversal since dogs normally bully cats, not the other way around.

Teasing is not a perverse pleasure, but rather a marvelous way of killing time. Boredom can be so hard to bear at times that there's no better way to break the monotony than stimulating oneself by irritating another being. The endless satisfaction I gained by ragging Butch made my life as a teaser worthwhile. I never teased my human associates because that would have been disrespectful.

I offer the conclusion that a cat teasing a dog is *purr*-fectly acceptable behavior, even though a dog on the receiving end would likely consider it a bit much. So what, as long as it's in good fun! And it didn't damage our relationship at all as indicated by the scene below, which shows us mellowing out side-by-side, something we did every single day that we were housemates.

Butch and I had a couple of very important things in common. She was the first canine and I was the first feline to become Mom, Dad, Barb, Steve, and Brenda's lasting pets. Neither of us was a purebred. Unlike the three registered Akitas Peko, Chiro, and Koro that came after us, Butch's lineage was unknown and so was mine. Purebreds appear to be cut from the same mold, but crossbreeds like Butch and I are truly one-of-a-kind.

I was 2 years older than Butch, so, technically, she and I became seniors around the same time. That's because our veterinarian considered dogs reaching age 8 and cats at age 10 to be entering the geriatric age.

As the first canine to live long-term in Mom and Dad's household, Butch set the standard for the dogs to come. After being on the receiving end from Butch, Mom believes there is no mental health remedy as effective for humans as a face-licking by a dog. Butch was notorious for doing disgusting things with her mouth, but that didn't seem to bother Mom or the children. Dad, on the other hand, took evasive measures, thereby letting it be known he had second thoughts about allowing Butch to plant a big juicy one on his face.

Butch led by example. She taught Peko and Chiro to always run —never walk—when greeting each of the humans in our family every time they returned home. And, she taught them how to do it with the whole-body wag. I can attest that watching a trio of non-greyhounds jump-running in concert was an impressive sight to behold—just like true greyhounds breaking away from the gate in a dog race.

**

Two days after Butch's 12th birthday, the veterinarian diagnosed arthritis, and recommended reduction in calories to lower the stress on her joints. Mom had not previously followed the vet's advice to put her on a diet; however, this time, she was concerned for health reasons, so she lowered Butch's caloric intake. She prepared the same food, just lesser portions. It was hard because Peko and Chiro ate side by side with Butch, and they didn't have to count calories. It took a while, but she finally adapted to the modified meal plan. Weight loss occurred although it wasn't astronomical—52 pounds down from 55.

Three days after her 13th birthday, Butch suffered her first seizure. Although it lasted less than a minute, it was both disturbing and alarming to Mom. I can speak firsthand because I was there, and it scared the be-Jesus out of me. The experience was traumatic and extremely frightening to Butch. She was lying on her right side on the kitchen floor. Her body became rigid, eyes rolled back, and belly twitching. Drool gushed out the side of her mouth. It ended just as suddenly as it had begun. Butch got up, shook her rear end a couple of times, and then resumed routine activities as if nothing had happened.

The vet prescribed Phenobarbital to reduce the severity of the seizures, but it didn't put a stop to them. At first, they occurred about two months apart, and that frequency lasted for almost six months. Then they started happening once per month, and that went on for about three months. Each one lasted 30-60 seconds, but it sure seemed much longer. Butch snapped back quickly with short-lived disorientation following each episode. After relaxing for a few minutes in Mom's arms, she would jump up on her feet and return to her usual self.

She had two or three seizures per week during her last month. *Why you Butch?* Mom thought out loud after hearing from the vet that less than 1% of dogs suffer such seizures. Throughout the duration of each episode, Mom would clutch Butch with a hand on each side of her head and console her by talking in a calm, reassuring manner until the shaking finally stopped. Other than the seizures, Butch never seemed to experience an unhappy moment—never! It was as if she may have sensed there was a limit to her earthly life, so there wasn't any time to waste by being downhearted.

Butch really did love to eat—more than any human or any animal I ever knew. The day came, however, when she declined all food and didn't want any water either. It got to the point that Mom had to use a syringe filled with water to keep her hydrated during the final six hours. She managed to nibble a little bit on a piece of broccoli, her all-time favorite snack. Although she had no idea that the end was drawing near, she knew Mom would feel better if she ate something, so she did it.

A good face-licking was her final goodwill gesture to Mom, who would later say, "That sure did mean a lot." Thankfully, there were no more seizures during those final hours, and Butch was at peace in the end. Mom cradled her head while softly kissing her nose as her eyes closed for the last time.

Mom cried uncontrollably for hours saying such things as, "I am so sorry I couldn't stop the seizures Butchy… Remember our walks with Chappie and you guys chasing those nasty crows? So proud of you my bodyguard… I love you so much Butch."

She continued directing more words of sorrow at Butch's lifeless body, "You were not fat. Shame on the vet for saying that. You loved Steve's barbeques so much. Sorry about the fireworks scaring you. I will never forget the beautiful singing you and Steve did together my sweet baby." Her last words especially hit hard, "You didn't even know you wouldn't wake up."

Just before, and again right after Butch passed, I wondered what might have gone through her mind—what she may have been thinking about during her final hours. I didn't think she felt death was near, but there was no way to know for sure. She may have thought she was just going to sleep and she'd see Mom again when she woke up.

Butch had floppy ears, but after she had passed, both ears were straight up and erect and they stayed that way. It was indicative she had strained extra hard to hear Mom's final words in the form of a Japanese song called *Happy Doll Festival* that Mom had sung to her at least once a day every day of her life. She went peacefully looking at the face of her most beloved human while Mom stroked her head lovingly until the last breath. It was comforting for Dad and the children to know that the last thing she saw was Mom's face and the last thing she heard was Mom's voice. After all, *Butchy* was Mom's shadow and totally devoted to Mom her entire life.

Peko and Chiro sniffed Butch's body before Dad transported her remains to the vet's office for cremation. Mom carefully wrapped her in her treasured blanket, along with her favorite stuffed toy and a bouquet of flowers delivered by Brenda, before Dad carried her out to the car in a makeshift stretcher fashioned out of a cardboard box. While fighting back tears, Mom repeated over and over, "I love you Butchy. I love you so much." Petting the top of her head, she added, "I'll see you again someday. Just wait for me up there by the Rainbow Bridge, okay." Butch's mouth was slightly opened creating the appearance of a peaceful smile.

When Mom opened the door for Dad to carry her body out to the family van, a lively black butterfly fluttered excitedly alongside the walkway leading out to the driveway. It seemed to be dancing in a soft breeze. My first thought was Butch's soul may have transformed into the butterfly and came back to show off her new form to Mom, Dad, Brenda, Peko, Chiro, and me. The butterfly flew above the van and hovered there stationary facing down toward Dad as he placed Butch's body into the rear of the van.

When Dad pulled out of the driveway, the butterfly trailed hastily behind following the vehicle down the street until they were out of sight. I just knew Butch's soul had to be inside that butterfly's body. Mom must have thought the same thing, as I heard her muttering to herself, "There goes Butch flying away."

Unfortunately, Butch just missed seeing Barb and her children Ricky and Erika. They came from Japan for their yearly visit one week after she had passed. They arrived in the early evening and, as they were unloading suitcases from Dad's van in the driveway outside our house, a black butterfly circled over their heads. It was identical to the one that had appeared seven days earlier when Dad left to take Butch's body to the veterinarian's office for cremation. Mom blurted out, "Look! Butch came back to see you guys," as the butterfly nosedived toward Barb barely grazing the hair on the top of her head, after which it flew across the street and disappeared from sight. It happened so fast that Barb and the kids did not take seriously what Mom had said.

Despite the distraction and excitement of having family visitors from Japan, Mom did not merely chalk it up as nothing more than one among thousands of transient butterflies that had crossed her path. She recalled the earlier black butterfly incident and felt that Butch was returning to say hello.

The next morning, I was by myself out on the back patio looking for lizards, when a black butterfly suddenly landed on the screen door and peered at me through the wire mesh. I froze because it looked just like the butterfly that had shown up when Dad transported Butch's remains to the vet's office for cremation, and the one that came by while Barb and her kids were unloading the car the night before. I felt weirdly eerie and joyful at the same time—eerie in view of what appeared to be the supernatural effect of Butch's transformation into a butterfly, and joyful to see what may have been Butch in motion again, albeit in a totally different physical form. I felt Butch's presence! In a few seconds, the butterfly was gone as quickly as it had shown up.

The epitaph engraved on a life-like dog statute with add-on angel wings standing guard in Mom's garden reads, "Butch The Light Of Our Lives." Mom tears up when someone mentions her name. After all, Butch and she were bosom buddies for a whopping 5,015 days, and that wasn't even close to long enough for either of them. There are millions of true-love relationships between a dog and their main human, and some may match the relationship that Mom and Butch had, but there's no way any of them could be closer.

It's always too soon to lose a loved one whether human or animal. Mom experienced a profound sense of loss for the first time in 10 years when Butch passed—10 years and 4 months to be exact, which was how long it had been since Dad's mother had died. It was more than 13 years since her own mother had passed. For humans like Mom, the loving attachment to an animal friend comes close to equaling that of a human relationship, and that makes the loss of an animal nearly as devastating as the loss of a beloved human. Some people do not feel that the loss of an animal friend is comparable to losing a human family member or a friend; however, they are no longer in the mainstream.

My own grief over losing Butch was overwhelming. It was my first and only experience with heartbreak, and it was most evident late at night when I roamed the house alone. My crying was made up of an interweaving of howls and wails that often woke up Mom. I got carried away at times and just couldn't control myself emotionally because I had taken Butch for granted until she was no longer there. I sure did miss that dog a lot!

Before Butch died, I had experienced countless highs in the Herron household, and many of them were high highs, but this was my first low, and it wasn't just a low, but rather a low low. After I disturbed Mom's sleep with my howling and wailing, she always got out of bed to hold and comfort me by singing the *Happy Doll Festival* song that she had sung for Butch thousands of times. She sure made it easier for me to grieve by grieving alongside me.

Dr. Stanley Coren, Ph.D., DSc., FRSC, is a great writer on canine psychological issues. I especially liked an analogy he had made that dogs are like the fictional character *Peter Pan* because they remain as a child without ever growing up. Dr. Coren posted online November 10, 2016 in *Psychology Today* about whether dogs grieve over the loss of an animal companion (Coren, 2016). He referenced research on this topic that was recently conducted by a team headed by Jessica Walker of the New Zealand Companion Animal Counsel. Ms. Walker's team studied 159 dogs and 152 cats in New Zealand and Australia that had lost a dog or cat companion in the previous five years. One of the team's findings, mentioned by Dr. Coren, happened to fit me perfectly: increased vocalizing—whining and whimpering—following the loss of a dog or cat companion was not very common in dogs at only 27%; however, it was much more prevalent in cats at 43%. Based on all the vocalizing I did after Butch passed, compared to practically no vocalizing at all by Peko and Chiro, those findings were on the mark.

One late night about two weeks after Butch's passing, Mom was sitting in her favorite chair in the living room reading a book. I was lying on the floor close to her feet. Everyone else, including Dad, Barb, Ricky, and Erika, had gone to sleep. There was total silence. All of a sudden, I heard the sound of a dog lapping up water. The distinct noise was coming from the kitchen. Thinking it was Peko or Chiro, I did not pay much attention to the noise until I remembered that Peko and Chiro were in the bedroom sleeping with Dad at the time.

I got up to investigate by walking over to Peko and Chiro's water bowl in the kitchen doorway, but saw nothing. The bowl was empty. I instantly thought to myself, *Is that you Butch?* I know I heard the drinking sound, and there was no water in the bowl, so I could only conclude it must have been Butch stopping by to check on us. Mom didn't say anything, but at the same time I heard that sound, she looked up from her book with an inquisitive look on her face as if she may have heard it too.

***

Although the seizures were gone and she felt great physically, Butch was an emotional wreck while she waited in the meadow by the Rainbow Bridge. She was all by herself for the first time ever. Prior to her passing, I had communicated with her a lot, and attempted to make it clear that we would all see her again on our after-Earth journey. I wanted her to patiently wait for us, but had a hard time getting my message across. The look of desperation in her eyes told me that she realized something bad was happening, but I don't think she equated it to the end of her life. She did not know anything about death.

Among Mom's furry kids, I was the only one that understood the meaning of dying, and even though I knew Butch was unable to fully comprehend what I was trying to relate to her, I continued doing it as my way of offering comfort. She did not know what it would be like without Mom, and that would have been too much for her to bear. Nor did she know what it would be like without me. After all, I was in the home when she arrived, and I was still there when she passed. She and I spent more time together than any of Mom's other furry kids.

As previously indicated, I had taken Butch for granted and was devastated upon realizing she was gone. It was only right for Butch and I to be reunited soon, so only six months after Butch passed, she and I were together again. As mentioned earlier, after my arrival at the Bridge, it did not take long for me to bop her with my paw and swish her with my tail again—felt so good—and she genuinely enjoyed being bopped and swished. She's one heckuva canine!

I conveyed Mom's message of reuniting with her. We rejoiced knowing that we'd see her again, and all we had to do was wait. This time, we understood each other completely because, after life on Earth comes to an end, language becomes universal among all beings in the afterlife. And yes, she confirmed she had gone back as the black butterfly we had seen. She also divulged she was responsible for that water lapping sound Mom and I had heard after she was gone.

CHAPTER FOUR —CHIRO

"No animal I know of can consistently be more of a friend and companion than a dog."
-Stanley Leinwoll

Hachiko is the most famous dog in the history of Japan. No, wait—make that the entire world! He was an Akita Inu (*Akita* is a Japanese canine breed and *inu* is the Japanese word for dog). His given name contains two words—*hachi* is the number *8* referring to his birth order in the litter, and *ko* means duke (nobility).

The story of Hachiko was presented in a Japanese movie titled "Hachiko Monogatari" (*The Tale of Hachiko*) released in 1987 a few months before Butch came along. Mom, Dad, Barb, Steve, and Brenda were living in Japan when the movie came out, and they all saw it. Each of them was moved by the unmatchable devotion Hachiko had displayed to his human companion. As a matter of fact, the influence was so great that the next three dogs they would welcome into their home after Butch would all be Akitas, and that string remains intact as of this writing. Since Akita dogs are designated as a Spitz breed, and Butch was a mixed-Spitz, all four of Mom and Dad's canine kids were part of the same basic dog group.

Since I had heard everyone in the family talking about the Hachiko movie numberless times, I became intimately familiar with the story making me able to recap it in a nutshell. In 1924, when Hachiko was just a few months old, he started accompanying his human, a male college professor who went to and from work by train, on a walk each morning from their home to the Shibuya Train Station in Tokyo. Hachiko would go home after the professor left, and then head back to the train station by himself in the late afternoon to wait for the professor to return. This went on for a little more than one year.

One day, the professor died suddenly of natural causes at work. Like every other day, Hachiko was waiting for him at the train station, and knew not why he wasn't on the train. Hachiko was only 18 months old. He was given away after the professor's death, but he would regularly leave on his own for the next nine years (practically the rest of his life) and go to Shibuya Station in the afternoon just prior to the arrival time of the train the professor had always come back on. Each time, he waited there a while for the master who would never return.

In 1934, one year before Hachiko passed away, he was memorialized by a bronze statue of him erected in front of Shibuya Train Station. Hachiko's legendary faithfulness became a national symbol of loyalty in Japan, and his statue remains a famous landmark to this day. This story is especially sad because Hachiko never had closure regarding the professor's death since he never got to see the professor's body. He did not know anything about the concept of death, and had no way of knowing the professor would not come back, so he kept going back to the train station to wait for him—more than 3,000 times!

The famous deaf and blind American lecturer Helen Keller was on a speaking tour in Japan in 1937. On a visit to Akita Prefecture (the original home of the Akita breed), she stated she had been so impressed by Hachiko's story that she would like to have an Akita dog. The Government of Japan subsequently gave her an Akita male named *Kamikaze*, but he died of canine distemper less than one year later. Ms. Keller later wrote in the *Akita Journal*, "If ever there was an angel in fur, it was Kamikaze. I know I shall never feel quite the same tenderness for any other pet. The Akita dog has all the qualities that appeal to me. He is gentle, companionable and trusty."

After Kamikaze passed, the Japanese Government presented his brother named *Kenzan* to Ms. Keller. With those two dogs, Ms. Keller is credited with introducing the Japanese Akita breed to the United States. The photo below depicts Ms. Keller touching the statute of Hachiko in front of Shibuya Train Station.

Everyone in the Herron household has a special connection to Japan—Mom was born there and still has many relatives there; Dad and she met there and were married there; Dad spent more than 20 years working there; one of their nonfurry kids (Barb) was born there; all 3 of their nonfurry kids spent most of their childhood there, graduated high school there, and started their college education there; 3 of their 4 canine kids were born there; and although born in the United States, more than half of yours truly's lifetime was spent there. To merely state the combined Japan connections of all the Herron family members —both furry and nonfurry types—is noteworthy would be an understatement of the highest degree.

In setting the stage for Akita dogs to be introduced into our household, it would be remiss of me should I fail to mention a certain period in Japanese history long before Hachiko and Helen Keller's time. For 264 years between 1603 and 1867, the Tokugawa family ruled the samurai government in Japan. The shogun was the family's military ruler. Tsunayoshi Tokugawa—Number 5 in the long line of 15 Tokugawa shoguns—was famous for implementing the very first animal welfare laws in the world. Those laws known as the *Orders on Compassion for Living Things* existed for a 22-year period from 1687 to 1709, and were designed to protect all living things. They even authorized capital punishment for humans who abused animals (Tsuruoka, 2016).

This shogun made sure that dogs, in particular, were covered under the laws, owners were punished if their dogs were injured, and a large monetary reward (up to approximately $30,000.00 U.S. dollars at the exchange rate as of these writings) was paid to anyone making a report about the killing of a dog (Tsuruoka). Born in the Chinese Zodiac's Year of the Dog, the shogun was a dog person and the Akita breed was his favorite. He spent a lot of money to build large kennels for rescued dogs (Tsuruoka). His successor abolished the animal welfare laws that had been in effect for over 20 years. Regardless, Tsunayoshi Tokugawa went down in history for being the first government ruler in the world to have laws created for animal well-being (Tsuruoka).

***

During the winter months of 1992-93 at Misawa, Japan, Mom worked part-time for Mr. Hiroki Yamamoto, the Japanese owner of a small shop that sold snow ski equipment to U.S. military members and their families. Since he didn't speak English well, he needed someone like Mom to interpret and translate for him.

Barb met Mr. Yamamoto through Mom. One day, while Barb and he were discussing dogs in general, Barb told him about Butch's remarkable devotion to Mom. Hachiko's story came up in the conversation. When Barb said her wish was to acquire an Akita dog someday, Mr. Yamamoto indicated he could make that dream come true. He told her that one of his associates was a local Akita breeder with a litter of puppies. She quickly accepted Mr. Yamamoto's offer to see the pups, so he took her to the breeder's residence while Mom stayed behind to mind the store.

Small-scale carbon copies of Hachiko is what Barb thought when she first laid eyes on the litter of purebred Akitas. There were 8 puppies in all: 1 male and 6 females with reddish fur that not only closely resembled their dam, but also made them look like miniature Hachikos. Oh yeah, that's only 7—the other pup was totally different, a female, not red like the others but pure white just like her sire. Upon viewing photos of the sire hanging on the wall, Barb marveled at his appearance—a majestic show dog and grand champion award winner.

When Mr. Yamamoto told Barb she could take her pick of the litter, except for one—the only male was off-limits—she rejoiced, but the choice was not any easy one. She had to pick from the 7 females. He explained to her that approximately 90% of Japanese Akitas are foxlike red in color and only about 10% are white. The white pup was tempting because white Akitas are rare, and that was the first time she had seen a white one. On the other hand, the red ones were desirable because they were the same color as Hachiko, and that turned out to be the selling point for Barb. She ended up selecting one of the little Hachiko lookalikes.

Upon seeing the puppy Barb brought home, Mom was a bit disappointed. She had heard about the white pup and was hoping Barb would have picked that one. She didn't push the issue, but

THE DOGS' BEST FRIEND: A CAT'S EYE VIEW

Barb sensed her disappointment and decided to take the puppy back and exchange it for the white one.

Brenda went with Barb and Mr. Yamamoto to trade the red pup for the white one. While the deal was being negotiated, Brenda became attached to the white puppy after getting licked all over her face. Brenda would not put the little girl down. The pup became so excited that it seemed as if she sensed they were going to take her home.

In the meantime, one of the other red pups had caught Barb's eye because she kept trying to continue feeding from the dam's breasts without the dam's concurrence long after the other pups had finished. Barb and Brenda laughed as the mother brushed the pup away and the pup crawled back to feed, and the mother pushed her away again, and she crawled back. Barb said wishfully, "Aah, I wish we could take her too."

Upon overhearing the girls talking, Mr. Yamamoto told them they could take both puppies, and they did! However, their second trip to the breeder's location did not end there. When Barb mentioned to Mr. Yamamoto that one of her college instructors named Diane also wanted an Akita puppy very much, he said they could keep the first pup she had taken home and give it to Diane. Remarkably, in the end, not only did they get the first pick of the litter—they got the first 3 picks! Brenda became the main human companion of the little white pup, while Barb got the Hachiko look-alike she wanted, and Barb's teacher got the other red one. They later found out that the breeder previously borrowed a large sum of money from Mr. Yamamoto and had not repaid him, and that's how and why they got three full-bred Akitas for free (part of the repayment to Mr. Yamamoto).

After Butch, Mom gave all her dogs Japanese names. She could easily have named the white pup *Yuki*, the Japanese word for snow, since her fur was pure white. However, she selected the name *Chiro* because the pup reminded her of a white dog by that name that her family had during her adolescence. She named Barb's puppy Peko, a dog she had when she was a child. (Incidentally, Barb's teacher named the third pup "Reba" after the red-haired, American country music singer Reba McEntire)

Some stuffed animals are so realistic they appear to be alive. Conversely, Chiro and Peko were so doggone cute that even up close they could have passed for stuffed animals, that is, if someone would have been able to do the impossible—make them stop moving! Their individual hyperactivity channeled through each other and that resulted in near constant high-strung behavior between them.

Chiro and Peko's B-day was easy to remember—Halloween Day (1993). Their pedigree was registered in Akita Prefecture in Northern Japan (the original home of the Akita dogs for which the breed was named). Barb and Brenda brought them home 10 days before Christmas when they were 6½ weeks old.

At the time Chiro and Peko were added to the family, Barb and Brenda were making plans to go back to the United States to attend college. Dad had been thinking about acquiring a good guard dog—emphasis on singular—to serve as the girls' protector in his absence. He was spellbound by the Hachiko movie and knew the Akita breed was recognized as the national dog of Japan because of intense devotion to their humans. Hachiko's story was an inspiration to Dad. He was particularly impressed by the unsurpassable faithfulness that Hachiko had displayed even after several years of separation from his deceased human.

On the day the girls brought Chiro and Peko home, Dad was out-of-town on a business trip. The night before, Barb had informed him on the phone that they might get an Akita puppy with Mr. Yamamoto's assistance. When Barb subsequently disclosed to him that they had brought not one but two pups home, he almost dropped the phone before replying "Nuh-uh! [*No way!*]."

Realizing he was about to have a conniption fit in front of his boss, who happened to be standing next to him at the time, Dad regained his composure. Determined to maintain control of his emotions, he bit his lip, got a slight taste of blood, and continued to speak on the phone in the Mon Valley Pittsburghese dialect that always becomes more noticeable when he isn't pleased with what someone is telling him. "Hey Boorb, did yew-unz rilly git two a dem? [*Hey Barb, did you guys really get two of them?*]," he managed to say in a relatively calm voice. "How's come two? [*Why two?*]" "Are dey da same keller? [*Are they the same color?*]" His voice speed accelerated and he started running his questions together. Fearful that he might say something he would regret, he abruptly ended the conversation with, "Gots ta go. See yew-unz tamarra. [*Got to go. See you tomorrow*]."

It all went down so fast that, except to say the pups were both female and they were free, Barb wasn't able to get another word in.

After cooling off and thinking about it throughout the day, Dad sorted out the good and the bad of the situation. He knew that full-grown Akita males can be aggressive, and cost more to feed since they are considerably larger than the females. He was also aware that the males are strong-willed and can be difficult to train. Hachiko was a male; however, he convinced himself it was good that both puppies they got were females. After all, he had already given thought to maybe getting an Akita dog, plus there was no way he could complain about getting two purebreds free of charge.

Upon returning home the next day and nearly getting knocked down by two of the cutest and most playful fur babies he had ever seen, Dad was quick to dismiss any thought he might have had about trying to get rid of one of them. "Jusee that? [*Did you see that?*]" he exclaimed excitedly as the frolicsome duo tried to outdo each other by climbing on top of him and licking his face as he rolled around on the floor. "Looky dare! [*Look there!*]" he blurted out when they shifted their attention to each other and

153

began bite-wrestling. "They smell just like you guys did when you were babies," he babbled to Barb and Brenda.

Playing with the two teddy bear lookalikes was a true source of enjoyment for Dad—not only that first time, but every one of the 10,000+ other times he would romp around with them thereafter. Here they are with Mom at the end of their first month as Herron family members.

***

Butch had a harder time than me accepting Chiro and Peko. That was partly because I had prior experience dealing with a new dog as a housemate (in the form of Butch). Since they had come directly from the breeder, Chiro and Peko's introduction to me was undoubtedly their first encounter with a cat; however, it wasn't my first up-close meeting with a dog. So, I had a distinct advantage over Butch, whose experience with furry housemates had been limited to me. Up until approximately one year before Chiro and Peko showed up, Butch had spent a considerable amount of time interacting with a certain dog—Chappie, the Shetland Sheepdog in our neighborhood who Butch had mentored chasing crows. Since Butch and Chappie did not live under the same roof, their relationship was a lot different than what Butch was about to experience with Chiro and Peko.

The puppies wanted to play with Butch and me, but I wanted absolutely nothing to do with them, and neither did Butch. The best way I could convey my desire to avoid them—without causing physical injury—was through body language. My direct stare into their eyes, coupled with my hunched back, resulted in both of them backing away and leaving me alone, and I didn't even have to hiss.

Upon showing her teeth and adding a low growl, Butch was able to send a loud and clear paws-off message to the pups and got the same reaction as me. She knew she needed to establish herself as the alpha-dog; hence, she wisely added the oral touch of growling, and that worked by making the pups quickly retreat. Butch had prior experience in doing the same thing to Chappie, and even though she was a girl and Chappie was a boy, he backed off every time when she demonstrated her domineering skills.

Just like Butch, Chiro and Peko enjoyed playing in the snow. Our house was in Northern Japan where it snowed so much every winter that Barb, Steve, and Brenda would jump out of Steve's second story bedroom window into snow drifts against the side of the house. The snow became compacted, so they were able to slide all the way down to the ground. During their first six months of life, Chiro and Peko got a lot of play time in the snow. After accompanying Barb and Brenda to the United States while still puppies, they would never see the white stuff again.

***

Chiro had to endure a string of bad luck beginning in April 1994 when she was only six months old. Barb, Brenda, Peko, and Chiro were temporarily staying at Grandpap Russ's house in Bentleyville, Pennsylvania. Dad had left them there while he, accompanied by Grandpap Russ, went to Florida on a house-hunting trip.

On the day after Dad and Grandpap Russ left, Dad's sister Carol and her son Lee took Barb, Brenda, and the pups to their home to meet their dog *Mr. Bodacious*, aka: *Bo*, a black, male Labrador Retriever. Lee had warned them not to touch Bo's blanket because Bo was highly protective of it. For a reason known only to Lee, he had named the blanket *Brenda* after a character on an old TV show. Every time someone called the real Brenda by name, Bo took offense, and when she came close to him or the blanket, he growled. It was a soft, low intimidating growl, but a growl nonetheless. He was sending a message that he did not like her having the same name as his beloved blanket. Bo was okay with Barb, but he did not take a liking to Brenda. It was a dog thing that centered on Bo's passion for an old, cruddy blanket.

Bo was one year older than Chiro and Peko. He was full grown and outweighed the pups by more than 40 pounds. Peko fell for Bo at first sight, and it didn't take long for him to bond with her after only one or two *mew*-tual sniffs. Bite-wrestling was a favorite pastime of Chiro and Peko, and it didn't take long for Peko to teach Bo how to do it. That was Peko's rambunctious nature. They rolled around bite-wrestling all over Aunt Carol's house. Neither of them bit hard enough to hurt the other. Bo would let Peko win by allowing her to eventually get the best of him. Chiro enjoyed the rough and tumble play as much as Peko, but did not have an outgoing *purr*-sonality like Peko, so she became the odd dog out and just sat nearby watching Peko and Bo play.

On Barb and Brenda's follow-up visit to Aunt Carol's home two days later, Aunt Carol asked them, "Jawant sumpin ta eat? [*Do you want something to eat?*]. Hows 'bout a chipped ham sammitch? Yew-unz er rilly hungry, aren't yew-unz?" [*How about a chipped ham sandwich? You guys are really hungry, aren't you?*] Bochins worsh your hands. [*You both wash your hands.*] Yew-unz can git a can a pop outta da icebox [*You guys can get a can of soda out of the refrigerator*]" Aunt Carol rambled on. She was always the loquacious host, and the girls loved to hear her deep Mon Valley

Pittsburghese accent.

While Aunt Carol was making sandwiches for the girls, Peko was quick to resume play with Bo, and they were at it again bite-wrestling on the living room floor. Chiro remained impassive and walked through an open door outside onto a second-floor balcony situated off the living room. All of a sudden, Peko and Bo raced together through the doorway out onto the balcony. As they ran by, they bumped Chiro knocking her off the rail-less balcony. She fell feet first down onto the gravel driveway 12 feet below. Her bloodcurdling yelp upon hitting the ground sent Barb, Brenda, and Aunt Carol rushing downstairs to her aid.

"Oh no, she broke her leg!" Aunt Carol shouted. "Yew-unz [you guys] can see the break."

Barb and Brenda were horrified. The fracture of Chiro's right front leg was clearly visible due to a split in the skin where the shin bone was protruding. The bone had snapped completely into two pieces. The onslaught of intense pain was sudden and acute. There was absolutely no doubt the pain would not subside until medical treatment was obtained. And there was no way of knowing if she may have also sustained internal injuries.

It was Saturday evening and the local veterinarian offices were all closed, so they had to transport Chiro to the only animal hospital open on weekends within driving distance. It was located near Pittsburgh one hour away by car. Chiro cried all the way in the back of Aunt Carol's SUV, while Brenda and Barb tried their best to comfort her. The on-duty veterinarian was able to repair the fracture by setting the leg bone. She had to stay overnight for observation.

When they picked her up the next day, Chiro had a full-leg cast. What an image that was—a bright red cast on a little white dog! Even though one of them had only 3 mobile legs and they had only been separated for 12 hours, the way Chiro and Peko jumped around on top of each other was a sight to see. They were 6 months old and it was the happiest day of their lives so far.

The veterinarian determined there were no internal injuries, and prescribed pain medicine and antibiotics for her leg. For the first two days, Brenda and Barb took turns carrying her outside to potty. She was quick to adjust and by Day 3 was able to squat and relieve herself despite the inconvenience of the cast. She tried to walk on her own, but it was a struggle, so the girls kept carrying her outside when she needed to go.

They stayed in Pennsylvania three more weeks. Brenda cracked up on the day before they left when Barb asked Grandpap Russ and Dad's brother Bob, "Yew-unz goin' up Aunt Curl's? [*Are you guys going to Aunt Carol's (house)?*]" She didn't speak exactly like a Mon Valley native, but her attempt was close enough since there was no need for Grandpap Russ or Uncle Bob to ask for clarification.

Fully comprehending what Barb had said, Grandpap Russ replied, "Nuh-uh, Curl annem'll be comin' dahn in a hour er so on the way back from Worshington. [*No, Carol and them (her family) will be coming down here in an hour or so on their way back from Washington.*]"

Thanks to Dad's relatives, besides Mon Valley Pittsburghese, the girls added a few new words to their vocabulary during their stay in Western Pennsylvania. For instance, Grandma Nellie did not permit the use of profanity in her house, so Grandpap Russ would use the term "son of a brick" (substituting *brick* for another 5-letter B-word). Grandpap also used the word "doohickey" a lot when he couldn't readily remember the name of an object. Once, when he wanted the TV remote control, he said, "Hey Boorb, gimme dat doohickey ober dare [*Hey Barb, give me that thing over there.*]" He continued by saying, "Mash is pertineer over [*Mash (a popular television sitcom) is pretty near (almost) over.*]" Other examples new to the girls' ears included *doozy* [something extraordinary, one of kind] and *humdinger* [an extraordinary person or thing]—both of which can be used to describe this cat to a T!

The 1,000-mile car ride to Florida wasn't easy, but Chiro did not complain. The SUV Dad had bought, along with the trailer he rented, provided enough space for both dogs and four adults—Dad, Barb, Brenda, and Aunt Carol's son Lee, who went along to help them get settled in their new home—plus all their baggage. By then, Chiro was able to lie down on her belly with the casted leg extended straight out in front of her, and Peko had enough room to stretch out in the back of the vehicle. They were on the way to their new house that Dad had bought in Orlando. Here's a photo showing Chiro with her leg cast and Peko *chillin* on the first day in their new house (7 months old).

Chiro got rid of the leg cast one month after they moved to Florida. The broken leg healed nicely and she didn't limp, so there was no crimp to her mobility. Brenda massaged the leg regularly until the following year when Mom arrived in Florida and took over by giving her daily massages. That's when the bonding process between Chiro and Mom accelerated.

Unfortunately, Chiro was destined to have more bad luck than all of her housemates combined. The broken leg was just the first incident in a long list of physical problems she would have to deal with. It made Mom a believer that purebreds are more likely to have health problems than mixed breeds. She also believed that white purebreds are destined for more health problems than any others.

***

Chiro was a chewer. Having at least a dozen chew toys didn't stop her from chomping down on furniture, carpet, and other things, including every family member's shoes multiple times. She chewed more things than all the other Herron dogs combined. She probably loved shoes because they were a twofer: (1) each one contained the widest possible variety of scents picked up while Mom, Dad, and the kids walked around outdoors, plus (2) the lingering odor of smelly feet was present in them all.

By far, Chiro's biggest chewing escapade was a fabric sofa that she attacked with a vengeance and totally destroyed. The picture below shows her on the sofa a few days before she tore it up.

Peko was the only other one at home when Chiro ate the couch. Barb and Brenda discovered the mess upon their return from shopping. All the cloth material had been ripped and chewed to bits and pieces, and spit out onto the floor along with most of the cotton stuffing.

Speechless was Brenda. All Barb said nonchalantly was, "Dogs will be dogs," as she walked away leaving the discipline to

Brenda. There was no doubt as to the identity of the culprit, as Chiro was a chewer and Peko was not. Anxious to find out what form of punishment Chiro would be subjected to, Barb listened out of sight from an adjoining bedroom.

Brenda did not raise her voice. No one ever elevated their voice when talking to mild-mannered Chiro—never ever! At the time, Chiro was only three weeks shy of her first birthday, and, by then, she had cleverly mastered the extra worried look —sad eyes and droopy head—upon realizing someone was not pleased with something she had done. As Chiro's main human, Brenda was on the receiving end of that look far more than anyone else. She mistakenly took the look as a sign of guilt, but it actually meant fear.

The worried look worked for Chiro every time and the sofa disaster was no exception. Brenda immediately thought she would chide Chiro, but was unable to go through with it. As soon as they made eye contact, any admonishment she may have intended came to an abrupt halt. All she could say in a non-elevated, empathetic voice was, "Goodness gracious Chi-chi [Chiro's nickname)]". Barb knew right then that any thought of disciplinary action had gone out the window.

Pointing toward what was left of the sofa in the family room, Brenda said, "You know better than that," in what sounded more like a huggy tone than an angry ring. There would be no scolding—only hugs.

When Mom heard of the sofa incident, she recognized that dogs have a different thought process than humans not only because their emotions are far less complex, but also because they live in the moment with no thinking about the past or planning ahead. She knew that what's happening right there right now is all they care about, and whatever happened in the past—even the very recent past—had been forgotten.

What Brenda did not realize is that since Chiro was not caught red-handed in the act, she had no idea why Brenda may have been upset. Like all dogs, she had no regrets about anything that had previously happened because she did not dwell on the past.

Mom tried to reinforce to Brenda that dogs do not have short-term memories. She added that attempting to take disciplinary action after a dog had done something wrong—even soon after — was ineffective because the dog's concentration had already shifted to something else, and they would not understand why the *purr*-son trying to discipline them was unhappy. According to Mom, discipline would work only if applied when the dog is caught committing the act or with no delay after the tail end of the act.

Like Brenda, Chiro was a shoe freak. There was a major difference—Brenda didn't chew shoes and Chiro did. Their veterinarian, along with some of Brenda's friends, thought the chewing behavior was likely due to separation anxiety, which would indicate Chiro felt abandoned every time Barb and Brenda left the house without her. That sounded as good a reason as any, especially when taking into consideration that time passes slowly for dogs—one hour for humans equates to approximately seven hours in doggy time. After all, she did not chew things while Brenda and Barb were at home, only when they went out. When a friend made mention of their dog pooping on the carpet due to separation anxiety, Brenda was grateful Chiro didn't act in that way.

It did not surprise Brenda or Barb that Peko did not react the same way as Chiro when no humans were in the house. The girls thought that since Peko wasn't in need of human companionship as much as Chiro, she was probably glad to see them leave the house and, in all likelihood, never suffered from separation anxiety.

Digging was also something that Chiro liked to do, not only outside, but inside the house too. When she started digging into the carpet, Brenda or Barb would tell her to stop. Since she was scolded while in the act, there was no doubt in her mind as to why the girls were upset, so she stopped digging immediately. However, she didn't stop *purr*-manently and was quick to do it again—like the next day! *No big deal*, the girls thought since the only damage done was just a few loose carpet threads.

About three months after tearing up the sofa, again when no one else was at home except Peko, Chiro started digging into the family room floor near the back door. This time, she dug with a vengeance. There was no stopping her until a patch of carpet disappeared. She also tore up the pad beneath the carpet. She quit only because the carpet layer and pad were gone, and even a super digger like her could not put a dent in the exposed concrete floor. Separation anxiety had struck again!

When Brenda and Barb returned home and discovered the hole in the carpet, there was no doubt in their minds that Chiro, not Peko, had done the dirty deed. When it appeared that Brenda was going to make an attempt to scold her, Chiro looked puzzled because she had no idea why there was a problem. The carpet-digging was over and done with a few hours earlier. Even before hearing, "Cheech (another nickname for Chiro), you know better. This is a no, no!," the eyes turned sad and her head dropped, which caused Brenda to react as usual by giving her a ginormous hug. After Dad used a 10 x 12-inch piece of spare carpet material to repair the damage, Chiro was forgiven, and the incident was forgotten.

Digging and chewing were Chiro's only bad behaviors. After she outgrew both habits shortly before her second birthday, she was as close to *purr*-fect as any dog could be. In addition to her great *purr*-sonality, she was beautiful physically.

Her thick, white fur coat looked particularly good upon being brushed to a sleek finish. When stopping to rest outdoors on a walk, she displayed pride by looking like a military canine standing at attention with her ears erect and tail upcurled above her back. Her features nicely combined to make an impressive sight that readily stood out next to her sister Peko, who preferred to stand loosely at ease, tail down more often than not, and ears sometimes drooping.

Mom grinned upon observing Dad when he made himself stand extra tall, forced his chin down, and threw his shoulders back like he frequently did while walking alongside Chiro. When they were out together in public, it was as if Chiro's pride percolated through Dad regenerating his military bearing and appearance.

When it comes to dogs in general, Chiro was as placid and docile as they come. That does not mean she was weak. On the contrary, she possessed the hunting spirit for which her breed is well known.

During a walk one day, a large (3-foot) snake slid away from the bank of a small pond toward Dad as he was walking by with Chiro three feet ahead and Peko 10 feet behind. Dad's eyesight was incapable of seeing the big snake, but Chiro saw it coming. She quickly turned and lunged in a single motion catching the snake's midsection in her mouth. While she was shaking it vigorously side to side, the snake's head curled around and took a swipe at Chiro's head narrowly missing her snout with its poisonous fangs. Chiro reacted by shaking extra hard causing it to fly out of her mouth about 10 feet in the direction of the pond. Chiro gave chase, but before she could get to it, the snake had escaped by slithering into the water.

If Dad had not pulled back on the leash with his left hand, Chiro would have jumped into the pond after the snake. It's a wonder he kept his hold on Chiro's leash, as he was holding Peko's leash in his other hand and had to tighten that grip because Peko lunged in an attempt to follow Chiro on the snake chase. The attacker was identified as a poisonous Water Moccasin (Cottonmouth) through a picture in a North American wildlife book in the home library. To make a long story short, Chiro had saved Dad from a venomous snake bite.

Although Chiro had proven herself equal to the task of taking on a dangerous reptile, she was unable to defend against a tiny insect. Taking into account the vast amount of time the dogs spent on paths in the park close to wooded areas, it's a wonder that Chiro was the only one to attract a tick. The little bugger had embedded itself in the skin just above her right eye. It was a Black Deer Tick that was clearly visible since its rear end was sticking out on Chiro's thick, white coat. Mom spotted it while they were heading back to the car. They always carried a first-aid kit in the car, from which Mom obtained a pair of tweezers. Knowing that ticks embed themselves headfirst, she was able to ever so carefully grab the tick's back side with the tweezers and slowly extract it without breaking off its head or blood-sucking mouth.

The first-aid kit contained a lot of other things, including a small bottle of rubbing alcohol into which Mom dropped the tick. She kept it just in case Chiro showed symptoms of Lyme Disease (fever, swelling, rash, loss of appetite, etc.). Fortunately, no symptoms occurred, so there was no need for veterinary treatment; however, the tick had left a permanent scar above Chiro's eye. If it wasn't for Mom's knowledge of dreaded ticks and how to extract them safely, Chiro may have suffered worse permanent damage.

***

Around humans, Chiro was a gentle giant with the absolute kindest tem-*purr*-amental makeup *paws*-sible for a canine. Her disposition was characteristic of a Japanese heritage—considerate, noble, easygoing. The description that Helen Keller wrote in the Akita Journal of her Akita dog fit Chiro to perfection: "The Akita dog has all the qualities that appeal to me...

gentle, companionable and trusty."

Chiro was highly affectionate and exhibited a strong maternal instinct around Mom and Dad's first two grandchildren, Ricky and Erika, with whom she was quick to become attached. Her extra sweet nature, above average intelligence, and overly friendly, totally non-aggressive *purr*-sonality fit the so-called *nanny dog* mold to a T. She was the antithesis of Peko, who would tolerate, but not closely bond with any child—or any adult human other than Mom and Barb for that matter. Dad told Mom, "Chiro has all the right traits," adding, "I wish I could have half of them."

Mom and Dad had me spayed while I was a kitten. It didn't really bother me as, unlike Chiro, I wasn't the motherly type. Based on veterinarian recommendations, Butch, Peko, and Chiro were all spayed as pups, and Koro was castrated. That was something Mom and Dad had mixed feelings about. They had heard unneutered pets generally live longer lives than the ones missing body parts, but they also knew that females, in particular, would have to endure considerable discomfort while in heat if not spayed. The main reason they had us spayed was a veterinarian's claim that having a litter shortens the lives of female dogs and cats. They later learned they had gotten bad advice as having *multiple* litters—not just one—may shorten lives.

Mom regretted having Chiro neutered because she displayed the type of *purr*-sonality that would have made her a *purr*-fect mommy. She wishes she would have allowed Chiro to have one litter. Dad wasn't so sure about that because he would have wanted to keep just one of Chiro's puppies, but was certain Mom would try to keep every pup in the litter. After Chiro was gone, Mom and Dad were equally very sorry that they didn't have a descendant from her. She was that good.

***

Mom often took Chiro and Peko outdoors for a walk while Dad

was at work and the children were in school or at work. She couldn't handle them together, so they went separately. Peko was receptive to meeting strange dogs, but Chiro was not.

Chiro didn't have a mean bone in her body, except when it came to snakes and canine strangers. Oh, she would peacefully *purr*-form the customary nose-to-nose sniffing ritual with an unknown dog, but only for a few seconds and then walk away. Butt-sniffing was an absolute no-no. It took less than a minute for her to shift from peaceful coexistence to a posture of ready to fight toe-to-toe, so it was a good thing she'd try to turn away before violence erupted.

One day, Mom took Chiro for a walk in the park when a little old man allowed his little male Rat Terrier to approach them. Mom tried to pull Chiro away while motioning with her free hand for the guy to back off and yelling out, "Don't come closer!"

The guy refused to comply yelling back, "My dog doesn't bite. He just wants to say hello." Chiro stood her ground and went nose-to-nose sniffing with the other dog for about 10 seconds and Chiro was okay with that, but when the other dog walked around behind Chiro and attempted to sniff her rear end, all hell broke loose. Chiro's demeanor abruptly changed from tolerance to aggression as she jerked her head around and came very close to landing a neck bite. If that little mutt could have spoken English, he would have screamed out, "Oh shi _!," or if he were conversant in Mon Valley Pittsburghese, "Jeez-oh-man! [*Jesus C _ _ _ _ _!*]"

The man shouted at Mom, "Your dog is bad! You better learn how to control that dog!"

Mom was able to pull Chiro away before she did any damage, shouting back at the audacious numbskull, "Your dog is bad because you are bad. You're the one who needs to control your dog!" as she pulled Chiro away.

That dog was only slightly larger than a Chihuahua. That made Mom think Chiro may have aggressed due to a flashback of the hostile environment that Grandpap Russ's Chihuahua Ginger had created for her and Peko a few years earlier (Ginger's escapades are detailed in the next chapter).

That dog was a Rat Terrier, which made me wonder how *rat* became part of a canine breed's name. Then it came to me—since dogs are only slightly higher up than rats on the low end of the all-animal totem pole, Rat Terrier is an appropriate name for a canine species.

Mom was well aware that she had to do her best to keep Chiro away from strange dogs. She also knew that if a strange dog was able to come close, she would have to break away before something happened to cause Chiro to think about turning belligerent. She didn't have to worry about Chiro trying to approach strange dogs because that would never happen. Mom could not stand the way some humans permitted their dogs to behave.

Numerous times after the Rat Terrier incident, an owner had allowed his or her Chihuahua or Dachshund, or whatever to run up to Chiro. Stranger after stranger thought nothing of approaching Mom and her. They would babble about how friendly their dog was, or mumble about their dog being non-aggressive, while *purr*-mitting their dog to try to get close to Chiro without even asking if it was okay. They may have had good intentions, but ignorance is no excuse, so their actions were just plain rude and disrespectful. After all, if they were alone and not with a dog, they would not accost a person they did not know in public. They seemed to think it was okay just because they had a dog and Mom had a dog.

Every time Mom saw someone with a dog coming toward Chiro and her, she reacted by turning away, and then it wasn't uncommon for the other person to start verbally abusing Mom as if she had done something wrong—like walking a well-behaved

Akita dog on a leash? Or, they would indicate they thought their dog was just being cute, and Mom was being snobbish. Their thoughtlessness galled Mom to no end, and the agitation it caused was out of consonance with her usual calm demeanor. This infuriated her a great deal because she knew it annoyed and upset Chiro.

Mom wasn't mad at the other dogs, just their humans, and she didn't hesitate to let them know in pithy terminology what she thought about their lack of pet etiquette. Often, it was as if they blamed Mom for the way Chiro acted toward their dogs, and nothing could be further from the truth. They failed to understand that even a human, who understands dog behavior and treats them with love and affection, can have a dog that reacts unfavorably toward unwanted advances from a dog they don't know. It's a no-brainer to Mom that a dog's reaction to unwanted advances from a strange dog is no different than a human's reaction to unwanted advances from a strange human.

Mom scolded Dad every one of the umpteen times he went up to a strange dog and put a hand down for the dog to smell as a way of greeting. He kept it up until he learned the hard way not to do it.

One day, he was walking alone and came upon an old lady with two yelping Chihuahuas, when the woman said, "They might calm down if you say hello." So, he put a hand down, at which time one of the little dogs immediately snapped and drew blood from his forefinger. The woman responded, "Oh, he does bite sometimes," and she went along on her merry way with her little biter. Dad told Mom what had happened adding, "I wish she would have told me before I put my hand down there," to which Mom bluntly replied, "See, you should listen to me."

From then on, Dad has been following Mom's advice by always verbally greeting strange dogs with no attempt to touch them, even if the dog's human says it's okay. Conversely, strange dogs instantly sense the large amount of oxytocin that Mom has built up through her furry kids over four decades. That makes it fairly common for a strange dog to actually encourage her to get up close and personal with no worries. And, much more often than not, Mom accommodates them.

Dr. Evan MacLean, Ph.D., Director of the Arizona Canine Cognition Center at the University of Arizona's School of Anthropology, was quoted as stating, "For a lot of dogs that have aggression problems, the owners report that the onset of the aggressive symptoms happened after some sort of traumatic experience (MacLean, Gesquiere, Gruen, Sherman, Martin, & Carter, 2017). Often it was that the dog was… in a hypervigilant state after that event, almost like a post-traumatic reaction" (MacLean et al.).

The findings of MacLean et al. may help explain the role that certain life experiences could have played in Chiro's behavior around unfamiliar dogs. For instance—the harassment she had endured from Grandpap Russ's Chihuahua Ginger, and Ginger's vicious attack of Peko that she had witnessed, followed by the broken leg she suffered when knocked off the balcony by Aunt Carol's Labrador Retriever Bo after observing Bo romance her sister Peko. Those incidents all took place in a one-week period while Chiro was only 6 months old, so there's a good possibility they may have left a lasting impression and contributed to her temperament around any dog outside her pack.

Although she lacked social skills with other dogs, Chiro was *purr*-fectly well-behaved around humans. She never met a human she didn't like. Her extra calm, friendly manner made her a hit with guests in our home.

At two years of age, she began to howl as a means to beg for food. Her howling seemed to articulate the Japanese word *gohan* [a meal of rice]. Mom, Dad, and the children all started prompting her to beg just to hear her howl that 2-syllable word. They all enjoyed showing her off in front of visitors by offering her a food item and not giving it to her until she vocalized *gohan* in her whiny, high-pitched, uniquely doggy voice. She was then rewarded not only with the food, but also with a round of applause from spectators.

The monkey-organ grinder *purr*-formance was a source of enjoyment for Chiro. The more she did it, the better her lips, tongue, and voice box were able to pronounce the word gohan. I heard Barb and Brenda each start a verbal joust with unknowing guests on at least a half-dozen occasions by exclaiming, "I bet your dog can't speak Japanese like our dog can!" When the other *purr*-son replied they didn't believe any dog could speak Japanese, Barb or Brenda would back it up by having Chiro *purr*-form, and she never let them down. It resulted in an *ooh-aah* moment for every human who heard it for the first time. She seemed to really have fun showing off her linguistic talent.

Mom spoke in Japanese a lot to the dogs and me. We recognized as many words in Japanese as American English. Every day at mealtime, Mom would shout out, "*Gohan da yo!* [It's time to eat!]" prompting the dogs and me to take off running to our individual food bowls. So even though we all knew what the word gohan meant, Chiro was the only one able to verbally articulate it. Impressed was I!

Dad and the children usually spoke to Chiro and the other dogs in English mostly using the S-words—*Sit! Speak! Shake!* The dogs were able to learn those simple one-word commands and respond accordingly by sitting down on their rear ends, barking, or raising a front paw, but they couldn't comprehend conversational American English like me. Their willingness to learn 100 words or so was not due to their intelligence, but rather their dopey eagerness to please for the sole purpose of soliciting a treat. To put this in *purr*-spective, cats are less interested in obedience training than dogs because we resemble certain smart human kids—the ones who underachieve in school due to boredom.

Dad actually came up with the most liked English term for all the dogs when he concocted *LB*—short for "last bite." Butch would always get in Mom or Dad's face toward the end of a meal and give them her unmistakable, inquisitive look, *Are you going to eat all of that?* At the end of dinner one day, Dad held up a bite-size piece of food and inquiringly said, "LB?" Butch barked in response and was rewarded with the morsel. From that time on, she recognized what Dad meant—even if he didn't show her the food. She let out a single, loud bark every time he asked "LB?"

Peko and Chiro were quick to learn the meaning of *LB* by listening to Dad and watching Butch. Dad gave them the LB by hand; however, despite his repeated warnings about contracting worms, Mom fed it to them right off the tip of her fork. Her demands for pro-*purr* etiquette always apply to humans, but not so for pets.

***

The trio of Butch, Peko, and Chiro (and me) shared home space for the better part of eight years. We all went to the vet's office at least annually for required shots and a checkup. The combined cost when we were all in good health was approximately $1,200 per year—that's 8,400 dog dollars if figured at roughly the same 7-to-1 ratio as dog years versus human years! When Chiro became sick, the cost skyrocketed.

At age 6½, Chiro underwent surgery for removal of both ovaries and her uterus. The vet advised the procedure was necessary due to his diagnosis of pyometra—an infected uterus. Dad, in particular, was amazed that she showed no sign of pain and did not need any medication to control pain, not only after being spayed, but also following major surgery for the pyometra. She was one tough girl!

Two months after the surgery, Chiro was diagnosed with

pancreatitis—inflammation of the pancreas. According to the vet, the earlier surgery had nothing to do with the pancreatic problem, which Dad and Mom found hard to believe. Anyhow, pancreatic powder was prescribed. From then on, Mom had to carefully mix the powder with canned prescription dog food every day for the rest of Chiro's life (six more years). The stuff emitted a god-awful odor even to the human nose, so you can imagine how bad it would have been to Chiro's keen sense of smell. My nose caught the repulsive odor of that stuff as soon as Mom poured it into Chiro's dish the first time and I immediately felt nauseous. Chiro never complained about her meals before or after she got sick. She became accustomed to the prescribed food right away, ate the same thing every day for the last six years of her life, and was grateful for it prolonging her life.

Dad suspected the veterinarian might have been overcharging and scheduling more visits than necessary. When Dad saw him driving a new BMW one day, he directed a few expletives toward the driver, only one of which is fit for print in a book of this nature—"Quack!" That's all it took for him to start looking for, finding, and eventually switching to another veterinarian, who just happened to drive an old, beat-up Ford pickup truck.

Mom and Dad both wondered how many pets do not get medical treatment solely because of incredibly high vet fees. Mom told Dad, "If we could find a pet doctor as good as Dr. Kovats is a people doctor, dogs would be lined up out the door and down the street every day to see him" (she was referring to their family physician Dr. Christian Kovats in Sanford, Florida with whom she could not find a single fault). It was lucky for them that the guy driving the old pickup truck proved to be just as good with pets as Dr. Kovats was with humans, so he became their go-to vet.

***

Chiro not only shared Mom and Dad's house—she also shared

their bed. She slept horizontally across the bottom of the queen-size mattress. Not even a square kick in the snout from Dad, while he was sleeping and moving around, would cause her to vacate that position. For reasons unknown to this cat, she favored Dad over Mom and slept with her head on his side of the bed at his feet. I never slept in their bed, but rest assured that if I had gone there to sleep, it would not have been on his side!

I often watched Chiro jump up on the bed and sidle around the bedding before curling up in the space where Dad's toes would be. She always pretended to be sleeping until he plopped down and kicked her in the head a couple of times. After that, except to adjust her position while on the receiving end of more kicks, she would drop off to slumberland and barely move until her regular morning wake-up time. That's when she licked Dad's toes to signal him it was time to rise and shine.

The only break in Chiro's sleep routine took place when Barb's kids, Ricky and Erika, came to Mom and Dad's house from their home in Japan on vacation every year. Around 2 o'clock in the morning on each day of their two-week visit, while Mom and Dad were sound asleep, Chiro sneaked out of their bed ever so quietly, went to the bedroom next door, and gently sprawled out at the children's feet on the bedding. It was as if the motherly instinct, which she never got to use on her own brood, kicked in and made her feel the need to watch over the children. This picture depicts her side by side with Erika right after they woke up.

After observing construction workers replacing the sidewalk near our house, as soon as they left for the day, Mom walked Chiro and Peko through the wet cement to save their paw prints for eternity—or so she thought. Realistically, the prints will only be preserved for as long as the three segments of concrete walkway bearing their prints remain intact. Not once has Mom given thought to the sidewalk being replaced someday, and Dad elected not to break the bad news to her. As of these writings, 15 years after the Akita sisters had left their prints in that wet cement, they were undisturbed, but time may be running out.

***

Peppermint, spearmint, any kind of mint—Chiro was fond of the taste of mints. Since dogs rely much more on smell than taste, it was the minty odor that got to her. She searched countless times through Dad's briefcase, which he usually left opened on a dining room chair, and often found mint candies. She'd tear off the wrapper and chew up the contents. She hardly ever got caught in the act. Most of the time, Dad didn't realize she had taken something until he observed remnants of candy wrappers on the floor next to his briefcase. She was caught red-handed one time with a wrapped piece of candy in her paws.

To say she loved mints would be an understatement of the highest degree. It's a good thing Dad didn't buy sugar-free mints, as one of the ingredients in that kind of goody—an artificial sweetener called xylitol—is highly toxic to dogs. Mom always checked to make sure he did not have the bad mints.

Chiro not only used her teeth to tear the wrappers off candy mints, she also tore wrapping paper off gifts on birthdays and other occasions, especially Christmas time when she had the most presents to rip open—not only her own, but everyone else's gifts too. Mom insisted that everybody allow her to assist them in opening their packages. No one had to tell Chiro when to begin—she did so on her own upon seeing wrapped gifts. Once underway, she did not hesitate while going from package to package. She was extra careful not to damage anything inside the packages, and spit out tiny, shredded paper pieces as she moved along.

"What a girl!" exclaimed Brenda. "What a girl!" echoed Barb.

Chiro was the center of attention while opening packages and she darn well knew it! It gave her a sense of joy by pleasing everyone who was watching. She possessed an innate desire to pleasure people, not only Mom, Dad, and the children, but every single visitor to our home, every single passerby in the park, every single customer she saw in the pet store, and every single occupant of cars passing by on the road. She truly thrived on interaction with humans and the attention she got from them. She genuinely loved to make people smile.

***

Canine saliva contains a healing agent that enables a dog to treat its own wounds—by licking. Chiro not only licked her own bug bites and paw bruises, but used her tongue to cleanse Peko and Butch's wounds too. She would also try to lick small cuts and bruises on Mom, Dad, and the children's arms and legs. Trying to help others was part of her nature. She didn't do it to me—no need as I never had a wound, but if I did, I'm sure she would have tried to lick it, and I would not have objected. A furry nurse was she!

Despite the excessive bad luck and associated pain she had to physically endure, Chiro invariably displayed a happy disposition. After suffering a debilitating injury (fractured leg), a serious illness requiring major surgery (pyometra), followed by a condition requiring lifelong treatment (pancreatitis) and a special diet, along with a deer tick bite that left a scar, she was diagnosed with terminal cancer in the form of a malignant nasal tumor that prematurely took her life only three months after it was detected. She was just as good at hiding the pain accompanying her illnesses as she was at showing joy when she felt pleasure. Having her around was a blessing to every single furry and nonfurry being in our home. I wish I could have given her some of my 9 lives.

The only time in her life that Chiro showed pain was when she fell off the balcony and broke her leg at 6 months of age. That pain was acute and unbearable. The chronic, cancerous pain, however, developed slowly over a period of time making it relatively easy for her to gradually tolerate and live with, and that made it difficult for Mom and Dad to notice that anything was wrong. She was unable to tell Mom or Dad that she was in pain, and her Akita pride would not allow whining to signal something was wrong. Since she did not complain or otherwise draw attention to her illness, when it was finally diagnosed, it was too late for a cure.

The next month brought a series of difficult treatments that tested Chiro's iron will to the max, and her strength remained steadfast. The vet was able to surgically remove a portion of the malignant growth in her nose during two procedures, but the disease was too far advanced to get it all. Despite all the aches and pains associated with prior illnesses and the current one that would eventually end her life, no dog ever wagged a tail with greater vigor every single time when Mom, Dad, or Brenda came home after being gone for even a brief period of time.

One night during one of the many barbeques at our house, a guy remarked to others in attendance, "No one in their right mind would spend thousands of dollars on surgery for a dog." Mom was within earshot and the insult caused her to be beside herself for the rest of the evening. She wasn't personally insulted, but felt bad on Chiro's behalf, as she considered Chiro to be in the Top 3 sweetest beings of her life (Dad's mother and her own mother were the other two). The guy later displayed two faces by going out of his way to hug Chiro and saying he wished he could pay whatever it takes to rid her of the cancer. Mom wanted to confront him, but decided to bite her lip rather than make a scene. Needless to say, that guy was never invited back to our home. To Mom, this was another example of an undesirable trait common among humans that does not exist in dogs—hypocrisy.

At the last home barbeque Chiro attended, upon hearing about her condition, someone pitifully remarked, "Poor, poor girl." Mom immediately responded, "She's not poor, she's rich," which drew the response, "What do you mean?" Mom's comeback was priceless—"Her heart is pure gold. That's what I mean!" End of discussion.

The results of a canine DNA project conducted at the Institute for Genomic Research in Rockville, Maryland, clearly indicated distinct physiological similarities between dogs and humans (National Institutes of Health (NIH)/National Human Genome Research Institute (NHGRI), 2005). Prior findings included the fact that dogs were susceptible to inherited diseases common in humans, such as cancer, rheumatoid arthritis, heart disease, epilepsy, autoimmune disorders, blindness, and deafness, to name a few. Subsequent research determined that the leading causes of death in dogs are a variety of cancers that are biologically similar to human cancers, and that although the assorted dog breeds have significant physical diversity, they share large segments of DNA that is indicative of their shared origin—evolution from the gray wolf (NIH/NHGRI).

The life expectancy of Akitas and other large canine breeds is much shorter than smaller breeds. Mom reasons that if everyone wanted a small dog because they live longer, the big dogs would become homeless. Generally speaking, mixed-breed dogs live longer than pure breeds. Mom also reasons that if everyone wanted a mixed breed because they live longer, the purebreds would become homeless. Chiro was a large purebred with a lifespan of 12½ human years (a little higher than average for big dogs).

It was emotionally painful for Mom to watch Chiro's condition deteriorate during those last three months. Despite the cancer and all her other ailments, Chiro had remained vibrant. "She's only 12 years old," Mom repeated over and over out loud to herself, but often within Dad and Brenda's earshot. She was medicated with a steroid (Prednisone) and didn't appear to be in pain, but recurring hard sneezes and occasional nose bleeds were irritants. She was frustrated too because the nasal tumor had adversely affected her sense of smell.

Although she gradually weakened and dropped from 80 to 70

pounds, she remained full of love for life, and still looked forward to a walk in the park every day—until her last week when she was unable to keep up with Peko and Koro. She still went on rides to the park but became weak, and due to her restricted movement, she laid down in the grass as soon as she got out of the van and waited with Mom for Dad to bring Peko and Koro back.

At the end, she had little energy left and, during her final day, she did not go outside except to pee, the last time only 18 hours before she died. She barely had the strength to squat down and empty her bladder one last time, but somehow her pride took over and she managed to do it without losing her balance.

The dreaded refusal to eat anything or drink water signaled the end was near. Mom laid beside Chiro on the floor at home in the front foyer during her last 10 hours. She stroked her head, moistened her lips with drops of water, all the while singing the *Happy Doll Festival* song over and over. Like Butch, the last sounds Chiro heard were the lyrics of that song while Mom sang it to her. She was Daddy's girl too and the last visions she had were Dad and Mom's faces. He kneeled down to say goodbye and kissed her on the nose while Mom held her head before she peacefully closed her eyes for the last time. "You are so brave Chichi," Mom whispered at the end.

In her final few moments, she gave Mom and Dad a relieved look as if to convey the message, *Don't worry about me. Everything's okay.* Her physical ailments never affected her mental health, and she remained calm while lying there beside Mom. I noticed a teardrop starting to form in the corner of each eye, but she held them back so as to not further upset Mom. She may have sensed what was happening. Such grace was totally in character for a dignified being like Chiro. If she could have picked her own way of passing, let there be no doubt she would not have changed a thing.

Right after she died, Mom trimmed all her toenails explaining to Dad, "Now, she can run faster with Butch in Heaven." With tears flowing down her cheek onto Chiro's lifeless body, Mom said, "Say hi to Butch and Chibi for me. I will see you all someday at the Rainbow Bridge."

Mom wept while holding Chiro's lifeless head in her lap saying, "Oh how I loved walking with you and showing you off in the park. You were so beautiful. And gentle. Chewing up my shoes and the sofa, it was okay."

The emotional pain of having watched her put up with so much adversity throughout her life had gotten to Mom, and set her off talking more to Chiro's body, "You suffered way too much with surgery and taking that medicine dog food. When you broke your leg, it must have hurt really bad. I am so sorry Chichi." She went on, "You saying 'gohan' with no accent was so cute. You were very tough fighting that big snake. You playing with your sister was so much fun to watch every day. I love you Chiro." Except for soft sobs, Mom then went silent with her chin on top of Chiro's head until Dad was finally able to ease her away 30 minutes later.

The discomfort accompanying her severe nasal and digestive problems did not interfere with Chiro's passion to live life to the fullest. Some canines may enjoy life as much as she did, but there's no way any dog could enjoy it more. Mom and Dad were in total agreement that only a handful of humans they knew possessed genuine compassion equal to that of what Chiro had displayed.

The one time that Chiro stayed overnight at a pet hospital for the broken leg at 6 months of age was the only time Peko and she had ever been separated. Peko got a final sniff of her sister's remains just before Mom and Dad took her to the crematory in the back of the van. She gave a gentle nose nudge on the neck and then walked away. Peko did not appear distressed or depressed.

That was not surprising to Mom since she clearly understood that dogs live for whatever is happening in the moment and, unlike humans, they do not dwell on the past or look ahead to the future. They do not think about aging.

Mom felt Peko knew her sister was no longer in that body and had gone to a better, pain-free place. Although dogs know nothing about death per se, Peko sensed Chiro would not be coming back.

Two weeks after Chiro passed, Dad swears he saw her apparition materialize at a certain place in the park where Mom and he took the dogs on walks. He described what he saw as "shadowy." It appeared in a clearing of the woods along the pathway they always took. Mom was there and although she didn't see it, she believes Dad did.

That was the one and only time Dad claimed he had seen Chiro come back, and he never had that type of experience with Butch, Peko, Koro, me, or anyone else. As one of the most matter-of-fact human beings imaginable, Dad couldn't help but question the basic nature of what he had personally observed. He has an extremely hard time dealing with anything he cannot explain.

As I described earlier, I did not see Butch after she passed, but I did hear water-drinking sounds I believe were made by her in our house. Many people say that after the loss of their pet, they can still feel their pet's presence, or detect their footsteps walking around the house, or hear their bark or miaow, or even see them in familiar places. Mom is a firm believer that her deceased pets are still with her in spirit and come regularly to pay her visits.

Right after Dad claimed he saw Chiro's image, Mom noticed a white butterfly in the air coming toward her from the very spot where Dad said he had seen the apparition. The butterfly flew directly at her, passed about 6 inches above her head, and kept going until it was no longer in sight. "Bye-bye Chiro. See you again someday," Mom muttered softly to herself while watching the butterfly disappear from sight.

***

I admired Chiro as much as Mom, Dad, Barb, Steve, and Brenda. Not even one time during our eight years together did she try to antagonize me. On the contrary, she left me alone, and on those occasions when I got up close and *purr*-sonal with her, she merely gave me a non-threatening look as if to say, *Hello. How are you?* She and I shared brief moments of *mew*-tual gazing into each other's eyes—a form of bonding and reciprocal stimulation made possible by each other's oxytocin. Yes, pets not only bond with humans and other animals within their race (dog on dog and cat on cat, for example), but also with other animals of another race (e.g. dog on cat and cat on dog).

Chiro was the perfect role model for trustworthiness, loyalty, love, perseverance, and selflessness rolled into one. I could add more, but let it suffice to say she had all the good personal qualities and not even one irritating trait. As a cat, the highest tribute I could pay to any of my canine roommates would go to her—*If I should be reborn a human, I would hope to have a pet dog exactly like Chiro.*

Butch and I were all over Chiro as soon as she arrived at the Rainbow Bridge. Chiro didn't care when Butch got up close and personal and went nose-to-nose with her. She even let Butch sniff her butt—for the first time ever—with absolutely no sign of agitation. All three of us have been beaming with smiley faces ever since Chiro got here. Seeing her pain-free was absolutely awesome.

CHAPTER FIVE—PEKO

> *"Anybody who doesn't know what soap tastes like never washed a dog."*
> -Franklin P. Jones

Peko's line of thinking was cat food is for dogs. I cannot begin to guesstimate how many times I caught that dog with her mouth in my food dish. I don't think she ate out of my dish because the items in it were particularly palatable for her. There is no doubt in my mind she did it only because she knew it was something she wasn't supposed to do. There is a single word that describes Peko to a T—*mischievous*!

December is the absolute worst time to acquire a pet in Northern Japan. That's because harsh winters are the norm and December is smack dab in the middle of winter there. Under normal circumstances, housebreaking a puppy is a pain in the you-know-what for humans, but when you add wind, snow, and ice every day, the nuisance becomes at least ten-fold. Butch came into Mom and Dad's home in December and so did Peko and Chiro. Since they didn't learn anything by adding Butch to the family in the middle of winter, they had to pay the price a 2nd and 3rd time with Peko and Chiro.

As mentioned in the previous chapter, when they were only six months old, Peko and Chiro accompanied Barb and Brenda from Japan to the United States. What a change in climate that was— icy temperatures and frozen turf to hot weather and warm sand! The girls wanted to go to college in Florida. They stayed with

Grandpap Russ temporarily at his home in the small, coal-mining town of Bentleyville, not far from Pittsburgh, Pennsylvania. Dad was with them for three days before heading to Florida on a house-hunting trip.

Grandpap Russ had an adult female Chihuahua named *Ginger*. Despite her extra small physique, she wasn't afraid of anything. She regularly patrolled the top of the hill where Grandpap Russ's house was located in search of any dog, cat, or critter of any kind that dared to tread into *her* territory. Every time she found a trespasser, Ginger attacked. She had the heart of a wolf and acted more like a Doberman Pinscher than a Chihuahua. The neighbors often marveled at the sight of her chasing dogs 2, 3, 4, and even 10 times her size and weight. The element of surprise was key for her, as bigger dogs would be startled and run away as soon as she went on a hostile offensive. Grandpap Russ referred to something President Dwight Eisenhower had once said: "It's not so much the size of the dog in a fight, it's the size of the fight in the dog!"

Ginger, who was 4 years old and weighed 9 pounds (same weight as me by the way), laid down the law to the 6-month-old, half-grown 40-pound pups right away. She would growl and lunge toward them, and come very close to their heads narrowly missing contact. Her smaller size didn't matter because she was on a mission to assert herself as the alpha figure. She did not like the diversion of human attention away from her toward the younger dogs. She hid all their toys, stole leftovers from their food dishes, and yapped at them incessantly with the most annoying barks they'd ever heard.

"Dang nabbit! Cummere! [*Doggone it! Come here!*]" was what Grandpap Russ yelled in Mon Valley Pittsburghese a dozen times a day to keep Ginger away from Peko and Chiro. Every time he yelled at her, she stopped dead in her tracks and, with head down, walked slowly toward him. Then, a little while later after things had cooled off, the scene would be repeated.

On Day 2, Dad bought three identical, gravy-laden bones and gave one to each dog. They chewed on their own bones relentlessly until their jaws tired. Afterward, Ginger took Chiro's bone without Chiro's knowledge and hid it behind Grandpap Russ's recliner chair in the living room, where she had already stored her own bone. Then, Peko caught a glimpse of Ginger sneaking toward her bone. Peko had already concluded that Ginger was evil and decided she would not take any more *hounding*. She had *a bone to pick!*

As soon as Ginger emerged from behind the chair after de-*paws*-iting Peko's bone, she noticed Peko was watching from five feet away, and that *purr*-turbed her. When Peko indicated she was about to growl, Ginger decided to go on the offensive. She rushed straight toward Peko, jumped up, and tried to bite her neck. Peko saw her coming and was able to send her flying by sharply jerking her own head to the right at the precise moment Ginger jumped and tried to get a grip. That move prevented Ginger's teeth from penetrating skin, and sent her rolling like a little bowling ball on the carpet.

Despite giving up 30 pounds in weight and six times in size, Ginger did not concede defeat. She got right back up, broke into a jump-start run, and cleanly leaped 18 inches off the floor grabbing for Peko's throat with her mouth. This time, she was able to sink fangs into flesh. She hung on tightly while Peko unsuccessfully tried to shake her off.

Upon hearing the commotion from the adjoining dining room, Barb came running and hustled over to assist Peko, but no matter how hard she tried, she wasn't able to pry open Ginger's mouth. Grandpap Russ came from the kitchen and motioned Barb to move away, at which time he scooped up Ginger with one hand and disengaged her teeth from Peko's throat. Yelling at Ginger, "You son-of-a-brick!" (a phrase Grandpap Russ popularized by modifying *son-of-a-b* _ _ _ _ to avoid cussing), he held her by the back of the neck, carried her over to the stairwell, and shoved her down to the cellar.

"Cussid dang dog!" [*Cursed damn dog!*]. "For cryin' out loud, what's wrong witchew?" [*For crying out loud, what is wrong with you?*], he mumbled angrily as he tossed Ginger's bone down the stairs after her. "Sure as heck, yewer gonna stay down there! [*Sure as hell, you are going to stay down there!*]" he yelled out.

The skirmish between Ginger and Peko was cause for concern. Peko could have badly injured Ginger due to their size difference, and Ginger's teeth latched onto Peko's neck could have done major damage. Fortunately, neither dog was seriously hurt. Peko had minor, teeth-mark lacerations on her neck, and Ginger was only slightly banged up following the rough handling by Grandpap Russ.

Peko and Chiro would not be moving out until three weeks later. Since Chiro had never challenged Ginger and would not likely change, no one was concerned about her. Peko seemed okay with the living arrangement as long as Ginger kept her distance. And since Ginger did not want to go any higher up on Grandpap Russ's poop list, she made no attempt to escalate the friction between Peko and her. As a result, no more incidents occurred; Peko and Chiro moved to Florida on schedule; and Ginger was happy again since she did not have to share the human attention in Grandpap Russ's house with the pups—at least not for the next seven months.

To Ginger's chagrin, Peko and Chiro returned with Barb and Brenda to visit again later in the same year at Christmas time (1994). Sensing that Grandpap Russ's displeasure with her had carried over, Ginger was on her best behavior the whole time they were there, so the entire visit went by with no trouble. To Ginger's delight, that one-week period was the last time she had to share time and space with Peko and Chiro, who were *mew*-tually elated by the prospect of no further contact with Ginger.

Barb and Brenda have been quick to bring up the Peko-Ginger debacle in conversations with their friends. The manner in which they tell the story—slightly embellished—makes it sound hilarious to anyone hearing it for the first time. They likened it to David and Goliath—the Biblical story about a boy and a giant engaged in mortal combat.

***

Peko kept us all tittering at her antics on a regular basis. Playing dumb was a common tactic for her. In no way was she a dimwit, but rather a stubborn creature, and smart like a fox.

It didn't take long for Peko to copy the manner in which Butch resisted bathing. In a feeble attempt to hide, she would first squeeze her extra-large frame under the extra-low, Japanese-style coffee table in our living room. After someone was able to dislodge her, she employed butt power to resist. She was pig-headed every time she disagreed with what was happening around her—especially bath time! When Mom or Dad wanted to give Peko a bath, they knew they were going to get wet too because she would drench everyone within splashing distance as soon as her paws hit tub water. Bathing her meant tasting soap!

Despite all the resistance, after every bath, Peko appeared joyful—probably because it was over. She went nuts running all over the house, stopping every 10 seconds to violently shake her whole body. After finally tiring herself out, she'd roll around on the carpeted floor to dry her fur.

She acted the same way when caught outdoors in a rainstorm, but instead of shaking off outside, she'd wait until she had gone inside to do it. Barb, Steve, and Brenda cracked-up watching her, but only after they learned the hard way to keep a safe distance to avoid getting soaked. More than once, Mom thought out loud, "I need to make a doggie umbrella just for Peko," only to learn later than someone had beaten her to it by actually inventing such a contraption.

Ordinarily, Peko was as laid back as any dog could be—or any cat or any human for that matter. She wasn't nondescript. It was just that nothing fazed her. For example, when an electrical storm approached, Butch and Chiro scurried about, each acting like *a cat on a hot tin roof*, while Peko could care less. Butch and Chiro voluntarily followed Mom to a walk-in closet in the master bedroom to ride out a bad storm, but Peko had to be coaxed to go along and usually resisted any attempt to have her accompany them. Butch and Chiro were *scaredy-cats*, as the sound of nearby thunder always raised fear in them, but Peko merely rolled over and slept through it.

Peko's apparent lack of energy and nonchalant attitude—*take life as it comes*—gave the impression to some human observers that she was dispirited. Seemingly without a care in the world, she went her blithe, lighthearted way.

Even during one of the largest storms to ever strike Central Florida—Hurricane Charlie in August 2004—Dad had to literally drag her into the master bedroom closet. That was where everyone else was already squeezed together to ride out the dangerous storm, which ripped off large portions of the roof and made it feel as if the whole house might lift off its foundation. Barb and her kids Ricky and Erika were visiting at the time, and all of us were tightly jammed in the walk-in closet—3 adults, 2 children, 2 big dogs, and 1 medium-sized dog literally piled on top of each other inside a confined space that was already filled to near capacity with articles of clothing, suitcases, and other assorted items.

***

All dogs naturally take their time in finding a good place to pee and poop; however, Peko would take up to three times longer than Butch, Chiro, or Koro. It wasn't uncommon for her to stop and take five minutes to search for the *purr*-fect place to do #1, and double that amount of time to find the right spot for #2. Locating and properly smelling a certain place where an unknown dog had previously peed or pooped, and then peeing and pooping on that very same patch of ground must have been her weird method of networking.

Peko was a tomboy and her slanted way of thinking of herself as a male was highlighted by the manner in which she tried to pee, not always, but much of the time. She would lift up her left hind leg like a male, tottering and nearly losing her balance every time, and peeing a little without ever coming close to emptying her bladder. Those antics were a constant source of fun for Barb, who sometimes copy-catted Peko, and almost fell over with laughter a few times while watching and mimicking Peko's attempts to pee like a male.

All too often during playtime, Peko would mount Chiro and start humping. Since they were both females, she didn't do it in a mating way. She exhibited this type of behavior just to show anyone who happened to be watching that she was dominant over Chiro. Granted, they were siblings, but Peko was definitely the leader and Chiro basically followed Peko's lead her entire life.

From puppyhood all the way through seniorhood, Peko and Chiro regularly vied with each other, competing to get the most attention from humans. Chiro's occasional attempts to emulate her sister's dominant *purr*-sonality were always short-lived, and never once did she try to mount Peko or attempt to pee like a male.

On their 1st birthday—Halloween 1994—Brenda tried to coax Peko and Chiro to allow her to carry them piggyback. Chiro refused—it was a pride thing—however, Peko was okay with it. One of the funniest sights I ever saw was Brenda actually carrying Peko piggyback, as she wasn't very much taller than Peko when Peko stood up to climb onto her back. Hilarious!

At least twice every day, without fail, Peko would prostrate her 80+ pound frame beneath the small coffee table in the living room. Here's a rare photo of her on top of the table instead of under it (and yes, she posed for this).

Squeezing beneath the table was Peko's way of securing a little privacy. Everyone knew that when she was under that table, which was only 12 inches high, she did not want anyone to look at her, talk to her, try to coax her to come out, or otherwise acknowledge her presence. When she was ready, she emerged on her own terms.

It was not unusual for her to spend up to four hours at a time lying flat as a pancake under that table, probably thinking she had made herself invisible. Upon crawling out, she was ready for one of two things—either a bonding session with Mom or a bite-wrestling match with Chiro.

***

Dr. Miho Nagasawa of the Department of Animal Science and Biotechnology at Azabu University in Kanagawa, Japan, along with her colleagues, published a paper in April 2015 regarding landmark research regarding human-dog oxytocin bonding (Lees, 2015). According to Lees, Dr. Nagasawa and the other researchers concluded that oxytocin levels in urine specimens collected from the humans and their dogs, who had participated in the study, were higher following episodes of the humans and dogs gazing at each other, and also after durations of petting and other forms of touching by the humans.

Dr. Nagasawa and associates observed the interactions between 55 dogs and their owners in a controlled setting, and concluded that a dog's gaze, as a factor that contributes to social bonding, has a particularly strong effect on its owner's neuroendocrine system, which includes hormones that affect behavior (Nagasawa, Mogi, & Kikusui, 2009). The experiment by Nagasawa et al. also suggested that dogs and humans have a common attachment style that may explain, in part, why dogs are able to adapt to human society.

In contrast, *mew*-tual gazing by domestically raised wolves and their humans, who had also participated in the experiment by Nagasawa et al., was observed, but there was no increase in urinary oxytocin of the humans or their wolves. This experiment was similar to the one previously described in Chapter Three. Moreover, nasal spray of oxytocin on female dogs had led to longer periods of time by the dogs gazing at their humans, and, in turn, resulted in higher concentrations of oxytocin in the humans' urine samples—indicative of relationships similar to that of human mothers and their babies. As a believer that a famous saying, *Eyes are the windows into the soul,* had originated in the Bible, Dad wasn't at all surprised upon hearing about the significant role that eyes played in the oxytocin experiments.

Mom and Peko's relationship was like mother and child since Mom was, by far, the one at whom Peko gazed the most. During the first two years of her life, Peko spent more time bonding with Barb than anyone else, but Barb moved out into her own place, after which Peko latched onto Mom for the rest of her life. She occasionally gazed at Dad, Steve, and Brenda, but with less intensity than she did with Mom. This meant that even though Peko exchanged oxytocin with Dad and the kids, her interchange with Mom exceeded the levels reached with the others by a wide margin.

On occasion, Peko would stare just because she wanted a bite of something that Mom or someone else was eating; however, that was not always the case. Much of the time she was using eye contact to communicate for another reason—bonding, albeit with less frequency than her sister Chiro due to the difference in their personalities. She also regularly engaged in *mew*-tual gazing with Chiro, and that too resulted in tight sibling bonding.

***

All through puppyhood and beyond, Peko had a propensity for mischief that she never outgrew. She loved to softly bite shiny earrings and bracelets, or anything else that sparkled. She did not damage the items—she was merely attracted to them. Mom, Barb, and Brenda each lost a few pieces of jewelry while Peko was around, which made me wonder what an x-ray of Peko's stomach might reveal, but that is something we'll never know.

Standing up on her hind legs and thrusting in close to a *purr*-son, face-to-face, was Peko's way of saying *Hello*. Chiro followed Peko's lead and they tried to outdo each other when greeting —more like startling—guests at the door. Here's an example of them welcoming Miyuki (Mom's nephew Jun's wife) with Peko, as usual, taking the lead.

JIM HERRON

Exuberantly trying to bowl over visitors became Peko and Chiro's joint trademark. Barb and Brenda let them get away with it while the four of them were the only occupants of the new family home in Florida for the first 18 months. It took a while, but after Dad moved in, he was finally able to break them of that habit by lifting up one of his knees to create an obstacle to block their lunges. A knee coming up to meet their chests wasn't something they expected. It didn't hurt, but was sufficiently uncomfortable and served as the means to get them to stop lunging at people.

Peko had another bad habit that took much longer to correct— goosing visitors in the front and back with her nose. After goosing them, she would sniff their crotch or backside, whichever presented itself to her first. She had mastered the *shake* command at an early age, but favored sniffing body parts like dog-to-dog over the less *purr*-sonal hand-to-paw shakes preferred by humans. Unlike her sister, Peko liked smelling the butts of unknown dogs she encountered out in public. Nothing unusual about that, but Peko even tried to sniff human butts. She must have wondered why humans did not smell each other in the same manner.

The goosing and butt-sniffing caused embarrassment to Mom. The blame goes to Peko's nonfurry sister Barb for allowing her to get away with such antics for so long. Constant scolding by Mom and Dad while Peko was in the act of goosing or sniffing human body parts finally paid off, but it took several weeks to break the ever-pig-headed Peko of those bad habits.

Peko routinely displayed her own types of body language. She would jerk her head to the right or left a few times in an attempt to signal Chiro to come and follow her in that direction. Peko was a rebel, so when she acted that way, she was usually up to something no-good, such as trying to sneak off through a backyard fence gate that someone had forgotten to close. Altogether, she escaped at least a dozen times either out the front door after someone opened it and gave her enough time to run out, or through an open fence gate, or under the fence through a hole she had dug deep enough for her to squeeze through. She ran off with Barb usually close behind trying to catch her, and managed to get further away a couple of times with Mom, who wasn't as fleet afoot as she once was, the only one in pursuit.

Peko had ample opportunity to go far, but always stopped short —no more than 100 yards away from the house—and then she would hop around back and forth daring whomever was in pursuit to come closer. She didn't give up until she was dead-tired, after which Barb or Mom would have to drag her back home. She wasn't easy to latch onto because she did not wear a leash while inside the house or outside in the backyard, so they had to grab the fur on her neck.

Peko was friendly, but strangers didn't know that, and quite often while on the loose, due to her large size, she scared people by running up to them prompting an immediate apology from Mom or Barb. Mom wished she could put Peko in timeout as she had done with her own biological kids to curb misbehavior when they were toddlers, but that doesn't work with dogs. She often dreamed of having a bigger backyard someday so her dogs would feel less constrained; however, even a larger yard would not have stopped Peko from exiting if the opportunity should present itself.

I heard Mom mumbling to herself, "Oh dear Peko, I wish you and I could have a conversation about your behavior so I could ask you why you do the things you do." My best estimate of how many times I heard her say that, or words to that effect, would be in triple digits.

When Dad told Mom that he had heard about a Japanese company inventing a collar that supposedly could interpret dog barks into human words, she directed him to research it. What he learned was disheartening, as the accuracy and reliability of the device—called the *Bowlingual Voice*, was iffy to say the least (Bond, 2009). But Dad was optimistic saying he believed that future technology would someday produce something to enable humans to actually converse with their dogs by translating words to barks, or barks to words, or both.

Rolling over on her back and exposing her belly was one way that Peko displayed contentment. Although Chiro often copied Peko's antics, she stopped short of showing her tummy since her *purr*-sona was dignified and always commanded respect. Peko had far less pride, but she didn't lie on her back and show her stomach due to a lack of self-esteem. Rather, she did it as a way to show her total confidence in the furry and nonfurry beings with whom she cohabitated.

Peko's confidence in her domination over Chiro was evident the most when she would rollover on her back and expose her belly making her appear vulnerable, a position she assumed at least once a day to keep getting Chiro's attention. In an attempt to goad Chiro to play-fight, she would go belly-up while looking at Chiro directly in the eyes, after which Chiro always took the bait. A true instigator was she!

***

Although six years her junior, as an adult, Peko outweighed Butch by 30 pounds. Between her first and second birthdays, Peko often tested Butch in a number of ways, all the while attempting to show dominance. She liked to run up to Butch face-to-face, bark once or twice, back up a few feet, and then repeat the scenario.

Butch hated the teasing, but put up with it until Peko got too close for comfort one day, at which time Butch suddenly responded by nipping her with a short, quick bite just above the right eye. Peko yelped while running away with no thought of retaliatory tangling with Butch. From that day forward, she never tested Butch again during their remaining 6-year coexistence. Thanks to Butch, Peko had a permanent scar above one eye that made her appear tougher than she really was. Her scar looked a lot like the one that an embedded deer tick would later cause above Chiro's right eye.

There's a lesson to be learned here: a dog and a cat can sometimes get along better than two dogs living in the same household. That's because there is no struggle over pecking order. Butch and I lived together in three separate homes with the same humans over a period of 14 years—longer than any of our housemates lived with us or each other—and never once did we get into a heated exchange or altercation like the one Butch and Peko got into, or the knock-down drag-out fight that Peko and Koro had later on. Butch had a pack mentality, but not so for me. The animosity level between us stayed at zero!

As descendants of wolves, dogs are social animals with a pack instinct. The main difference between wolves and dogs is that wolves hunt for food in packs, while there is no need for dogs to hunt (except under human control). My feline ancestors (sabretooth tigers) lived and hunted alone, not in packs. As a result, cats do not possess the pack mentality, so that was never an issue between the dogs and me.

As far as Mom was concerned, pack and family are synonymous—the seniors in a human family lead the juniors, and one of the seniors is generally recognized as the head leader. So, there is usually a hierarchical order in a human family that makes it somewhat similar to a wolf or dog pack. Mom understood that packs are not part of the feline nature, so she did not hold my lone wolf manner (pardon pun please) against me. Dad didn't get it though as my solitude and non-submissiveness made me appear aloof to him. What can I say?

***

When they first brought Peko and Chiro home, Mom and Dad were not aware that it was inadvisable to keep together same-sex siblings from litters of dog breeds considered aggressive (Akitas included). Fortunately, Peko and Chiro never aggressed toward each other, nor were they ever aggressive with Butch, Koro, or me. In the one incident that Koro and Peko got into a fight, Koro was the aggressor by attacking Peko for getting too close to his food dish, and Peko merely acted in self-defense.

Once or twice per week until age 10, and with less frequency after Chiro got sick, the play between them was rough. Knowing the limitations, they each engaged in bite inhibition to avoid hurting the other. It was common for them to show off by putting on their *dog and pony show* for visitors, all of whom became filled with excitement while watching them *purr*-form. Their fake biting became so heated on occasion that one of them would inevitably become undisciplined and accidentally draw a small amount of blood from the other, at which time they would instantly break apart as if a bell had rung to end a round during a boxing match.

They would start bite-wrestling on the spur of the moment.

It was restrained biting accompanied by playful yelps that occasionally changed to furious sounding growls. It was nothing more than innocent sibling roughhouse competition. They'd abruptly stop after a few minutes to companionably hydrate by sharing a water bowl, and then the show would resume. Both of them always knew when to call it quits before the situation got out of control, and that precluded any serious injury to either of them. It was just a way for them to attempt to outdo each other while vying for attention.

Chiro's softheartedness was detailed in the previous chapter. Peko was nowhere near as compassionate as her sister. For instance, at least once a day, Chiro gave Peko a massage by gently nibbling on her jaws, throat, and neck. It was her way of grooming Peko, who laid there with eyes closed and enjoyed being the recipient of Chiro's loving care. Not once did Peko reciprocate.

This picture of the Akita sisters was taken on their 2nd B-day—Halloween 1995.

***

JIM HERRON

Despite our veterinarians repeatedly recommending commercial dog food, Mom believed human food was best for the dogs, so that's what they got. *Purr*-haps, she thought Dad may have been right when he suspected two vets of being on the take by getting something in return for pimping dog food. The dogs got a wide variety of human foods, but Mom avoided certain ones knowing they were bad for them, including chocolate, grapes and raisins, onions, and anything containing caffeine, among many others. She fed all of them extremely well by giving them lots of protein in the form of grilled boneless and skinless chicken breasts and 100% pure ground beef. She mixed in small portions of carrots, cabbage, and rice. Their meat intake was much larger than the vegetables so no one could ever accuse them of being vegan dogs.

Mom made all their meals from scratch. She tirelessly cut the chicken, along with occasional all-beef hotdogs, into bite-sized pieces, and chopped the veggies for better digestion. Their carefully prepared meals, which also included small portions of no-grain dog food on the side, were rich in basic nutrients. She believed in feeding them the best she knew how because dog lives are so very short compared to humans. Nothing could shake her resolve that they would get the best meals *paws*-sible.

Dad often remarked, "They eat better than me!" He could have been joking, but based on what I saw, the dogs may have actually eaten better than him in the long run.

If you ask me, all the dogs ate far too high up on the food chain. If Dad could hear me say that, he'd come back with something like, *She's only a cat, so what does she know?* Well, I'll tell you what I know! Not only did Mom spend more money to feed each dog than me, she also spent a lot more time fixing their meals than she did opening a can for me. Sorry for getting sidetracked. I love her to pieces and realize she knew I was low maintenance when compared to the dogs, and that was flattering. I just didn't like it when they got more attention than me at mealtime. I am not whining, as that might imply the B-word and, as I have unequivocally stated before, in no way does the B-word fit this cat! It's just that I did have feelings.

Peko was a fussy eater. She performed an annoying ritual about twice a week by sniffing the meal Mom had prepared, after which she'd suddenly tip over the dish with her nose spilling the contents, and then nonchalantly walk away with an apparent disgusted look on her face. The rest of the time, she ate Mom's food offerings without incident and seemed to love everything. So, the type of food wasn't what bothered her, nor was it the quantity or quality, as there was nothing to be desired in that regard. Maybe, it was the lack of variety, but only Peko knew for sure.

Other times, Peko would tip over her food dish when it contained something new, *paws*-sibly because the smell was unappealing, or maybe only because it was an unknown odor. In an attempt to make her feel bad about spilling food and refusing to eat, Mom always spoke softly to her saying something like, "Don't you know a lot of homeless dogs have nothing to eat and they would love to have your dinner," but it was to no avail. Whatever Peko did not consume would later be replaced with doggie treats, so that may have been her motive all along. Although Peko was silent when she did it, I would liken her acts of tipping over food dishes to temper tantrums commonly displayed by human toddlers. A brat was she!

Peko sure wasn't finicky when it came to cat food, as she would sneak *my* food into *her* digestive tract every chance she got. There was never a reason to suspect either Butch or Chiro of stealing my food, only Peko—I could smell it on her breath! Butch ate everything Mom or any other nonfurry being gave her, usually so fast she didn't taste or chew it. Despite having an awful smelling digestive formula added to her food every day for 50% of her life, Chiro never complained. And then there's me, who was not only the easiest to please at mealtime, but also the easiest to prepare meals for since my foods all came in a can —something that never seemed to bother Peko.

The treasured snack of Peko and Chiro was not a dog treat, but rather a human one in the form of popsicles. Not just any popsicle would do though—only banana ones! They got hooked because Barb and Brenda regularly snacked on banana-flavored popsicles to beat the heat in the hot Florida sun. The girls would hand-feed them one popsicle per day in bite-size pieces. Not just any banana-flavored popsicle mind you—only *Blue Bunny Banana Pops* would do.

One day, their favorite brand was sold out, so the girls bought another popular brand with assorted flavors. When they tried to feed orange, cherry, grape, and lime-flavored popsicles to them, they sniffed and then walked away in refusal. They even rejected all other brands' banana popsicles. The Blue Bunny Company could've employed Peko and Chiro to produce possibly the greatest banana popsicle commercial ever. I don't know why they made such a big deal out of Blue Bunny Banana Pops. I cannot comment firsthand because I never tasted any kind of popsicle and there is a good reason for that—a cat's tongue is su-*purr* sensitive to cold objects and mine was no exception.

Mom and Dad's favorite snack is the apple fritter found in donut shops. One day, Mom gave a piece to Butch, and she loved it (of course, there wasn't any kind of food that Butch didn't like). Upon observing Butch beg for more bites, Peko and Chiro mooched for it too. All three dogs developed a liking for the apple fritter, as did Koro soon after he came along. It became a favored snack for all of them. Mom was aware that too much sugar was not good for them, so she limited them to 2 or 3 small bites twice per week.

***

Mom not only loves domesticated animals, but the wild ones as well. She doesn't hesitate to let everyone know about her animal rights conviction—*Just like humans, every animal has the right to live in a world where they are free to do what comes naturally*. The Sandhill Crane, in particular, receives her utmost respect because a male-female pair mates for life, a monogamous arrangement that two other birds—swans and turtle doves—have in common. This is something that Mom considers a *purr*-fect model for the human species.

Sandhill Cranes are plentiful in Florida, and their cousins, known as Red-Crowned Cranes (also called Manchurian Cranes or Japanese Cranes), are common in Northern Japan where Mom grew up, so she is familiar with both species. She's fascinated about their devotion to their mates, and upon observing a pair of them out in public, she's quick to remark about their fidelity. Sometimes, 3 cranes are observed together—parents with their single offspring until the young one is able to find a mate and go off on its own. There have been a couple of times when she saw 4 of them—the parents and twin offspring—a sight that brought an instant smile across her face. Observing a single crane by itself, however, brings instant tears to Mom's eyes because she suspects its mate may be deceased.

Loyalty and devotion are synonymous, and that makes the cranes just as admirable as Akita dogs. It's no wonder the cranes and the Akitas are both considered national treasures in Japan. While on the topic of monogamy, domestic animals, like dogs and cats, do not mate for life, but wolves are among a handful of wild animals that are life-long monogamous.

Mom made it a habit to feed the wide variety of birds, turtles, and fish that congregated in and around the pond across the street from our Orlando residence about the same time each morning waiting for a handout. She usually got there on time; however, should she fail to show at the expected time, as many as 10 Mallard ducks would waddle across the street and march right up to our front door, loudly quacking in unison to remind Mom that she was making them wait. After going outside to feed the ducks in our yard, she would then serve as traffic cop by stopping passing cars to allow the birds to slowly meander safely back across the street.

Feeding breadcrumbs to baby Mallards has given Mom great pleasure over many years because she is often their very first human contact. In one instance, she started feeding bread to a mother Mallard and her babies by the pond across the street. In the beginning, there were 8 ducklings, but only 7 the next day, then 6, 5, and so on until the babies were all gone—8 babies in 8 days! This scenario repeated itself two more times with other mother ducks and their broods.

Feral cats were often seen roaming around in our neighborhood, and Mom suspected they were responsible for the disappearance of the ducklings. Unlike strays, feral cats tend to avoid human contact and do not depend on supplemental food from humans to survive. They are predators that feed on smaller animals and birds—like Tommy, the feral cat befriended by Mom and the kids before they got any pets. That's why it was logical for Mom to think feral cats might be the culprits since a large number of them were living in nearby wooded areas.

Mom couldn't take it any longer, so she sent Dad out on a nighttime mission to conduct a surveillance of the pond in an effort to ascertain how the baby ducks were disappearing. Feral cats hunt at night, so Mom ordered Dad to begin his observations after dark and continue into the wee small hours. After three straight nights and many long hours of watching, he had observed nothing suspicious. All the feral cats he saw merely passed by the pond on their way somewhere else.

Baby ducks kept vanishing and the mystery of their disappearance remained unsolved for more than a year. Then one morning, by chance, Mom happened to observe the real villain in the act. Just as she was about to feed breadcrumbs to a mother duck with 2 ducklings, a hawk swooped down no more than 10 feet in front of her, and brutally seized one of the babies in an instant by grabbing it with its talons. The attack by the screaming banshee projectile in broad daylight was swift and without warning. It broke Mom's heart to witness it. Peko was by her side, but there was absolutely nothing that she, Peko, or the mother Mallard could have done to stop it from happening.

Mom fully understands nature's role for the hawk and the duckling in the cycle-of-life food chain; however, that did not make it any easier to watch something as horrible as a baby's life come to a violent end. Having had a lot of practice in trying to think like an animal, she presumed that because Peko and she were standing very close to the mother duck and her babies, the hawk may have viewed them as competing predators with duck on the menu. She believed the hawk had reacted instinctively by dive-bombing to capture the duckling and beat them to it.

The hawk took the fuzzy, brown baby bird straight to the top of the tallest tree across the street where a second hawk was perched waiting to share lunch. The duo became extremely vocal with screams that could have been heard a mile away. Since Mom got a close-up look, she was able to *paws*-itively identify the attacker as a Red-shouldered Hawk from pictures and a description contained in a North American wildlife book in our home library.

It was difficult to accept, but Mom finally realized the truth in the old adage, *Whatever will be, will be*. I heard the following monologue after she got home while she was talking to Peko about the horrible event they had just witnessed. "Oh Peko, why couldn't you stop that bad hawk from taking the baby ducky? Why did you just stand there? Did it happen too fast?" Mom rambled on.

A stunned Peko locked eyes with her and listened intently. She concluded by saying, "It's okay. I'm sorry Peko. Don't worry. I know there was nothing you could do."

Years earlier, Butch had gotten the best of a flock of crows, but a lone hawk was too much for Peko to handle. It's just nature's way of telling us that strength in numbers is not always the case, and that a lone predatory bird relies on the element of surprise to succeed in filling their intestinal tract with fresh kills. Mom used the term *Mother Nature*, which prompted Dad to tell her that it sounded as if there is a *goddess* controlling the environment. Looking back to Chapter Two, there wasn't supposed to be any further mention of religion; however, Dad said something else to Mom in an attempt to simplify things: "Nature is everything that is God-made, not man-made."

After being an eyewitness to the big bird killing the little one, Mom frequently observed the same hawk—or its lookalike partner—perched high above in a tree or on top of a streetlight waiting to pounce again on an unsuspecting creature along the bank of the pond. They screamed at their partners in such a loud tone it hurt Mom's eardrums. Ironically, the hawks had hung around to feed off the ducks and other pond creatures that she was feeding, something quite troubling to her because she felt as if she was fattening the pond inhabitants for the hawks to eat.

The hawks not only took critters on land, as Mom had seen one of them zoom down to capture a small fish swimming near the pond's surface. She wished she could feed the hawks to stop them from killing, but knew that would not be *paws*-sible because the hawks are birds of prey and instinctively have to kill a live bird or mammal before eating it—unlike the vultures in our neighborhood that favored devouring animals that were already dead.

Without fail, Mom averts her eyes to avoid viewing a dead animal on a roadway, but not so for black vultures with their eyes constantly scouring the landscape in search of dead critters. Most humans describe these birds as gross and ugly, and despise them for feeding on the carrion left behind by motor vehicles. Mom thinks differently. In her mind, the vultures are a wondrous sight flying in tight circles while using their keen senses of sight and smell to locate a decaying animal carcass. And then they soar together above the spot where carrion is found before making a group landing to dine.

Mom fully respects the role designed for the vultures in the overall scheme of things—roadkill feeders, which makes total sense, hence, there is no way they deserve the widespread disrespect directed their way. She told Dad, "Think about what would happen without them"—the rotting flesh of dead animals piling up on all the highways and back roads would result in the spread of serious diseases infecting not only other animals, but humans too.

As a retired cop, Dad is far better at being aware of his surroundings than Mom, so he can always see coming what I am about to describe. Every single time they drive by a construction site, where trees are being cut down to make way for apartment buildings or an office complex, which is quite common in the Orlando area, Mom blows a gasket. She hates it when wild animal habitat is destroyed to benefit humans. The animals' continuing loss of precious turf is near the top of her list of pet-peeves.

In our neighborhood, deer, raccoons, opossums, armadillos, squirrels, rabbits, and alligators, along with turkeys and a wide variety of other birds, have less cover for their nests and dens. Most troubling is the fact that wildlife is helpless because there is not a single thing the animals and birds can do to stop humans from displacing them from their territory.

Not only does Mom empathize with animals in the wild, she also feels sorry for trees since they are living things too. Seeing multiple trees being cut down to make way for human development bothers her to no end. Dad once had to physically restrain and pull her away from two men who were in the process of sawing down an oak tree that had to be close to 100 years old. They were killing that tree to make room for a new pathway in the park where Mom and Dad walked the dogs. Mom had already begun to give the guys a piece of her mind and didn't back off until Dad intervened. He told her those men did not make the decision to cut down the tree, someone else did, and they were just ordered to do it.

If you have never seen a human being shed tears over a tree being killed, and somehow, someday, you are able to spend time with Mom, that's something you may get the chance to witness. She has shed more tears for trees she saw killed and natural habitats she saw destroyed than a torrential downpour has raindrops. She was doubly upset over that very old oak tree in the park because two families of squirrels had nested in the tree and their homes were destroyed.

***

If she had been named *Pokey* instead of Peko, it would have suited her. She was never in a hurry, not only on daily walks, but in everything she did in and around the house. She ambled along and spent as much time as *purr*-mitted on every scent along the walking path. Conversely, her sister Chiro did not saunter, but insisted on hastily leading the way as if she was on an important mission with a short deadline. Chiro's nose was constantly on the ground to briefly savor the multitude of odors available as she scurried along.

Dad handled both Peko and Chiro on separate, retractable, 12-foot, nylon leashes, while Mom walked behind them with Butch on a shorter leash. I never went on the walks, but from what I heard Mom say, the sight was often comical—Dad's arms outstretched fully in two directions (forward and reverse) with

THE DOGS' BEST FRIEND: A CAT'S EYE VIEW

Chiro pulling ahead to speed up and Peko pulling back at the same time to slow down. Since both dogs weighed up to 85 pounds, one can visualize how hard-pressed Dad must have been trying to maintain his balance and keep his armpit sockets from popping out.

Unlike Chiro, Peko was never injured. Unlike Butch and Chiro, Peko never got sick. That was a good thing because Peko had an extra hard time swallowing any kind of pill, especially the large heartworm variety. Mom gave all the dogs an expensive heartworm capsule every month, but Peko was tricky. She would hold the medicine in the back of her mouth and later spit it out when she thought Mom wasn't looking. After Mom caught on, she started shoving the capsule as far down Peko's throat as *paws*-sible and then held her snout closed until she swallowed it. That was the only way it could be done. Snacks containing pill pockets didn't fool Peko—she spit them out.

I once overheard Mom telling Dad about the red-fur mutt she had as a child. His name was Peko too and he was her first pet. She had Peko #1 since he was a baby and fell in love with him. He was always the first one to welcome her home every school day. He was the only one to hear all about everything that had happened to her. She watched him grow to adult size.

Mom was heartbroken on the day she came home and discovered Peko #1 was gone. Neither her mother nor her brothers and sisters wanted to talk about his whereabouts. Finally, her mother disclosed she had given him away because he had gotten too big to feed. Mom demanded to know the address of whoever took him, but no one would tell her. After overhearing her mother telling her older brother that the person who got Peko may have wanted to eat him, Mom cried continuously, and went on a hunger strike for a week. When she heard that red-fur dogs were especially favored by people who ate dogmeat, disgust was added to her distress. That situation emotionally harmed her more than words can describe. It happened when she was 9 years old and Peko #1 was only a year old, and it hurts her to this day to talk about it.

There is no doubt that Peko #1's misfortune started Mom down the path of animal rights advocacy. Her mother had tried to explain by telling her that, at the time—shortly after the end of World War II—there was a food shortage in Japan, and that's why some people ate dogs. In Mom's mind, that explanation did not come close to justifying what was happening.

With Japan's economic growth and development, the people there stopped eating dogs a long time ago; however, occasionally hearing in the news about people in other Asian countries still eating dogs makes Mom cringe. Just listening to Mom and Dad talk about humans eating dogs turned my stomach. Then, when Dad brought up cat meat being considered a delicacy in some places in Southeast Asia, I lost it—my previous meal, that is.

Like Mom, I cannot comprehend the rationalization for humans eating pets, whether it's of the canine or feline variety. People in countries where dogs and cats are eaten would fall back on the fact that cows and pigs are also domesticated, and since humans eating certain other mammals is generally acceptable, it comes down to the level of domestication—pets versus farm animals. I will leave it at that, as this is a deep topic of discussion directly involving me and my canine housemates—something that could fill the pages of a separate book and then some.

***

Back to the Peko that I knew—she finally grew old. She was always emotionally mellow, but became even more laid back upon entering the geriatric stage. Physically, she developed stiff, arthritic joints around age 10. That's when Mom started giving her over-the-counter glucosamine (the stuff humans ingest for the same problem to relieve the pain). She showed signs of hip dysplasia at age 12, a condition that is fairly common among senior Akita dogs. Her hip condition gradually worsened, and by age 14 it had debilitated her to the extent that she became wobbly after standing for only a few minutes. She was ambulatory, but unable to jump into the family van so Dad would have to lift her up when they went on rides.

Peko's hearing started to diminish around her 14th birthday, so Mom had to sing the *Happy Doll Festival* song louder for her. Something that did not diminish was Peko's appetite and she ate well to the very end. Unfortunately, she lost partial control of her bowels about 10 months before she passed. Mom took her outside five or six times a day to potty. She had an occasional accident inside the house, and Mom cleaned it up without ever complaining about any mess that Peko had made.

Like Butch, Chiro, and me before her, Peko chose her own time to head up to the Rainbow Bridge. Mom made sure that no one picked that time for her. She passed away with Mom in attendance just 10 days shy of her 15th birthday—an exceptionally old age for a big dog. Her longevity can be attributed, in large part, to Mom's meals, regular exercise, great companionship, and a stress-free, loving home environment.

Seconds after Peko's passing, Mom spoke while lying on the floor beside her stroking her head, "You were such a good girl Peko. I wish everybody could go through life with no cares like you did." She went on, "You and Chichi looked just like teddy bears the first time I saw you. You were my little Hachiko. I am so glad you got to play in the snow when you were little. I loved watching you guys playing. You got to play with Bo too." Mom became overwhelmed with emotion and couldn't say another word because so many fond memories of Peko's life were flashing through her mind.

***

Peko and Chiro were not just siblings—they were bosom buddies. There was never a disagreement between them—not even a mild one—during their 12½ years together on Earth. Their reunion upon Peko joining us in the meadow by the Bridge was an event to behold! Chiro and she spent the first hour rolling around on the ground and play-biting just as they had done nearly every day before Chiro passed. There is no way a bystander could tell which one was more excited. After all, they were blood, and the obvious joy that each of them felt was indescribable, even for a prolific storyteller like me.

Something Mom said while lying next to Peko after she had passed—wishing everyone could go through life without any cares like Peko had done—made me think. She had a good point: dog people could all benefit by reducing stress should they live life vicariously through their dogs.

CHAPTER SIX—KORO

> *"If you get to thinking you're a person of some influence, try ordering somebody else's dog around."*
> -Will Rogers

It was Mom who decided that the family's 4th canine addition—their first and only male—would be known as *Koro*. "It's like Zorro with a *K*," Dad replied when someone asked for his name. As was the case with Peko and Chiro, Koro doesn't mean anything in particular—it's just a Japanese name reserved for canines (like *Max* or *Buddy* in English). Mom's older brother had a dog named Koro when he was in high school and she was in elementary school. She liked the name and revived it.

Dad couldn't resist the male Akita puppy he saw in the pet store window. Why? Because he looked so much like Chiro when she was a baby. Since Chiro and Peko were already seniors (almost 11 years old), Dad had been thinking for a while that the time had come to look for a puppy, and his mind was set on a pure white Akita resembling his beloved Chiro.

As was the case for certain bungled decisions Dad had made in the past, he should have done something other than what he actually did. He should have heeded Mom's advice about purebreds—"They have more health problems than mixed-breeds." He should have also taken her advice about pure white dogs —"They are more likely to develop health problems than blacks, reds, or any other colors." He should have suspected something was amiss upon finding out the price had been cut by one-third. Furthermore, he was aware that the best age to take in a puppy is 8-weeks-old and this one had already passed that timeline six weeks earlier, so he should have suspected something was wrong. He should have done all those things, but did none.

Dad may have been having a senior moment and forgot that male Akitas are typically much more aggressive than the females. Chiro and Peko were females and in no way aggressive, but this pup was a male and, even at the young age of 14 weeks, his genetic makeup displayed signs of aggression and dominance. He growled—not softly but loud; he bit—not lightly but hard; and he nudged—not gently but forcefully.

Everything Dad knew or had heard went out the window. The pup was a Chiro lookalike and that's all that mattered. He envisioned what he would look like when full grown—a rare, pure white, full-blooded Akita male with a large physique that would closely resemble Chiro's grand champion sire. What Dad did in this situation could be used to liken him to one of Pavlov's experimental dogs—he acted impulsively to get a reward. He took the pup home the same day he first laid eyes on him.

Koro was filled with excitement in the car on the way from the pet store to our house. He couldn't sit still. As soon as he got inside the house, he ran through every room. His enthusiasm after finally being let out of a crate and free to move around was so great that it caused him to pee on the floor in front of the TV in the family room after only one minute in the house. Dad didn't care and gladly cleaned up the puddle on the carpet.

While still a puppy, it didn't take long for Koro to show the family that his tem-*purr*-ament was more typical of a Pit Bull than an Akita. He had an overly protective *purr*-sonality that enabled him to quickly replace Peko as the alpha dog and become the chief guardian of the home. The wolf within him remained near the surface. Typical of a large guard dog breed, he aggressed toward strange canines and other species, such as stray cats and trespassing humans, who came within a certain distance of our house that he considered too close—50 feet. In his mind, the mission was absolutely clear—defend the dwelling against would-be home invaders, especially the ones wearing FedEx, UPS, or Amazon uniforms and driving big trucks! They couldn't fool him, as he saw right through their masquerade and knew they were up to no-good.

What he lacked in sociability, Koro made up for in a fierce determination to make sure no stranger would ever enter the house without Mom or Dad's *purr*-mission. He took his job seriously. There was no doubt he would risk his life to stop an intruder and protect the home from anything he *purr*-ceived as a threat. Literally, the only way a burglar, or anyone else with the intent of *purr*-petrating a crime, could gain entry would have been over his dead body. His rugged appearance was so imposing that no one in their right mind would ever try to get past him.

An absolute pecking order mentality highlighted by a strong instinct to be leader of the pack paints a succinct word picture of Koro. At only 4 months old, he was already pushing around Peko and Chiro who were more than 10 years his senior. Mom recognized the situation early on and knew what had to be done. Knowing that alpha figures in the canine world are only males, she made sure that Dad assumed the lead role quickly male-to-male with him. By doing so, he was able to suppress and hold Koro's domineering personality in check.

Mom and Dad grew up in the 1940's and 1950's, but 1960's music was their favorite. Mom refreshed Dad's memory of a 1964 hit song *Leader of the Pack* by a group called The Shangri-Las as a theme song for keeping Koro under control, after which they played it over and over on a CD in their car as a constant reminder.

Koro's philosophy seemed clear—with proper manipulation,

humans could become subservient to a dog. His focus on moving up in the homestead hierarchy remained deep-rooted, as he would roughly nudge Dad's hands, nibble at his belt, and push his snout hard against his legs constantly. Recognizing such actions as genuine attempts to test him as part of a vision of taking over the alpha position, Dad always put him in check and never allowed him to get the upper paw. He sternly backed him away trying to make sure there was no doubt in his mind that the leadership position would not be relinquished. It did not matter that Dad had won, as the scenario would repeat itself the next day.

Dogs have a different thought process than humans because their emotions are quite simple and they live in the moment, and Koro was definitely no exception. He was as strong-willed as any canine could be, so he would never allow his determination to be permanently suppressed. Even though he was destined to fail, he kept on trying to take over the top spot for the rest of his life.

During double careers in the military and law enforcement, Dad attended several leadership training classes and held multiple leadership positions, so that may have helped enable him to win the battles with Koro. Dad frequently remarked to Mom, the children, and his friends that he had never known or encountered any dog, or human for that matter, as wayward as Koro. The adjective I heard him use most often was "bullheaded." Koro would have been flattered.

Unlike Peko and Chiro who were born and registered in Japan, the United States was Koro's birthplace and he was registered with the American Kennel Club. He was purchased from a pet store chain in Orlando, Florida, and came with a five-generation pedigree marked by a gold seal. A registration certificate simply identifies a pup as the offspring of a known sire and dam born on a known date. In no way does it guarantee a dog's quality or health. Dad and Mom knew Chiro and Peko's breeder was reputable, but that wasn't the case with Koro.

The papers provided by the pet store showed the breeder's name and that the business was located in the state of Georgia, but the address did not appear on the certificate. Dad's keyword search on the Internet for the breeder, by name, suspiciously failed to turn up any information. The Certificate of Pedigree listed the names of Koro's sire and dam, along with the grandparents, great-grandparents, and even the great-great-grandparents, but again, no address or location for any of them was available.

Mom's first thought that Koro may have come from a puppy mill seemed like a *paws*-sibility since puppy mills are a known source for pet stores. Her biggest concern about puppy mills was that some were known to in-breed. She knew that the conditions in many puppy mills were deplorable, and some of them were only in business to make money with no intention of properly caring for the dogs they used for breeding. She found out it wasn't uncommon for them to mate brothers and sisters from the same litter, and even mothers and sons in order to mass-produce puppies to sell to pet stores. The long and short of it: puppy mills are revolting.

***

A little historical information regarding Akita dogs is in order to shed light on their general disposition. Historically, they go back many centuries to feudal Japan. The shogun and samurai lords owned Akitas for two reasons: to guard their castles and to hunt large wild game, including deer, boar, and bear (activities that Koro undoubtedly would have been good at if he had gotten the chance). The tale of the infamous Akita dog Hachiko and Helen Keller's infatuation with Japanese Akitas occurred in the 1920's and 1930's. The American Akita resulted in the late 1940's from crossbreeding, mostly with Siberian Huskies and German Shepherds, after numerous Akitas were taken to the

United States by members of the military returning from Japan after World War II.

There is a distinction between Japanese and American Akitas. The American Akita (of which Koro was one) is officially recognized by the American Kennel Club as a separate breed from the Japanese Akita (of which Peko and Chiro were two) because they have slightly different looks. The American breed is more muscular with a stouter physique, broader head, shorter snout, and black face mask rather than a white mask common to the Japanese breed. Despite the slight physical differences, two unmistakable similarities stand out: American and Japanese Akitas proudly hold their tails up above their backs, and they both derived a strong hunter mentality from their ancestors.

Koro's hunting instincts took over the first time he had an encounter with the infamous Florida vultures. His disdain for vultures was identical to how Butch felt about crows. Abominable behavior by the vultures caused him to go berserk on several occasions.

One day, when Koro was only 6 months old, while heading out with Dad on their morning walk, as soon as Dad opened the front door, Koro took off at lightning speed. Dad was facing the door trying to lock it so he had his back to Koro. The force was so great that the leash nearly pulled him down backward onto the sidewalk. Somehow, he was able to stay upright and keep his right hand on the leash while his right arm was jerked back on to his left waist. Koro had been stopped abruptly in his tracks at the end of the retractable 12-foot leash, but he still kept trying to pull away. Not yet knowing why Koro had charged down the sidewalk, Dad let out a loud "son-of-a-brick!" (parroting Grandpap Russ, the church-going man who wore out that phrase to avoid using profanity).

Upon gaining his composure and keeping Koro in check, Dad shortened the leash as he inched down the sidewalk to get within 10 feet of what had triggered Koro's anxiety. A black vulture was standing alone on top of the hood of the family van parked in the driveway. It was using its beak to shred the rubber weather stripping around the windshield. The vandal wasn't eating the rubber, just spitting it out. The big ugly bird ignored Koro's loud barking and lunges toward it while Dad struggled to hold him back. It just kept fearlessly pecking away at the strip of rubber sensing that Dad would keep Koro under control.

Koro eagerly wanted to take a big bite out of the bare-headed tormentor, and after observing the bird in the act of damaging his vehicle, Dad was ready to let him go. At the precise moment he fully slackened the leash allowing Koro to attack, the vulture jumped off the hood to the ground on the other side of the vehicle and hopped across the street to get away. Koro became further infuriated because the bird took off on foot instead of by wing. If the bird had gone airborne, the episode would have come to an end; however, it became prolonged because Koro wanted to give chase. In view of the big bird's slow ground speed, Koro would have caught it if Dad had not pulled him to a halt before he crossed the road due to an approaching truck.

The bird stopped across the street, turned around, showed its 3-foot wide wingspan, and looked straight at Koro as if to mock him for not continuing the chase (similar to what the nasty crows had done to Butch). While making a combination of hissing and grunting sounds, it slowly flapped its wings, flew up to treetop height (about 30 feet), looped around, and then quickly swooped down passing directly over Koro's head at a low altitude of no more than 10 feet. It had mocked Koro again, this time for his inability to get off the ground, before finally zooming upward and disappearing over the tree line behind our house.

As Dad and Koro watched, a group of vultures numbering at least 10 flew up from the roof of our house where they had been perched, and followed the tormentor beyond the tree line. Dad and Koro were unaware there was an audience watching their comrade make fun of Koro.

Koro, head down, was obviously in deep dejection. "It's okay boy. Don't worry. You'll get another shot at him some day," Dad consoled Koro after the bird had vanished. Koro would get several subsequent chances to chase vultures, and although he never caught one, like Butch with the crows, he deserved an A for effort by collecting shiny black tail feathers from two of them.

In the bird world, the vulture is known to be gregarious and naturally hangs with a flock. It is a scavenger that cleans-up roadkill. In Florida, a group of them are frequently seen on the side of a roadway, or even out on the road surface, jointly feeding on the carcasses of animals that had been run over by motor vehicles. They do not carry food back to the nest in their beaks or with their feet, but rather inside their stomachs, after which they regurgitate to feed their young.

Florida vultures—mistakenly called buzzards by humans not in the know—often appear to have white legs; however, this is actually due to a coloring that occurs when they squirt feces onto their black legs and feet to cool themselves. If they aren't the raunchiest birds in the world, they surely rank very near the top. No wonder Koro thoroughly despised them and gave chase every time they got within eyeshot or, more accurately, nose-shot. Their body odor was far more nauseous than his nasal passageway could tolerate.

I heard so many stories about a wide assortment of birds, including Butch's crows, Peko's hawk, Dad's hawk, and Koro's vultures, that I occasionally entertained the thought of going bird-hunting myself. However, I never got involved in an incident with a bird, and neither did Chiro. I guess there's no surprise that mild-mannered Chiro steered clear of birds, but there doesn't seem to be an excuse for me. My unsung protégé, Tommy, did not discriminate between rodents and birds, and neither did I for that matter—the difference being he hunted them, and I avoided them.

I previously admitted to not being a mouser, and I would also admit to not being a fowler (oh my, I may have just invented a new word). I saw a whole lot of birds perched in the trees in our backyard every day, albeit much smaller versions than the ones Butch, Peko, and Koro had run-ins with, and I cannot deny that they sure looked much more palatable than disease-infested rodents. But, as was the case with mice, I never attempted to catch birds. I was tempted though when Dad brought home a couple of lovebirds in a cage, but with family harmony at stake, I decided it was in my best interest to leave them alone, so I did just that. I was able to remain content by sticking with lizards and certain insects to satisfy my hunting instincts.

***

Although he was born in the United States, Koro's looks were more closely aligned with the Japanese Akita than the American breed. He had Japanese eyes (almond-shaped), and his long snout was similar to Peko and Chiro's. His muscular frame contained hardly any fat. Maxing out at 104 pounds and standing erect with his chest out and prominent snout well-displayed, he exemplified the finest specimen among Akita dogs, Japanese or American. His round head was huge, and he had massive jaws to match his magnificent physique. His paw prints were extra-large and could have been mistaken for bear tracks by park rangers or other humans in the know. When at rest, he laid down flat on his belly, body fully extended with his hind legs tucked under his rear end, and both front legs stretched out parallel in front of him. While sleeping, he could have been likened to a polar bear rug.

Like Chiro, Koro drew awestruck looks from 99.9% of the humans who saw him. His coat was white as snow. His rugged, powerful physical features could easily have passed for a wolf-Akita hybrid. When Chiro and he stood tall side-by-side, they looked strikingly alike. Chiro was 2 inches shorter in stature and 20 pounds lighter after Koro became full grown, but their coat color and facial features so closely matched, many strangers asked if they were related. It wasn't uncommon for someone to inquire if they were siblings or even a dam and her pup. Except for rude, strange dogs, Chiro wouldn't hurt a flea. Not so with Koro, as it didn't take much to bring out the wolf in him when he was at home or in the family van, both of which he claimed as his territories with no trespassing permitted.

Koro's Akita heritage was dominant in terms of physical appearance. When he came to a halt while walking outdoors, his stance was nearly *purr*-fect—head high, ears erect, chest out, back straight, tail curled up on top of his back, all four legs perpendicular, entire body rigid with absolutely no movement, and an air of superiority all about him. He looked like a larger scale of Chiro. He could have been likened to a Special Forces soldier standing at attention for a ceremony, or a thoroughbred horse standing in the winner's circle after a race. It came natural to him and he did it every time he came to a stop from the day Dad brought him home until his very last walk. A stud was he!

Koro demonstrated he was highly intelligent. For example, Chiro was able to vocalize a single word in English, but Koro outdid her, as he not only recognized the word "ride," but he knew how it was spelled. Dad taught him by repeatedly spell-inquiring, "R I D E ?" It took a while, but he finally responded affirmatively by running straight to the front door. Previously, Dad was proud of himself for teaching Koro the spelling of the word "go." He would spell-inquire, "G O ?" and it didn't take long at all for Koro to master that spelling. Mom finally told Dad that hastily spelling G O sounds almost like the pronunciation of the whole word.

It was Mom's idea to add a more difficult word to Koro's spelling capability. She came up with "ride" because it was a word they used every day. Dad showed him off spelling *R I D E* a number of times to his friends, as if making it appear that he might be God's gift to dogs who want to learn difficult tasks. He went on to teach him a few other spell-commands— *S H A K E*, *S I T*, and *S P E A K*.

Koro loved daily trips to the park, but that wasn't his favorite pastime—rides in the family van gave him more pleasure. Peko used to ride shotgun in front while Mom sat in the back with Chiro, but that all changed shortly after Koro arrived on the scene. Despite the huge age difference in the beginning (3½ months compared to 10½ years), it was only a matter of days for him to convincingly get his way by switching seats with Peko.

After Koro moved to the front passenger seat, Dad had a hard time seeing out the windshield on that side because it didn't take long for the glass to become smeared with Koro's nose prints. And the vents on the dashboard were constantly smudged with his drool. The big boy made a big mess! Wanting a cleaner car, Dad wished that Peko and Koro would switch back to the original seating arrangement, but there was no way Koro would allow that to happen.

While riding shotgun, Koro attracted a tremendous amount of attention from rubberneckers. It's not uncommon for dogs to stick their head out an open window while riding in a car. It is uncommon, however, for a dog to sit facing straight ahead and place its elbow on the open window edge halfway out the window like a *purr*-son might do while cruising. That is exactly how Koro rode, and he would turn his head to the right to observe something he heard that he wanted to see. Although his style was unorthodox, the feeling he experienced while riding along was not unlike any other dog because he never cared where he was going—he simply enjoyed the journey.

One evening, a highway patrol car pulled up alongside the family van on the right side. As always, Dad was driving, Koro was sitting beside him, and Mom was alone in the back seat (this was after Peko and Chiro had both passed away). When they stopped at the next traffic light, the police car was beside them. Koro's window was almost always opened, but it was closed for a change on that occasion due to unseasonably cold weather. Dad complied with the officer's hand signal to roll down the front passenger window. The officer commented, "Glad to see he has his seatbelt on," motioning his left forefinger at Koro.

When outside the house, Koro wore a shoulder harness attached to his leash, and while he was sitting in the van, it appeared he might be wearing a seatbelt, although he was not belted in. Dad wasn't sure if the cop was serious or not and replied merely by nodding his head affirmatively. The cop wasn't done speaking. "How does he rate getting to ride up front and she has to sit in the rear?" referring to Koro riding shotgun with Mom in the back seat.

Forced to say something because the light was still red, Dad jokingly responded, "Would you like to try to order him around?"

Just then, the light changed to green and the police officer pulled away with an extra wide grin on his face. Koro always cocked his head sideways when he was trying to understand something said or done by a human, and that's what he did while the policeman was paying close attention to him. Mom called it his "question mark" look, which was fitting in view of the inquisitive expression to match his head leaning to one side. Koro displayed that look a lot because he was cerebral—instead of reacting spontaneously like most dogs, he would first size up the situation and then act accordingly.

Koro also got tons of attention while walking in public. One morning while Mom and he were in the park, a young lady approached and asked if she could take some photos of Koro. Saying she was a college student studying photography at the University of Central Florida, she explained that she had a class assignment to find a subject—human or animal—displaying a unique quality, and take at least 12 pictures to display that quality. She told Mom that upon observing Koro strutting with his head and chest held high, she was immediately reminded of *Bolt*, a dog with superpowers in an animated movie she had seen two weeks earlier. Mom knew what she was talking about because Dad had taken her to see that movie, and the Bolt character had reminded her of Koro too, so she heartily agreed to the photo session. While the girl was taking photos, Koro stood at his tallest as if he seemed to enjoy being the center of attention. He made Mom proud. A ham was he!

***

Koro seemed to be thirsty all the time. He took in more water per day than Butch, Peko, and Chiro combined. Mom surmised that his thirst anxiety stemmed from his days in the puppy mill where he was likely neglected, and after that at the pet store where he stayed longer than the average puppy and got bigger than most of the others. Due to his size, she is convinced he probably got water only after the other animals in the pet store got theirs.

Koro growled when Peko or Chiro came anywhere near his food bowl, thereby demonstrating that he was overly possessive of food. Mom suspected that his defensiveness around food likely originated during the time he had spent in the pet store where chances are he got fed last, and then only if there were leftovers.

While out on rides, Koro cringed every time an 18-wheeler got too close, which indicated he may have been transported interstate in a large truck from the puppy mill in Georgia to the pet store in Florida. When a big truck came close, he displayed raised hackles, something that can be likened to a human who easily gets red in the face with aggravation. Just like the hackles on Koro's back rose with anxiety when he was in a heightened security mode, the short hairs on the back of Mom's neck bristle when she suspects someone of animal abuse. That was precisely what happened when she told Dad about being convinced that Koro had been mistreated during the first 14 weeks of his life, initially in the puppy mill and then at the pet store.

Buying Koro from a pet store turned out to be a learning experience. Later on, Dad found out through online research that many pet stores are supplied by puppy mills, and that abuse and neglect are not uncommon in puppy mills. He also learned that pet stores hire mostly young people with little or no experience in properly handling baby animals. Plus, it became apparent that unscrupulous veterinarians may be contracted by pet store management to attend to animals in their store with the stipulation that store employees steer buyers to them for follow-up care.

Customer reviews of the pet store where Koro ended-up and the office of the veterinarian working for that pet store—which Dad should have read before buying but didn't—were overwhelmingly negative. In short, what he discovered about both the pet store that had Koro and the animal doctor affiliated with that store was mostly unfavorable. He learned the hard way, but at least he learned, as ever since, he checks the customer reviews for every commercial establishment he is thinking about doing business with before contacting them.

***

Steve was Koro's best friend, and Koro treated him like a pack equal. He was more playful and affectionate with Steve than anyone else. *Purr*-haps, they were able to closely relate to each other because Steve was born in 1970—the Year of the Dog in the Chinese Zodiac (like the Japanese shogun Tsunayoshi Tokugawa mentioned in Chapter Three, who was also born in the Year of the Dog, and who established laws to protect dogs and other animals). There is a 12-year cycle in the Chinese Zodiac, and humans whose mothers birthed them in the following years were born in the Year of the Dog—2018, 2006, 1994, 1982, 1970, 1958, 1946, and so on every 12 years. It is believed that humans born in these years have a deep sense of loyalty and empathy, and will do everything they possibly can for whom they consider most important to them—just like canines.

Here is something to ponder while on the topic of Chinese astrology—there are 12 animals in the Zodiac, and although no cat per se, the tiger is among them. That made me wonder why the dog was included instead of the wolf since scientists have concluded that dogs evolved from gray wolves. This Zodiac goes back to ancient times, and there is no way of knowing why or how the 12 animals were chosen in the following order—rat, ox, tiger, rabbit, dragon, snake, horse, goat, monkey, rooster, dog, and pig. It is believed that each animal has certain personality traits that will be embodied in humans born in the year of that particular animal.

Mom was born in 1940—the Year of the Dragon—noteworthy because the dragon is the only imaginary animal in the Zodiac (all 11 others are real). By demonstrating the ultimate of enthusiasm and confidence, the dragon is considered the most powerful among these creatures. When I heard Dad occasionally referring to Mom as "bright-eyed and bushy-tailed," I wondered what he meant, but now it makes sense. Dragon years for humans are 2012, 2000, 1988, 1976, 1964, 1952, 1940, etc. In case you didn't know, humans born in the Year of the Dragon (like Mom) are called *dragons*, humans born in the Year of the Dog (like Steve and his wife Niki) are dubbed *dogs*, and so on. Enough said about the Zodiac, as the rat being chosen first is quite troubling.

Koro didn't like to be teased, but he usually let Steve get away with it. He did lose his temper once though and snapped at Steve during a teasing session when Steve became overly doggish. That incident left a mark, not only of the physical variety, but also an emotional one. That's when Steve abruptly learned the hard way that there was a limit to how far he could push Koro during play sessions. They both *purr*-fectly understood each other from then on, so there was never a problem between them after that single incident.

To say Steve is known to become excited and loud during certain sporting events on TV, especially Pittsburgh Steelers football and Pittsburgh Penguins ice hockey games, is an understatement. Dad and Steve regularly subscribed to pay-per-view so they could watch every one of their favorite teams' games. To cheer for a team other than the Steelers and Penguins in Steve's presence is blasphemous.

As soon as Steve would start yelling during a game, which happened every game, Koro would begin inching toward him, head lowered, obviously thinking he had done something wrong to cause the shouting. Koro didn't even watch the games, but he was there in front of the TV from start to finish. He suffered more stress than Dad or Steve while the games were in progress since Dad and Steve felt strained only when their teams were losing, but Koro felt it every game regardless of which team lost.

By a slip of the tongue, Mom has called her nonfurry kids by her furry kids' names hundreds of times. She does that most often with Steve, whom she has called "Butch," "Peko," "Chiro," and

"Koro" on separate occasions, both before and after the dogs had passed. Thankfully, for his sake, she's never called him by my non-masculine given name (Chibi—*Little One*).

***

Lots of things have changed since Mom and Dad's childhood. For instance, dogs are not free to run around anywhere they please —the way it used to be. And, most dogs stayed outside the house when Mom and Dad were young, unlike nowadays when they mostly stay inside except to go outside to pee, poop, or go on a walk. Since they do not have the freedom their ancestors knew, when some dogs get loose, they don't know how to act, so they're apt to create havoc and get into trouble, or maybe even injured.

Mom's biggest pet peeve is the humans who ignore leash laws and let their dogs run around in public without any constraint. The county park, where Mom and Dog took their canine kids on daily walks, was posted with signs referencing a county ordinance requiring dogs to be on a leash at all times; however, that did not deter some people from breaking the law. When referring to a rude, ignorant, or law-breaking human, Mom uses the word *idiota*—Spanish for idiot. Steve introduced that word to her and it stuck. In Mom's book, anyone who breaks the leash law is among those deserving of the idiota designation.

One day, a woman got out of her car and immediately released her female Beagle-mix off the leash approximately 50 yards away from where Mom and Dad were walking with Koro in the park. As soon as the dog was set free, she took off like *a bat out of hell* straight toward Koro. Dad saw her coming and braced for the attack that was quick and savage. The woman and a male companion had run after the dog, but couldn't keep up the pace. The guy got there 10 seconds too late and pulled the mutt away. By the time the woman got there, she was crying hysterically and screaming over and over again, "I'm sorry. I'm sorry. She's never done that before."

Koro did not have a scratch, but the same couldn't be said for the other dog that was led away whimpering and bleeding from the head and shoulders. Except to make a joint statement, "Keep your dog on a leash!" Dad and Mom had nothing to say. They turned their backs and walked away while the woman followed and kept trying to get them to accept her apology. Mom added in disgust, "Idiota! People like you shouldn't have a dog," loud enough for the woman and her friend to hear, after which her feet abruptly shifted from a routine walk to a not-so-routine stomp away from the scene.

Mom was furious because Koro had to protect himself and, as a result, the other dog got hurt. In her mind, it wasn't the other dog's fault, as all the blame lied with the woman for not keeping the dog on a leash. Looking back askance at the woman, Mom's face displayed scorn ear-to-ear because she wasn't dealing with an ordinary idiota, but rather a consummate one—an unmitigated jerk. Dad directed an uncomplimentary slur in the woman's direction, "*son-of-a-brick*," while Mom and he hurried away. (I wonder if the SOB terminology that Dad used might be as disparaging as idiota, or if it may even surpass it on the derogatory jargon scale; both terms are catchy, and I came to fancy each one)

After cooling off when finally out of sight of the woman and her dog, Mom mumbled softly, "Dogs don't live long enough and some people live too long," loud enough for Dad to hear. She had not meant for that remark to be within anyone's auditory range, and upon noticing the surprised look on Dad's face, she was quick to take it back exclaiming, "I didn't mean that like it sounded. Sorry."

Having already lost three dogs, whose longevity extended from average to above average but was still oh-so short compared to humans, Mom had said something she honestly felt, even though it wasn't politically correct. By flashing a quick smile out of the corner of his mouth, Dad was reassuring. The corners of Mom's mouth turned up slightly to partially expose her front teeth and create a grin-like expression reminiscent of the infamous Cheshire cat in the tale of Alice in Wonderland. Politically incorrect was she!

Since Mom and Dad used to go to the park with the dogs every day, they frequently encountered idiotas with unleashed dogs. Most of the time, the idiotas would say something about how friendly their dog was, or how he or she liked to run up and "say hi" to other dogs. What they failed to recognize was that another dog might not want to meet their dog, and if their dog runs up and invades another dog's space, their dog could get hurt by accosting and irritating the other dog, especially if the other dog is a full-grown Akita. Mom firmly believes there are no bad dogs, only bad humans who misguidedly influence their dogs and directly cause them to develop bad behaviors.

Koro could have been appropriately named "Rakki," which means *lucky* in Japanese, because he was fortunate to have been chosen to join Mom's family. In view of his overly aggressive nature, if he had gone someplace else, there's a very good chance he wouldn't have lived so long (12 human years). Mom looks at the situation differently, as she truly believes she was luckier than Koro because he became part of her family. She commiserated with Koro because there was no doubt that—unlike Butch, Peko, Chiro, and me—his earlier puppyhood environments had been abusive and neglectful.

***

Training usually pays off for dogs, as long as there's plenty of it. Most dogs enjoy being trained just because it gives them something to relieve the boredom of lying around and sleeping much of the day. Doggie schools are known to teach dogs to only respond to *paws*-itive instruction. If a trainer wants to teach them to fetch, they show them what to do over and over, and when they finally do it, they're rewarded. They continue to be rewarded with praise every single time they do it. Repetition is the key. They don't need a reward every time—sometimes all they need is a pat on the head or just a verbal "attaboy." Receiving praise for learning to react to certain voice commands engenders self-confidence in dogs.

Even a macho canine appreciates praise. Koro appeared to genuinely delight in the verbal kudos he received to accompany the certificates of completion he got from two training schools. Here's one certificate with Dad and the trainer.

When Koro was one-year-old, Dad placed him in an obedience training program at a police canine bootcamp for several weeks. At age 2, he stayed all day long for four weeks in a day care facility where dogs were integrated for play time, but he had to be segregated on the very first day after repeatedly attempting to dominate the other dogs in the caretaker's presence. Between ages 3-5, he spent six hours a day for more than 100 days at another doggie day care to work on improving his socialization skills with other dogs; however, unlike the other dogs, he could not be trusted off-leash.

He enjoyed the attention and rubs from all the attendants who worked at the aforementioned places—mostly young ladies—and showered each of them with kisses. However, it didn't work out anywhere because he insisted on trying to take over the alpha position every time he was with other dogs. He just didn't fit in. In short, his social skills with humans improved; however, despite all the effort to make him more amicable with other dogs, his social skill was essentially the same as it was at the start—*zero*!

At canine daycare centers, most dogs seem to fit right in. Some may take two steps forward and one step back, but with Koro, it was zero steps forward and zero steps back. After spending a lot of time and money, Dad finally admitted he had pursued a totally ineffective course of action, or as an old idiom goes—he was *barking up the wrong tree*! The way Koro acted was an indication that his earliest experiences—negligent care in a puppy mill and at the pet store where other dogs received preferential treatment—had played a key role in shaping his behavior as an adult. He was hell-bent on making sure he would get nothing short of *top dog* treatment after getting adopted.

Some dogs exhibit same-sex aggression, others opposite-sex aggression. Koro did not discriminate—he was not tolerant of either male or female dogs. He proved it when he got into a knock-down, drag-out fight with one of his female housemates. Dad had to break up that melee between Peko and him and, in the process, sustained a few minor bites from both combatants. The age difference was great—Koro was only 11 months old and Peko was 11 years of age at the time—proving that Koro did not age-discriminate either. Anyhow, that fight, which Koro initiated because Peko had come too close to his food bowl, may have ended in a draw, but Peko was quick to back down when Koro stood up to her from then on, so Koro had won psychologically.

***

Knowing that certain human foods can be toxic to pets, Mom was careful and always on the lookout for potentially dangerous stuff that someone had dropped on the floor. Bits of chocolate and whole grapes were common since they are among Dad's favorite snacks. Koro found a grape one day and ate it. He apparently liked the taste and began begging when he saw anyone eating grapes. He was given grapes until Mom became aware that they can be harmful to dogs, after which she made absolutely sure that no one gave him grapes anymore. Mom and Dad substituted doggie treats about the same size and shape as grapes. While they eat grapes, he consumed the look-alikes, and he was okay with that.

Koro was a little bit like Peko when it came to eating habits. If anyone gave him a treat he didn't like (one of Chiro's prescription snacks, for instance), he would spit it out, and then communicate via eye contact to let the *purr*-son know he was waiting for something he liked. His preferred treat was a crunchy granola bone. Frozen vanilla yogurt came in a close second—Edy's or Haagen-Dazs that he got in a large bowl every night. Dad and he also shared a daily handful of peanuts in the shell—minus the shell, of course, and always unsalted per Mom's order since salt, even in moderation, is not good for dogs.

Koro ate exceptionally well—the usual 100% ground beef, boneless and skinless chicken breast, rice, carrots, and cabbage mixed with grain-free dog food every day, along with an occasional all-beef hotdog—just like Butch, Chiro, and Peko before him. However, Koro had an eating disorder. Many times, while out on a walk, he chomped down on something he wasn't supposed to eat. A mouthful of sand was most common, and he also liked acorns. He learned to glance at Mom and Dad to see if they were watching, but it didn't matter. Even if one of them was looking, he'd still grab a bite of sand or an acorn with full knowledge that it would result in a scolding.

One time, something raunchy ended up in his stomach—he swallowed a toad! That cost him a nighttime, emergency trip to a 24-hour veterinary clinic. I should say it cost Dad since he had to pay for the x-rays that were necessary to identify the reason for the extreme discomfort in his digestive tract, along with follow-up treatments needed to cure him of the poisonous toxin secreted by the glands in the toad's skin. Ouch!

Koro regularly ate grass—lots of it—and immediately afterward, he would disgorge undigested grass blades. Mom said he intentionally ate grass to excess and then vomited as a means to self-cleanse his digestive system. To treat his occasional upset stomach, she sometimes gave him a dose of Pepto-Bismol that provided relief, but that was rare since chewing grass seemed to do the trick better than anything else. He ate grass steadily for up to 10 minutes at a time until it finally caused him to spew up the blades, all partially digested, that had changed in color from emerald green when they went in to slimy yellow when they came out. To keep him safe, Mom only allowed him to eat grass in a certain area of the park off the beaten path that was not sprayed with insecticide or weed killer.

***

Koro's hunter instincts kicked in while passing through the wooded area adjacent to the park path that Mom and Dad walked him on every day. The many wild critters that roamed those woods left their scents everywhere. Koro was especially attracted to the cottontail rabbits because he not only smelled them, he also regularly saw them during early morning walks. Dad ran with him tightly holding the leash while Koro chased them. In his younger days, he came close to outrunning two or three rabbits, but Dad made sure he never caught one. Baby rabbits were everywhere in the springtime when it wasn't uncommon to see a dozen or more out and about on a morning walk. That happened around Easter time prompting Mom to call them *Easter bunnies*. The young rabbits were slow to react and even slower afoot, so Dad had to be extra alert to keep Koro in tow.

All of Mom's dogs chased squirrels in their younger days, but

Koro despised the little nut collectors more than the others. Once when Dad was at work and Mom took Koro out for a walk, he jump-chased a squirrel so fast and hard that Mom lost her balance and fell headfirst onto a concrete sidewalk. He was almost one-year-old and nearly full grown, so she only outweighed him by a few pounds at the time, but it was enough to enable her to hold onto the leash as he ran after the squirrel. He pulled her over a curb and onto an adjacent paved roadway before finally stopping after dragging her approximately 6 feet on her stomach.

Miraculously, she suffered only minor injures—scraped and scratched elbows—but Koro became scared thinking she may have been hurt badly when she went over the curb. He forgot about the squirrel as it kept running away, went back to her with a concerned look on his face, and stood by her side until she was able to get back up onto her feet a minute or so later. They were lucky that no cars had passed by. All she said was, "Thank you Koro. It's that bad squirrel's fault."

From then on, Mom didn't have to worry when passing through squirrel-infested areas with him because he started staying close to her and basically ignored all the nutcrackers along the way. However, that was not the case if Dad was holding his leash as, on those occasions, he chased every squirrel that came into view forcing Dad to follow his lead and run behind.

Just as I never caught a rat, Koro never caught a squirrel, but if he would have caught one, there is no doubt the outcome would not have been pretty. I never wasted my time on the multitude of squirrels in our neighborhood. After all, they're nothing more than rodents with cute, fluffy tails—rats in disguise! They're just as deplorable as any other kind of vermin.

In view of the way Koro collected tennis balls like squirrels hoard nuts, Dad said to Mom in jest that he might have a squirrel or two in his family tree. They walked past tennis courts in the park every day, and that made it easy for him to add errant balls to his ever-growing collection.

His play with the tennis balls was basically solitary. He would approach Dad with a tennis ball in his mouth, draw back, approach again, and then back up again with absolutely no intent to give up the ball. So, the only chance Dad got to throw a ball for him to chase was when he found the ball before Koro, after which Koro would retrieve it but never give it back. He was fixed on keeping every ball exclusively for himself with no desire to share.

Mom attributed Koro's non-sharing nature to what he unfortunately had experienced in early puppyhood at the puppy mill and pet store. He had a lot of toys—mostly stuffed animals that he inherited from Butch and a few he stole from Peko and Chiro, and, like the tennis balls, he preferred to play with them alone. I could not begin to imagine how much canine saliva would have accumulated on those toys from four dogs over three decades. The very thought of it was totally repugnant. *Eww!*

***

As a huge proponent of daily walks for the dogs, Mom knew that as much exercise as *paws*-sible was the key to keeping them healthy. Twice a day sufficed on weekdays, but she insisted on taking them three times a day—morning, afternoon, and evening—on weekends, weather permitting. Even when Dad felt *dog-tired*, she was always able to coax him to go for a walk. They had a fenced-in backyard, but the area wasn't spacious enough for the dogs to run around at full speed.

For more than 20 years, they took their canine kids to Jay Blanchard Park on the east side of Orlando at least twice every weekday and usually three times on Saturdays, Sundays, and holidays. They did not mind a little rain, and unless severe, the weather never stopped them. Mom insisted on adapting to the mailman motto: *"Neither rain, nor snow, nor heat shall keep..."*

So, on really bad weather days—like just after a hurricane—it wasn't uncommon for them to have the entire park to themselves.

Although located within the Orlando city limits, Mom and Dad's favorite park consisted of hundreds of wooded acres, many of which extended close to the banks of the Little Econlockatchee River—a natural habitat perfect for a wide assortment of wild creatures. Besides what one might expect to find there, such as cottontail rabbits, red squirrels, and all kinds of birds, Mom, Dad, and the dogs saw a wild pig, a bobcat, a pair of river otters, a herd of 8 deer, a flock of more than 20 wild turkeys, quite a few snakes, and far too many alligators to count. The ever-present smell of those critters brought out the wild wolf psyche in Koro.

The results of the earlier mentioned canine DNA project conducted at the Institute for Genomic Research in Rockville, Maryland, clearly determined that although the assorted dog breeds have significant physical diversity, they share large segments of DNA that is indicative of their shared origin—evolution from the gray wolf (NIH/NHGRI). It just so happened that Koro had more than his fair share of his ancestors' DNA.

One hot, summer morning, Dad permitted Koro to walk along the riverbank closer to the water's edge than usual, and it almost resulted in a catastrophe.

THE DOGS' BEST FRIEND: A CAT'S EYE VIEW

A 4-foot alligator was sunbathing in high grass. Its head was facing down the bank toward the river with its tail extended up the bank away from the river. It wasn't visible to Koro or Dad until Koro got within three feet of its tail. The gator detected Koro in the same moment Koro saw it, and they were off and running. They were on a foot race to the water, a distance of about 10 feet for Koro and six feet for the gator. Koro lunged forward just as the gator slipped into the river barely missing the tip of its tail by a cat's whisker. He stumbled at the bank's edge, but regained his balance in the nick of time and was able to avoid going headfirst into the water. Somehow, Dad was able to hold onto the leash.

Koro will never know what would have happened if he had caught that alligator, nor will he ever know what would have happened if he had fallen into the river. Dad, Mom, and the rest of us can only imagine what it would have been like. The only sure thing is that it would not have been pretty, and Koro would have ended up on the short end of the stick. In this case, Koro's bark would have been worse than his bite, as if he had tangled with that alligator, whether on land or in the water, he would have been in over his head (pardon pun please).

From the tips of their snouts to the tips of their tails, Koro and the gator measured about the same length. The main difference in physicality was their weight and the size of their teeth, 2-to-1 and 10-to-1, respectively, in favor of the gator. Koro may not have learned anything from that incident, but Dad sure learned a lesson the hard way—never allow Koro to get that close to the river's edge again.

***

Since the park frequented by Mom, Dad, and the dogs had popular biking, jogging, and walking trails, it was fairly common for human passersby to see the dogs emptying their bowels. Like Peko before him, Koro took an inordinate amount of time to find the right poop place, and he wasn't the least bit bashful in emptying his bowels within eyeshot of strangers passing by.

One day, Koro was off the path pooping just as three women walked by. One of them yelled out, "Oh no! Not right here in front of us! That is soooo disgusting!"

Because it was directed at her furry kid in an unfavorable manner, Mom took umbrage at the woman's asinine remarks and responded loud enough for the trio to hear, "Buta! His unchi isn't as nasty as yours! [*Hey Miss Piggy! His poop isn't as nasty as yours!*]"

Dad cracked up because she mixed English and Japanese words acrimoniously. *Buta* means pig in Japanese, and *unchi* is a childish way of saying poop. The pig reference was an obvious reference to the obese physique of the woman, who should have kept her mouth shut. Mom's verbal assault drew only a shoulder shrug from the corpulent idiota, who couldn't fully comprehend what Mom had said, but definitely realized it was not complementary.

Instead of continuing on their way, all three women stood only 20 feet away watching her and Koro's every move. Mom used a baggie to pick up the two large stools Koro had deposited on the ground. When the idiota mumbled a few choice words about her aversion to dogs, that's all it took to make Mom decide that doing something to disgust her even more was in order. She tied the bag shut with both hands, held it up in front of her face with her left hand for the idiota to see, and then pretended to lick the fingers on her right hand.

The idiota suddenly appeared to be on the verge of doing something repulsive herself, so before she regurgitated whatever she last had to eat, Dad grabbed Mom by the arm and hurriedly led her away. They didn't see the woman throw up, but they did hear something coming from her direction—the unmistakable sound of stomach contents being discharged through the mouth.

The Miss Piggy incident would be as close as Mom has ever come to using profanity. It all happened unexpectedly and caught Dad off-guard. He didn't know whether to scold her or laugh out loud. All he ended up doing was changing the subject by blurting out, "Hey, look at that squirrel over there," making an effort to cool Mom down. While they continued their stroll in the park, he fought to resist the smiles that kept creeping onto his face. Mom obviously failed to see any humor in the situation, so Dad added, "Sure is a fat little nutcracker," pointing at the squirrel in a continuing attempt to divert Mom's attention away from what had just happened.

Dad had seen Mom that angry only one other time—when she found what was left of the sparrow carcass in his sock. He was glad that someone else had made her blood boil this time. Mom finally spoke about the ill-mannered idiota a few minutes later saying, "She doesn't deserve to have a dog." And, that was the end of it! Dad knew Mom was proud of successfully defending Koro from human verbal abuse as her gestural signs made it obvious—standing erect, head held high with a broad, beaming look on her face, and walking at a brisk pace. By putting that idiota in her place, she had tasted victory, while the idiota ended up tasting something else (*wink wink*).

***

Barb or Steve talked about a book they had read in school called *Gulliver's Travels* by Jonathan Swift. The word *yahoo* was used —no, not the popular Internet search engine that had not yet been invented, but rather a non-human race of creatures resembling men who were called yahoos. They were a crude, brutish lot, and Koro could have been likened to them. Barb and Brenda wished Koro would have been as sweet and gentle as Peko and Chiro, but unlike them, he was a male, and Mom was fully aware that an anti-social attitude is not uncommon among male Akita dogs.

A certain popular phrase was always in the back of Koro's mind —*every dog has its day*. It factored into his dominant attitude and aggressive *purr-sonality*. He was one of those rare dogs that can be subjected to continuous attempts at socialization for an entire lifetime with no success. Mom knew this better than Dad or anyone else. She was excessively indulgent and never scolded him no matter what he did.

Food, water, and shelter may take care of a pet's physical needs, but they need much more—support on an emotional level that only comes from hands-on, tender loving care every single day, all day long, which is exactly what Mom gave Koro. Doing everything she could for him, in an effort to make up for the horrible treatment he had been subjected to before joining our family, was constantly on her mind.

Next to Butch, Koro had the worst breath in the world, but that didn't matter to Mom. She was the only one he kissed, and he knew he could kiss her anytime he was in the mood—emphasis on *he*. She genuinely liked his slobbery smooches smothering her face, and if that doesn't exemplify unconditional love, I do not know what does! Koro selected all the kissing times, and since he preferred to give and not receive, she abided by his wishes and did not smooch back.

Koro loved rubs, especially behind the ears. Mom, Dad, and Steve rubbed those spots (Mom the most) and, without fail, Koro grumbled throughout every rub session. It was a happy grumble, the sound of contentment. Koro also liked back and belly rubs too, but he made very little noise while being rubbed on those body parts. The ear rubs were different and always generated grumbling that delighted Mom who declared it was his way of saying, "*It feels so good.*"

Like Butch and Peko, Koro freaked out at the sight of a bathtub. He didn't get many baths. Ever since Peko passed, Mom has been bothered by recurrent pain in her right shoulder that made it mission impossible for her to wash Koro in the bathtub. Dad's aging made it hard for him to lift more than 100 pounds and Koro weighed more than that.

Fortunately, Koro had cat-like grooming habits. I was impressed to find out he regularly licked himself clean like I did. Unlike Butch, who didn't have a doggy odor (except for her breath), Koro smelled like a dog, but, at least, he tried to clean himself, and I applauded him for that. However, his mannerly self-grooming was offset by icky drooling—he slobbered everywhere and, all told, dribbled more slimy saliva than Butch, Chiro, and Peko combined.

Koro was a dreamer. While asleep, it was fairly common for his whole body to quiver, his rear legs to twitch while he was fully stretched out on his side, and then for his rear legs to start rapidly moving as if he was running in his sleep. Mom wondered what he was dreaming about, and if it might have been the same dream recurring. Due to hip dysplasia, like Peko, Koro wasn't able to run at all during his last two years. Regardless, whatever he dreamed about triggered a running reflex. Mom was convinced he was chasing squirrels in his sleep.

***

Koro was not very vocal—he didn't bark a lot. He only barked at home or in the family van, and then only upon detecting a strange *purr*-son or an unknown animal coming near *his* perceived turf. To merely say he barked would be an understatement—his bark was extremely loud and ferocious. There were no false alarms. Mom or whoever was home at the time would first try to determine if there was, in fact, an unexpected visitor or would-be intruder outside. If a legitimate visitor was identified, communication would be made through a locked front door while trying to calm Koro down. Fortunately, only legitimate visitors were identified. There were a few others with unknown intentions, but they left in a hurry and were never identified. Koro was an absolute deterrent to any would-be home invader.

Koro's similarities with wolves were many, including physical looks and mentality; however, two dissimilarities stood out—wolves do not bark and Koro did not howl. Twice a week when the garbage truck pulled up in front of our house, without fail, Koro went berserk barking. He must have thought they were stealing property instead of picking up trash. He acted the same way when an occasional delivery truck stopped in front of the house, even though he should have figured out that, in the past, the FedEx, UPS, and Amazon drivers always left something and never took anything, but he never caught on.

Koro was okay with visitors and guests until he was about 6 months old. That's when he started becoming mistrustful toward persons unknown. Due to marring from the many bite marks he left trying to go through the woodwork to get at the mailman and other delivery *purr*-sons, Dad had to refinish the front doorframe. The first time he stayed by himself in the master bedroom with the door locked due to guests in the house, he bit and scratched the doorframe in the adjoining bathroom so hard that he almost dug out his nail beds. Mom found him licking his bloody paws while lying on top of wood shards scattered around on the bathroom floor. That's when they decided to buy a crate.

Mom did not approve of dog crates until Koro came along. She had no choice but to agree on getting one to ensure Koro's safety and the safety of visitors because he couldn't be trusted around strangers. Dad and she used to call them "cages" until employees at the pet store informed them that "crate" is the correct terminology.

They bought the biggest crate on the market and placed it in the master bedroom. It was large enough for Koro to stand up and turn around inside. That's where he stayed when visitors came until he finally began accepting guests, certain ones, that is, at age 3.

Peko and Chiro were party animals—Koro was not. He was highly suspicious of anyone he did not know who came to the door. He also challenged anyone outside the family who tried to approach our car. His testicles were removed at an early age, but the castration did not make him calm or otherwise change his alpha disposition one iota. On his first birthday, Mom gave him the Japanese nickname Kobushi [*Little Samurai Warrior*]. How fitting is that? For the rest of his life (11 more years), that's the only name she used to call him or talk about him, and it's still the only name she uses when reminiscing about him.

Koro was not aggressive because of a predatory nature or out of fear, but rather because he was territorial. At locations other than our house and car, such as in the park, or at the veterinarian's office, or inside a pet store, he behaved in the presence of other humans and pets. In the park, he ignored dogs passing by;

at the vet's office, he paid little attention to other pets in the waiting room; and in the pet store, his focus was not on other pets but rather on trying to shoplift a rawhide bone or another treat.

I did not choose to reference the work of Dr. Meghan Herron, Ph.D., just because she and I share the same surname, although that may have been a consideration (*wink wink*). I mainly chose her because she was recognized as an authority on animal behavior while working in my hometown Columbus, Ohio, where she headed the Behavioral Medicine Clinic at the Ohio State University Veterinary Medical Center. Dr. Herron identified aggression as the number one canine behavioral issue with which her clinic was dealing.

A certain case researched by Dr. Herron, which involved a dog with a history of aggressive behavior, caught my eye. Dr. Herron diagnosed the dog with territorial aggression displayed only in its home since the dog interacted in a friendly manner with clinical staff, humans, and other dogs outside the home (Herron, 2010). That was precisely the way Koro had acted—aggressive inside the home and in Dad's car, but nonaggressive outside the home and away from the car.

Some humans would have classified Koro as a cur. They would have been wrong because his junkyard dog *purr*-sona was reserved for on his turf only, and he did not have a vicious nature outside the house or car. Instead of cur, he could have been properly labeled a *black sheep*, which is how Mom refers to herself. She declared that Koro and she were black sheep because they both stood out from others by doing certain things most others would not do.

In human terms, Koro was an extremist that reached the heights of political incorrectness. He still acted tough and played rough, but finally began to mellow out around age 6 when he more readily accepted his position as a follower, and gave in little by little in recognizing Dad as the indisputable *top dog*. Even so, he never stopped testing Dad's hold on the leadership role, on the off chance he might start thinking about stepping down.

Peko and Chiro were gregarious Akitas—Koro was not. His overly protective, territorial behavior was atypical even among Akitas and the other breeds designated aggressive. Peko and Chiro got up close and personal with all of Mom and Dad's brood, relatives, and circle of friends, while Koro was far more independent and lived in a small world inhabited by only four humans—Dad, Mom, Steve, and Brenda. That made him particularly special to Mom. She often pondered, *If it wasn't for us, he wouldn't have anyone.* The thought of him being alone was discomforting to her.

Mom knew Koro couldn't help the way he was because he was born with dominant tendencies, and then he was wrongly influenced at an early age by the humans around him before Mom and Dad came along. She believes everything happens for a reason. Among her furry kids, he was the only male and that alone made him extra special. She never considered seeking professional mental health treatment for any of us just because we exhibited a behavior that could *paws*-sibly suggest the need for psychological care if we were human—had she done so, Koro would have spent an enormous amount of time on a psychiatrist's couch. She fully understands that animal behavior can be confounding, and that is not a bad thing.

In an effort to find out why some dogs are more aggressive than others, a group of American scientists, led by Assistant Professor Evan MacLean of the School of Anthropology at the University of Arizona, completed a study and published the results of their research. They reported that aggressive behavior in dogs toward humans or other dogs was the most common reason for owners leaving their dogs at animal shelters (Shaw-Becker, 2017). Their study involved two hormones common in humans and dogs—oxytocin (the bonding hormone that was discussed at length in prior chapters), and vasopressin that is secreted by the same gland that releases oxytocin, and is found in the kidneys to prevent water loss in urine (Shaw-Becker).

The experiments performed by Dr. MacLean's group involved several dogs of different age groups, genders, and breeds. According to Shaw-Becker, they used a number of dogs considered aggressive by their owners and an equal number deemed non-aggressive. The findings indicated the dogs that reacted aggressively during their experiments had significantly higher levels of vasopressin in their blood than those that did not react aggressively; however, there was no significant change in the oxytocin levels among any of the dogs (Shaw-Becker).

Dr. MacLean's group of researchers also found that the service dogs included in their study had significantly higher levels of oxytocin than the non-service dogs that participated, which could be an indicator that oxytocin may help inhibit canine aggression (Shaw-Becker). In short, it seems that vasopressin may play a role in causing aggressive behavior by dogs similar to how oxytocin leads to bonding. Veterinarians have been prescribing a synthetic version of vasopressin (desmopressin) to treat diabetes in dogs, so maybe the day will come when they can write prescriptions to manage aggression. Further research is needed to ascertain if vasopressin drives aggressive behavior (Volstad, 2017).

How vasopressin, which has a biological function of preventing water loss in the body, may also affect aggression in dogs is a cause for wonder. It goes without saying that other things may affect the level of aggression in individual dogs—existing aggressive tendencies, early environmental conditions, whether abuse or neglect could be factors, along with certain emotions such as anger and fear.

Like Koro, Chiro may have had a high level of vasopressin since she showed aggressive behavior toward strange dogs. Unlike

THE DOGS' BEST FRIEND: A CAT'S EYE VIEW

Koro, Chiro was never abused or neglected. Her aggression toward strange dogs may have resulted from the early encounters she had with Aunt Carol's Labrador Retriever Bo and Grandpap Russ's Chihuahua Ginger. Perhaps, by recalling her unfriendly experiences at a young age with a large dog (Bo) and a small dog (Ginger), Chiro viewed all unfamiliar dogs as hostile and capable of causing her harm, and that may have elevated her vasopressin level.

The research studies selected as references in this book are noteworthy for a couple of reasons: they shed light on two very important dog issues emphasized in these writings—*bonding and aggression*—and the results of experiments have aided humans to better understand canine behavior, which, in turn, helps dogs in need of help to get help. Furthermore, all the cited research involved not only dogs and other animals, but human participants as well.

***

Until Koro's blood tests came back out-of-range with a low thyroid number and he was diagnosed with hypothyroidism (an underactive thyroid gland) at age 5, Mom and Dad didn't know that thyroid disease can affect dogs the same way it does humans. Like Chiro, Koro was very stoic and had an extremely high pain tolerance. That's probably because he had more in common with a wild wolf than a pet dog. His physical looks were much more wolf-like than Chiro and Peko, and so was his frame of mind—showing pain was the same as showing weakness, and that would never *purr*-mit him to outwardly show it when he was hurting.

Although Koro took prescribed medicine for the thyroid condition, his physical state had gradually deteriorated by age 9. He started becoming lethargic and generally malaise. Patches of fur fell out and his coat developed bald spots. He continuously scratched his itchy skin that was greasy and oozy with a nauseating odor that clung to Mom and Dad's fingers.

Mom didn't want to use more prescription meds due to possible serious side effects, so Dad looked around on the Internet for something natural. The products he bought online and at a local vitamin shop worked—kelp (seaweed), iodine, and various herbal roots. The odor disappeared, fur started growing back, his energy level began to rise, and he was healed to the point of nearing his old self. Mom continued to give him daily doses of the natural products to keep him healthy. After all, he was her second son.

Like Peko, Koro's hips began bothering him at age 10 and lasted to the end of his life. It got progressively worse—he experienced more and more difficulty in moving from a lying position to standing up. Having cared for two Akitas before Koro, Mom and Dad were well aware that arthritis was quite common in that breed. Koro suffered more from frustration than pain as his rear legs gradually grew weaker. He still went on daily walks, usually once, but sometimes two times a day when he felt up to it; however, the duration became shorter and shorter. He still had his usual hearty appetite until the last two days.

On his final Friday night, Koro walked into the master bedroom for the last time. He stopped in the hallway, glanced over at Dad who was standing 30 feet away in the kitchen, looked around toward the front door as if he may have thought about wanting to go out on a nightly walk, then turned away and proceeded into the bedroom where he fell asleep on the floor. The next morning, he couldn't get up as his hips were too weak. Mom tried to hand-feed him, but he had lost his appetite. He still had a thirst and peed, so Mom changed his diaper twice during the day, once that night, and again in the early morning hours while he was half-asleep.

By noon the next day, he couldn't raise his head without assistance. Dad sensed the time was drawing near, so he went out and came back with one of Koro's favorite treats—a plain double cheeseburger from McDonald's. Mom could only get him to swallow two small bites. Steve spent four special hours with him that afternoon. That evening, he took his last breath. He passed in Mom's arms, and yes, she sang that familiar song *Happy Doll Festival* to him till the very end. So, like Butch, Peko, and Chiro, the last thing he heard was Mom's voice, and the last thing he felt was Mom's touch. Not once did he appear to be in pain, but as a strong-willed alpha, he may have been hurting and didn't show it.

As soon as he passed, Mom started recalling several events in his life. "You almost got that alligator before it made it to the river. You came so close to getting some vultures too. I'll never forget how you took care of yourself when that idiota's dog attacked you in the park. I couldn't count how many looks you got from people for having your arm out the window in the car," she reminisced.

She gave him tons of kisses, something she was unable to do while he was alive, as he, and he alone, chose the kissing times, plus he had insisted being on the giving rather than the receiving end. It was Mom's turn to give back.

"You made Daddy and me so proud Koro. I loved your wild side. I'll never forget you," she finished speaking overcome with tears as Dad helped her up from the floor where she had been lying next to Koro with both arms wrapped around his neck. He had been the only pet in their home after Peko passed away almost 8 years earlier.

The next morning, after placing Koro into the back of the van, Dad drove through Blanchard Park. They passed close to many of the pathways they had walked literally thousands of times with him. They stopped close to a spot where Koro had enjoyed eating tall grass so Mom could pick a handful, after which she placed the green blades with him inside his bedding saying, "So sorry Koro. I wish I can take you for more walks here so you can eat more grass and chase the bunnies. See you again at the Rainbow Bridge."

It was hard for Mom and Dad to leave him at the crematorium. His life of 12 human years may have been considered average for a big dog, but it was the shortest of all their furry kids. He came back home the next day inside an urn and took his place on top of the piano next to the ashes of Butch, Peko, Chiro, and me.

Within an hour of Koro's passing, Mom had trimmed his toenails, so he could run faster with the rest of us in the meadow next to the Bridge. Butch and I had passed before Koro joined the family, so Chiro and Peko introduced him to us. He was happy to see all four of us and his cheerfulness was instantly contagious. He was relieved because he was no longer a burden to Mom. The single maternalistic connection we all shared enabled him to fit right in with the rest of us. Mom's love and compassion were downright infectious.

EPILOGUE

> *"If there are no dogs in Heaven, then when I die
> I want to go where they went."*
> -Will Rogers

Mom once asked Dad, "What do you suppose they think I am, their maid or their mother? She was wondering about her furry canine kids' mindset.

Dad couldn't help chuckling to himself as he glanced at the wooden sign hanging on their kitchen wall that clearly showed, in writing, the answer she wanted to hear: "M is for Mom, not for Maid." She was pleased when Dad read it to her out loud with emphasis—"M IS FOR MOM, NOT FOR MAID!"

While continuing to wonder how the dogs *purr*-ceived her, she asked a follow-up question, "Do they think I'm a dog?"

I wish I could have stepped in to answer that question for her. It's simple—a dog does not view its human as a furless canine, but rather accepts him or her as a member of a separate species occupying the same living space (cats feel the same way). Dad's answer, "They probably think you're their mother," was even better.

Mom's voice was the sweetest *mew*-sic to the dogs and my ears. I admit I did not understand every single thing that she said to the dogs and me, and it goes without saying that the dogs comprehended far less. The fact that she took the time to single out each of us and say something several times every day made her a special human in our minds. We all vied for her attention and were glad that she often spoke to us individually, especially when there were four of us together for eight years. Although she chatted with each of us several times every day, she didn't talk incessantly. Rather, her gentle speech was relaxing, which made it clear she had our best interests in mind and, most importantly, it was just between her and us.

Her voice alone expressed a combination of pure love, loyalty, and gratitude—all in a singular, beautiful tone. Yes gratitude! She was utterly grateful to have each of us in her home. She was the one we could always depend on, so we were always there for her too. She possesses all the qualities each of us had—the exact, same ones she wishes all her human acquaintances could have. The love Mom had for us furry kids was *purr*-petual, that is, it was no different than the love she has for her nonfurry, biological kids. In a single word—boundless!

None of us could *speak* to Mom, but that did not stop us from effectively communicating with her through eye contact, barking, purring, and other various ways. All humans with dogs or cats talk to them, but very few *listen*. Mom heads up that listening minority. She encouraged each of us to keep doing whatever worked in communicating to get our point across. My body language was more distinct than what the dogs did—they relied more on vocalizing than non-vocal body expression to get what they wanted. Regardless, for all of us, actions spoke a whole lot louder than words.

Mom treated the dogs and me like her nonfurry kids by singing to us a popular Japanese children's song called *Happy Doll Festival*. It became our song. We heard it almost every day—thousands of times throughout our earthly lifetimes. It was the very last thing the dogs heard before passing, as she sang it over and over to them during their final hours. Mom chose that song because her mother had sung it to her when she was a little girl, and it was fitting for Butch because Butch was a little girl when

Mom began singing it to her. It also became fitting for the rest of us furry girls—Peko, Chiro, and me—and although Koro was a boy, Mom continued the tradition by singing it to him. Now, she sings it to all of her granddogs even though 3 out of 4 of them are boys. So what—it's a beautiful lullaby with lively lyrics.

The Doll Festival, known as Girl's Day, is held on March 3rd every year in Japan. The entire song with lyrics can be found on YouTube by searching for the Japanese title *Ureshii Hinamatsuri* [*Happy Doll Festival*]. The first verse goes like this:

Akari wo tsukemasho bonbori ni O-hana
wo agemasho momo no hana
Go-nin bayashi no fue taiko Kyou wa tanoshii hinamatsuri
Translation:
Let us light the paper lanterns Let us give flowers peach flowers
Five musicians with flutes and drums Today
is the merry doll festival

Besides the words of that song, Mom has a favorite phrase—*just a minute*. All of us heard her say it at least 10,000 times. She says it to her nonfurry kids, and she said it to her furry kids too. Her *mew*-sical tone combined with the way she utters these special words is unique—it's as if she uses a musical tone to express regret for not being able to do something for someone more quickly. It's her cute way of letting whomever is waiting for her to do something know that she will do whatever it is as fast as humanly *paws*-sible. The dogs and I heard it most often while she was preparing our meals—it sounded as if she was apologetic for the inconvenience of making us wait to eat.

Now, without any furry kids in the house, Mom is constantly busy doing something to make life better for her nonfurry kids and grandkids—both furry and nonfurry—all of whom are only a stone's throw away. They all keep hearing those delightful words—*just a minute*—as often as Butch, Chiro, Peko, Koro and I once did, and we heard them far, far more than any of the other words that were time and time again directed our way by all of our human associates.

Mom has learned practically everything she knows about dogs and cats *not* from books or word of mouth, but through a lifetime of *purr*-sonal, hands-on experience. She coddled Butch, Chiro, Peko, Koro, and me from babyhood to adulthood and all the way through seniorhood. Although we weren't her blood relatives, she treated us the same way she did her own kinfolk. Our affection for her had *zero* conditions attached. We respected her like one of our own; she reciprocated the same way. Our relationships with her could be described as *skinship*, a Japanese-coined English word meaning feelings of affection between two people, particularly a mother and her child—demonstrated by hugging, touching, and various other forms of physical contact. *Skinship*—not quite kinship, but very close.

***

There is a subtle significance of my careful distinction between dog persons and cat persons. The truth, of course, stems not only from which animal an individual human prefers, but also from how they choose to relate to the animal. Generally speaking, dog people—more men than women—don't seem to mind, and may even enjoy, being taken out of their routine way of life by their dog, while cat people—more women than men—welcome their cat into the emotional state of their life. Both types of bonding have value, but cat people treasure the quiet and *purr*-sonal nature of their relationship—occasional soft purrs instead of intermittent loud barks that dog people cope with.

In my mind, there is no doubt that the strongest bond between a human female and a feline companion can be just as solid as the strongest attachment between a human male and a canine pal. Please don't read me wrong, as I do not mean to imply in the slightest way that cats are more suited for women and dogs are best for men. I merely used these references in view of not only the widespread belief among humans that this is the way it is, but also based on *facts*. There is no doubt that millions of women prefer dogs and millions of men prefer cats—it's just that, in actuality, more gals than guys have cats and more guys than gals have dogs.

Mom has made it known to everyone acquainted with her that she does not like the terms *dog person* and *cat person*. She is among a minority with no preference for one or the other, and that is something I can give credence to, as there is absolutely no doubt that her love for me equaled the love she had for Butch, Chiro, Peko and Koro. She is by no means a dog person or a cat person, but rather a pet person who does not view pets as mere possessions, but as true companions. She doesn't just love dogs and cats, but every other kind of pet. During their childhoods, Barb, Steve, and Brenda (especially Barb) brought home assorted wild critters—birds, frogs, fish, and turtles. Mom welcomed all of them into her household as nonfurry kids of the feathery, slimy, shelled, etc. varieties, and taught the children how to care for them.

***

Mom was in her 40's when Butch and I came into her life; she had Chiro and Peko in her 50's and 60's; and Koro was there into her mid-70's. She's still full of vigor and only slightly slows down when occasional exhaustion sets in following overtime periods with her grandkids—both the nonfurry and the furry ones.

Recalling what it was like as a child in post-war Japan, Mom is parsimonious. Since she completely wears out every piece of her own clothing, she doesn't buy very many new clothes for her wardrobe. Although she rarely spends money on clothing for herself, frugality is not the reason, as she does not hesitate to spend freely on her nonfurry grandkids. She spends countless hours behind her sewing machine repairing and altering not only her and Dad's clothing, but also items belonging to family members. She repaired the damages that her dogs had done to their toys, and now she does the same for her granddogs. Assiduous is she!

Sharp eyesight enabled Mom to regularly spot tiny fleas on all the dogs, along with a tick on Chiro, and an occasional flea on me. Her eyes scanned our bodies every single day. She was able to quickly find and remove bugs before they caused any discomfort.

Over the years, her remarkably good eyes have also enabled her to find hundreds of four-leaf clovers, scores of five-leaf clovers, and even a few six-leaf clovers—all saved for *paws*-terity by placement between the pages of every book in the family library. She also has a keen eye for coins dropped on sidewalks or in parking lots. The number of pennies, nickels, dimes, and quarters she has found surpasses the number of four-leaf clovers in her collection, but not by much. There is no score sheet for the coins, but the total number of four-leaf clovers accumulated reached 1,997 (Dad counted them), so the coin total would exceed 2,000. Sharp-eyed is she!

***

Mom's baking made the dogs salivate to extreme. *Dogs drool and cats rule* (just couldn't resist inserting one of my favorite sayings). The smells of Mom's cooking *purr*-meated our house every day all day long. The dogs' noses—60 times stronger than humans (Keim, 2019)—did not merely smell which recipe she was cooking, but rather the eggs, flour, butter, etc.—every single ingredient that went into making it. Most dogs have a face that's basically defined by a large nose, and that's why their sense of smell and ability to detect and distinguish odors is at least four times greater than a cat. So be it, as I was relieved that my capability to smell wasn't greater because that would have made the doggy odors intolerable.

The dogs made me laugh almost every day. A cat's grin is not readily recognizable, and Mom was the only human who ever noticed me grinning. She caught me in the act several times, and always said to me, "Oh my Chibi, I just love your smile!" I also grinned a number of times in front of Dad and the children, but Brenda was the only one who ever caught on and even she wasn't 100% certain.

My sense of humor was more devious than any human. For example, I got a laugh out of seeing a dog drink from a water bowl and splash more water on the floor than they swallowed. That's because, even though I used my tongue to lap up water like the dogs, I thought Peko and Koro's messy drinking habits were hilarious—spilling more water than they drank by swishing it around in their jowls, and then walking away dripping it all the way into the next room—however Dad failed to see any humor while watching them do it.

Trying to humanize the dogs or me was something Mom never did. She believed that referring to any of us as "almost human" would have been a major insult to the canine and feline races. She never put clothing on us, or pushed us around in a stroller, or used baby-talk with us. On the contrary, she stooped down to our level. I don't mean she got down on all fours and sniffed. She merely allowed the dogs to be dogs and me to be a cat. That means she respected us for what we were, not what she might wish we were, which is something that many people with pets are guilty of doing.

**

Mom abhors humans who use strict disciplinary measures for training dogs, but even more so when they're just walking their dogs. Seeing someone use a choke collar or any other pain-inflicting device makes her cringe. She does not hesitate to rebuke a stranger whom she happens to observe causing the slightest discomfort to a dog. And her scolding will definitely become heated if the other *purr*-son tries to defend what they were doing by referring to it as a "training aid" (their most common response).

To anyone who doesn't know Mom well, she generally appears tractable; however, a stubborn streak of independence leads her to voice an opinion to anyone she feels is in the wrong. To her, any attempt to justify mistreatment of an animal is absolutely untenable. Even when it is advisable for her to bite her tongue, she usually blurts out a quick retort that imputes blaming a *purr*-son for wrongdoing when she has reason to suspect animal abuse or neglect.

When it comes to pet rights, Mom is dogmatic with a contagious ardor. Her inherent love of animals causes her to champion any pet she has reason to believe was treated badly. Her line of thinking is straightforward: just like humans, animals—domesticated and wild—possess certain inalienable rights that cannot be violated.

During prior walks in the park with her own dogs and now with her granddogs, Mom likes to greet each and every passing dog with a fond salutation, "How are you." She then chuckles to herself when the human accompanying the dog comes back with a greeting, not realizing that Mom had spoken to the dog, not to them.

More times than not, her initial impression of a human with their dog has been good; however, there have been a few occasions when she sensed something was not quite right. She subsequently kept an eye out for the ones considered suspicious, and upon spotting them again, she looked closely to see if there may be indications of abuse. She has not hesitated to notify proper county authorities of apparent animal cruelty in the past, and carries their phone number in her purse to call again as needed.

Turtles meandering across roadways in Florida are a common occurrence. Mom always provides assistance to them by making Dad stop the car and flag-down traffic in both directions, so she can make sure a turtle's slow mobility doesn't bring it harm.

While out with Koro one day, she saw a large snapping turtle walking up ahead on a sidewalk. A guy driving a white pickup truck stopped about 50 feet in front of them. Mom thought he was going to allow the turtle to cross the road safely; however, that was not the case. Instead, the guy jumped out of the vehicle, ran up to the turtle, snatched it up in both hands, placed it in the back of the truck, and then sped off before Mom could get close enough to question his intent. She later told Dad the guy appeared to be of a certain national origin and culture that considers turtles to be a culinary delicacy. She suspected the guy intended to have the turtle for dinner.

Not only does Mom vividly recall what the turtle snatcher looks like along with the truck's description, but she wrote down the first three letters of his license plate on the sheet of paper containing the phone number to call for animal cruelty that she keeps in her purse. She is still on a determined mission to find that guy. I don't know what all she'll do if she does locate him, but he will definitely get an earful about turtle rights, and undoubtedly a whole lot more.

***

Mom treated the dogs and me the same as she did her own biological children. She was unequivocally devoted to caring for us—we were lovey-dovey with her. She regularly rubbed our backs, ears, and other spots we couldn't reach on our own. She gave us soothing, head-to-toe massages because she knew it not only helped us relax, but it also played a role in solidifying the bond between her and each of us.

Countless other things that Mom did, with not a single condition attached, enabled her to match the love and companionship that us furry kids had for her. Hundreds of millions of people around the world have dogs and cats; however, identifying another human being like Mom, who displays *all* the favorable characteristics common to dogs and cats, may prove more difficult than *herding cats* (yet another misguided saying about felines). Talk about the ultimate dog parent—it's Mom!

She prepared and cooked every single meal for every one of her canines from their first day in her home till their last. She never failed to wipe their butts after they pooped, always making sure to remove the occasional dingleberry in order to keep our house and the car clean. She used eyewash to cleanse their eyes and wipe away tear stains. She brushed their coats daily to remove loose fur and make them as comfortable as *paws*-sible in Florida's hot climate. She brushed their teeth every day. She made sure their water bowls were always filled and added ice cubes to chill their drink. She wanted them to experience the same joys that her nonfurry kids and she shared, so they all got birthday parties, Christmas presents, and hardboiled Easter eggs (the same for me minus the eggs).

Keeping the dogs' nails neatly trimmed so they were short enough to avoid getting caught on the carpet, and to prevent discomfort while walking on cement sidewalks was a priority for Mom. She knew there was a fine balance between too short and too long. Her total trimmings numbered in the hundreds for each dog, and that would equate to at least 1,000 altogether. Miraculously, she cut into a nerve only one time—Peko was the victim, but her pain didn't last long because Chiro quickly fixed it by releasing her natural healing agent while licking the wounded paw. Even though it was only 1 in 1,000, Mom felt very bad. She never forgot about inflicting that pain and apologized to Peko at least 1,000 times for the rest of Peko's life.

Long fur was common in our house—'twas a whole lot of shedding going on. Most humans seem to prefer a non-moulting breed—Mom is not among them. She didn't mind displaying dog hair on her clothing back in the day, and still shows de-*paws*-its from her grandogs to this day. That's because it sends the unmistakable signal to strangers that she loves furry kids.

THE DOGS' BEST FRIEND: A CAT'S EYE VIEW

Peko and Chiro de-*paws*-ited generous amounts of fur on the carpet and furniture, especially under the coffee table (Peko) and on the sofa (Chiro) where they snoozed a lot. Mom could have vacuumed the house every day to suck up excessive dog hair, but instead she did it once a week because she didn't mind having the extra hair around, plus the dogs hated the vacuum cleaner. Even if she had vacuumed the carpet more often, the hair on the furniture would have emerged uncollected. Furthermore, even if the vacuum cleaner had picked up most of the pet hair and dirt that the dogs tracked into the house, it would have missed nearly all the dried dog drool. I got used to the loose dog hairs, but the dried drool odor build-up tested my nosebuds to the limit. *Eww*!

Mom was a big help to the dogs by keeping them groomed. When as many as 4 of us (3 dogs and me) were in the home together, she spent a considerable *purr*-centage of her time brushing and grooming us—far less time on me since I didn't really need any help and only let her do it to me out of courtesy. She would spend 2-3 minutes on me and 10-15 minutes on each dog every single day.

On a scale of 1-to-10, our quality of life was an 11. And if that doesn't make Mom the ultimate furry kid parent, do the math—it would take a score of 12 to beat her! Dad once jokingly said, "If our house was on fire and she [Mom] could only save me or the dogs, she'd go for the dogs." Even though he said it in jest—like he did when commenting about the dogs eating better than him—I'm inclined to believe it may have been accurate. After all, it comes down to priorities. Howbeit, only one person knows for sure and she did not say anything upon hearing her insignificant other make that statement.

***

The dogs and I knew very little about the world outside Mom and Dad's house. No big deal since we were supplied with all the material things we could ever need or want. In addition, we were given the chance to experience happiness, love, desire, and many other gratifying feelings.

I don't think anyone would disagree that dogs and cats are generally happy creatures with nicely balanced emotions. We love and defend one another. We feel sorrow and melancholy. We know nothing about greed, envy, or hate. We live our entire lives without committing sin. There has never been a war between animal species. Mom once said to a large bunch of attendees at one of the barbeque parties Dad and she hosted, "If humans would behave the same as animals, what a wonderful place the world would be."

More so than the average human, Mom realizes every pet is a lifetime commitment. In that regard, she gave us the security of food and shelter, protection, plenty of playtime and exercise, more companionship than most other dogs and cats come close to enjoying, and total emotional support. We also had the opportunity to go outside for fresh air on a regular basis. The dogs got to go to the park every day, and I was able to explore the backyard patio at my leisure. It was nice being able to go outside sometimes, but Florida's warm climate, especially the triple-digit summertime tem-*purr*-atures, made us all thankful our home had an air conditioner running virtually nonstop.

No one could possibly cogitate more than Mom over the short lives of furry kids. Since our lifespans in human years ranged from 12 to 16, to Mom, we were no more than adolescents or teenagers when we passed. Our life expectancies were constantly on her mind from our first day in her house till the last. We all entered her life as babies, and although she admittedly is not good at math, she calculated that her age had already quadrupled or quintupled the amount of time we would live on Earth. Assuming she would outlive us, she made sure to shower the dogs and me with a steady flow of love to make every moment count. Love cannot be purer.

Except for higher intelligence and a superior maturity level—not to mention a pleasant body odor—I really wasn't any different than the dogs. All of us had plenty of time to use our natural instincts, along with our special, God-given senses. We had many good days and an occasional bad day, along with lots of good moods and a few bad moods. There were times when we just wanted to be left alone—me much more than the dogs. Mom knew all this and made sure we were given time and space when we wanted it. Because of her influence, we all respected each other. I have high regard for all my canine housemates, and would not wish them anything dastardly—like coming back as a rodent in their next life—or any other ill will.

I gravitated to Mom because her bond with me was stronger than the ties I felt to any other nonfurry or furry family member. Like all my canine housemates, I chose her as my favorite human. She became a catalyst in bridging the gap between pets and humans mainly because she knew we experience many of the same feelings as humans, albeit with far less frequency and nowhere near the same emotional level. In a nutshell, she is a *purr-fect purr-son* (just couldn't resist adding this double inflection).

Mom would say the dogs and I gave her far more than she could possibly give us; however, the relationship she had with each of us was an even-up, two-way street. Mom taught me a lot and, in return, I taught her at least two important things: a human's relationship with a dog is adult-to-child, while their relationship with a cat is adult-to-adult—not to insinuate that one species is more advanced than the other (*wink wink*).

Mom frequently imagined how her canine kids were experiencing things around them. While out on walks in the park, she purposely went where she envisioned the dogs would like to go, not necessarily where she would have gone without them. She selected routes with the most natural smells—wooded areas instead of open fields. She got pretty good at putting herself in their *paws* and thinking like they did.

In Mom's mind, any human who merely puts dogfood in a dish once a day, opens a door twice a day so their dog can go outside to potty, and spends less than two hours a day playing and otherwise interacting with their dog does not provide sufficient companionship. Putting herself in their *paws*—if she were a dog left at home alone 8-10 hours a day five days a week, she would consider that to be intolerable and inadequate care. She knows that jobs and school necessitate many humans to leave their dogs alone at home all day five or more days a week, but that's a situation for which she has a simple solution—get a second dog! Two dogs can keep each other company during absences by their humans.

Mom's alternative solution—get a cat instead of a dog! Cats are better suited to humans who do not have an abundance of time to dedicate to a pet, and as my canine housemates and I have demonstrated, dogs and cats can live together harmoniously.

I think every human has probably experienced a hunch or gut feeling that drove them to act without reasoning in a certain situation. Mom goes beyond this—she's highly intuitive, an attribute she has in common with furry kids. If someone close to her tries to hide a negative feeling—worry, anger, etc.—she can quickly sense that something is wrong. Dogs and cats are the same as they can sense human emotions even when they are not openly recognizable.

I don't know if anyone close to Mom ever attempted to hide positive feelings—joy, happiness, etc.— but sometimes Dad or the children did try to hide negative emotions by pretending all was well. They couldn't fool the dogs or me, and they couldn't fool Mom. In that regard, the only difference between Mom and a dog or a cat is that she is capable of identifying the *cause* of negative feelings in others, while animals cannot reason since they know absolutely nothing about cause and effect.

To clarify by means of a slight play on words, a gut feeling to a human is comparable to a gut instinct to a dog or a cat. People and pets both experience perception; however, dogs and cats to a lesser degree as their reaction is quick without deliberation, while humans tend to give the situation some thought before reacting.

Mom believes her furry kids taught her nonfurry kids to be responsible and caring. There is no doubt in her mind that by feeding, bathing, walking, and communicating with the dogs (and me, minus the bathing and walking functions), her nonfurry kids became more sensitive to all living things. To her, the dogs and I also played a role in Barb, Steve, and Brenda gaining self-confidence, and best of all, caring for us was more like fun than a chore to them.

Mom and Dad's dwelling on Orlando's East Side was the final home to Butch, yours truly, Chiro, Peko, and Koro, in that order. It was the only house all five of us had in common. Koro lived there the longest at nearly 12 human years (almost his entire life), while the rest of us spent six or more years there, and it is where each of us took our last breath on Earth. Mom was always determined to make sure that life's end for each of her furry kids happened in a place with familiar smells and sounds, surrounded by family and housemates, and there was only one place that fit the bill. So, all of us died inside that house.

It didn't have to be that way, as Butch and Chiro had health conditions that could have resulted in veterinarian-recommended euthanasia. It happened that way because Mom firmly believed that's how her furry kids would have wanted it. Since we couldn't communicate our desires, she acted on our behalf, and she was not only right in this case, but in everything else that she did for our benefit.

Mom never uses the E-word, and because it disgusts me too, I have used it sparingly in these writings. She despises the E-word maybe even more than I hate the B-word. She finds the overused alternative—*put down*—equally offensive because of the disrespectful connotation it invokes. She taught her children that every life is precious whether it's human or animal.

The thought of dogs and cats being killed in shelters, solely due to a claim that there is no space for them, is deplorable to Mom. She isn't totally committed to never agreeing to veterinary-assisted termination of a furry kid's life, but has made it clear she would only acquiesce when there is constant and unbearable pain due to disease or injury, and absolutely nothing can be done medically. She felt an affinity with her furry kids. Their pains became her pains, hence she would have known if their pain came close to intolerable.

Opposition to the E-word and the overwhelming desire to engage in an extended goodbye to furry kids can be likened to hospice care made available to many humans with terminal illnesses. Mom was able to uniquely combine prescription medicine, dietary strategy, and *purr*-sonal interaction to make our end-of-life experiences as dignified as humanly *paws*-sible. It broke her heart each time because she knew we were dying while we were unaware that our lives were coming to an end.

The dogs and me had internal clocks that assisted in regulating our behavior on a daily basis. We knew what time it was in general terms, such as morning or night, and other specific times, like dinnertime, walk time, etc., but, otherwise, time and its passage did not mean much to us. The great French philosopher Voltaire summed it up nicely:

> "Animals have these advantages over man: they never hear the clock strike, they die without any idea of death, they have no theologians to instruct them, their last moments are not disturbed by unwelcome and unpleasant ceremonies, their funerals cost noth-

ing, and no one starts lawsuits over their wills."

Dad read an online article, written by a veterinarian, concerning humans who had taken their ailing dogs and cats to him to be euthanized over a period of several years. The vet estimated that 90% of them had refused to be in the room when he gave their pet the lethal injection. He related this upset him to no end because the dogs and cats would become scared and frantically look around the room for their owner who had brought them to him and then suddenly disappeared, so their final minutes had to be spent with only him and an assistant to unsuccessfully try to comfort them. When Dad informed Mom of this story, she broke down and cried uncontrollably. The thought of a pet dying without their owner present, solely because the owner *selfishly* chooses to not be there, is something Mom will never be able to understand. It's totally beyond her comprehension.

Cruelty is not uncommon among some humans, as indicated by something Mom overheard a woman say to her small son one day while waiting with Chiro and Peko at the veterinarian's office. The little boy was crying because their dog had just been euthanized, and the mother snapped at him, "Get over it! It was just a dog," as she pulled the youngster outside. Dad came in a few minutes later to find Mom in tears, and after hearing what had happened, all he could say was, "That just goes to show you how heartless some people can be."

I would bet many humans are just like Mom when it comes to staying out of pet stores on adoption days because the desperation on the faces of dogs and cats hoping for *fur*-ever homes is hard to bear. Unlike dogs, cats are generally incapable of showing emotion by facial expression, but the ones up for adoption feel every bit as desperate as the dogs. Many dogs and cats waiting to be adopted have something that interrupts or interferes with being chosen—old age, uncute, unfriendly appearance, etc. Looks can be deceiving, but there is no doubt that playful puppies and kittens have a much better chance of getting adopted than full-grown dogs and cats.

Certain statistics of late are highly encouraging for animal welfare enthusiasts like Mom—between 1973 and 2007, the number of cats and dogs living in households in the United States more than doubled, while euthanasia rates at shelters dropped by over 60% (Rowan, 2009). So. in recent years, Americans adopted more pets and abandoned less pets than ever before. The Japanese shogun Tsunayoshi Tokugawa—the first head of a government in the world to implement laws to protect dogs and other animals more than 300 years ago (previously mentioned in Chapter Four)—would have been elated.

***

Although there is nothing particularly remarkable about Mom's physical features, I thought it appropriate to devote a few lines here to describe her. I stole the following description of her on the day they met from *Dad's autobiography*:

> "Very pretty. Round face, Asian tone, slanted dark brown eyes, sparse eyelashes. Shiny, black, shoulder-length hair. Prominent forehead, brunette complexion, and rose-tinted cheeks. Petite, short stature, nicely rounded outline. Openly friendly, all smiles. Articulate, manners galore. Headstrong, high self-esteem. Abundance of Oriental feminine beauty. The take home to mother type."

Dad's description is right-on—and he did end up taking her home to his mother! His own writings shed a direct light on who's who (Mom or him) when describing the very early relationship between Mom and Dad as written in this book's Prologue—"Love at 1st glance—or 2nd depending on who you talk to."

Going back to Mom's description, her driver's license shows a height of 5 feet even—that would be a stretch! Her weight is listed as... (I know better than to go there). No need to say any more, as Dad didn't leave much else to the imagination.

Mom's way of thinking is basically ordinary and traditional, except for her prodigious attachment to dogs—she is convinced she can telepathically communicate with them. She goes out of her way to speak to and, if permitted, pet every dog she encounters. So far, each of them has been attracted to her, as indicated by countless strangers telling her that their dogs had never acted so friendly, so fast toward anyone else upon meeting for the first time. There is science to explain this phenomenon: an experiment involving 62 people interacting with unfamiliar dogs found that those participants, who had lived with four or more dogs in their lifetimes, had a positive increase in oxytocin after interacting with an unknown dog (Curry, Donaldson, Vercoe, Filippo, & Zak, 2015). Dad's an exception as he once put his hand down to greet a strange dog and got bit, so he doesn't do that anymore.

I decided to expose something here that I deleted from Chapter Three. An experiment conducted by a neuroscientist named Paul Zak, Ph.D., tested the oxytocin levels of pet dogs and cats before and after they interacted with their owners, and found that dogs secreted 5 times more oxytocin than cats at the end of the experiment (Dahl, 2016). Because the implication was that dogs love their humans 5 times more than cats, I removed that reference. However, I put it back in to set the record straight.

I do not doubt Dr. Zak's findings. However, I agree with Dahl that it must be noted that Dr. Zak's experiment was performed in a laboratory setting, and, unlike the dogs, the cats would have been stressed out in that type of environment. Believe me, the strain on the cats participating in that experiment would have adversely influenced what they did, or did not do, at the end of it. In short, unlike dogs, "Cats must be in their comfort zone to express their affection" (Dahl).

JIM HERRON

***

My main objective is to leave absolutely no doubt about Mom being a truly amazing human being—someone who is awesomely kind, awesomely loyal, awesomely devoted, awesomely awesome! It is accurate to state that these characteristics continually manifest themselves. She is special mostly because she truly knows her own self, and that self-awareness rubbed off on her furry kids just as much as it did on her nonfurry ones. For every human, dog, or cat, the most important thing in the world is to know one's own self. Mom has what it takes and she passed it on to Dad, Barb, Steve, Brenda, Butch, Peko, Chiro, Koro, and me.

The last breaths taken by Butch, Chiro, Peko, Koro, and me were in Mom's close presence. She made us as comfortable as *paws*sible until air was no longer being drawn into or expelled from our lungs. After each of us passed, she wept uncontrollably. To her, it was no different than losing a nonfurry family member. Every death left her disconsolate; however, some of her human acquaintances just didn't get it because they could not fully comprehend the depth of her loss. In turn, she failed to understand why they could not grasp the enormity of human-pet bonding.

Butch and Chiro succumbed to disease, and old age took Peko, Koro, and me away from Mom's tender loving care. She misses all of us equally, no more or no less than we individually miss being with her. Koro's passing marked the first time in more than 30 years that Mom and Dad did not have a furry kid in their house. They have talked about rescuing a shelter dog, but so far, their ages have been holding them back. For the first time in their lives, they realize a new furry kid may outlive them, and that is something they dread. So, since Koro's passing, they remain in a holding pattern. Their recent talks of possibly rescuing a senior dog indicates they are leaning in that direction.

Mom and Dad still stroll along the same pathways they used to walk with their furry canine kids, albeit not as often as before. They do it partly for the exercise, but mostly for the memories. There are many spots along the way that bring back recollections of many good times: the place next to a pond where Chiro fought and defeated a poisonous snake—the riverbank where Koro nearly latched his teeth into an alligator's tail—the fork in the path where Peko always wanted to go left and Chiro tried to go right—the clump of trees that was Butch's favorite poop place since she was the only one who insisted on privacy—the spot where Koro ate more than his fair share of high grass—the clearing in the woods where Dad claimed he saw Chiro's apparition not long after she had passed—the field where an idiota's dog attacked Koro and regretted it—and on, and on, and on. Mom and Dad relive these memories every time they pass by those spots.

Even though they are pet-less for now, Mom and Dad are by no means pet-free, as they still have furry kids in their lives. Absent a second generation from Chiro that Mom regrets not having, she couldn't wait until Barb, Steve, or Brenda acquired their first dog or cat so she could have her first grandpuppy or grandkitten.

Brenda and her husband Jeff were the first to oblige by acquiring a highly energetic, yellow Labrador Retriever puppy they named *Farley*, a prankster and relentless teaser who enjoys running off with hats, eyeglasses, keychains, and other stuff belonging to nonfurry relatives. Farley loves to go on long walks and Mom is always glad to oblige. Dad and she enjoy babysitting him every chance they get.

Then, Steve and his wife Niki rescued a yellow Boxador pup (cross between Boxer and Labrador Retriever) they named *Szekely*, who grew up to tip the scales at 125 pounds, cannot get enough car rides, erupts in loud howling every time a police or fire siren passes nearby, and hates thunderstorms as much as Butch and Chiro did. Mom gets lots of face licks from all of her granddogs, but Szekely has been giving her the most licks ever since he was a pup.

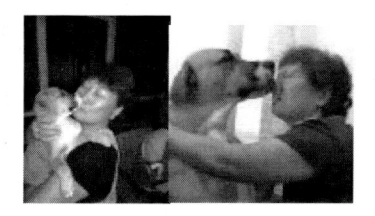

It was Barb's turn and she came through by rescuing a two-year-old Tabby tomcat named *Toby*, who I had my eyes on right away (*wink wink*); a couple of months later, Barb added a rowdy, white American Bulldog/Labrador Retriever mix named *Oliver James* (*Ollie* for short), a lovable, big body (135 pounds) with a gargantuan appetite. Ollie likes to cuddle with Mom as shown below.

Steve and Niki weren't done as they rescued a baby Golden Retriever with a broken leg named *Rina* (from ballerina) whose excitable tem-*purr*-ament makes her a constant source of delight to everyone around her. Rina begging for a treat below reminds Mom of Butch because she is every bit as much a food-lover as Butch was.

So, in a 3-year period, each of Mom and Dad's three nonfurry kids had adopted a furry kid or kids resulting in them having five furry grandkids, all of whom Mom spoiled, just as she's done with her six nonfurry grandkids. All four granddogs have boundless energy levels and do everything—play, eat, drink, run, and rest—in short bursts. At the beginning of every meeting, Mom allows her granddogs to give her a face-washing, and that's something they all push to the limit. No other human grants them totally unrestricted tongue access to the front of their head—forehead to chin—the same personal contact that Butch, Chiro, Peko, and Koro all had with her.

To boot, Mom has spent many days with Aunt Carol's black Labrador Retriever Sir Charles Michael (*Charlie* for short), a fun-loving pooch who enjoys long walks and destroying toys. This photo of Charlie was taken during one of Mom and Dad's trips back to Pennsylvania.

Mom also adored *PJ*, her friend Jackie's yellow Labrador Retriever, a kind-hearted male who loved car rides and walks in the park along the river, and gave Mom and Dad great joy during two years of babysitting.

And then there's *Picasso,* a gentle, well-mannered Beagle, and Safari, a highly sociable feline, who both shared a home with family friends Taeko, Atsushi, and Kyto. Mom thoroughly enjoyed the times she was able to spend with them.

Unfortunately, PJ succumbed to cancer in 2018, the same year that Mom's grandcat Toby died prematurely due to bladder complications common to tomcats. Safari and Picasso had previously passed after long lives in a happy home. RIP dear PJ, Toby, Picasso, and Safari! And, RIP to Butch's crow-bashing buddy Chappie who passed not long after Butch was gone, and to Peko's play pal Bo, who passed about one year before Peko. All of them left far too soon.

Right after Butch's demise, Mom created a shrine on top of the piano in the living room. That's where she put the urn preserving Butch's ashes. She subsequently placed the urn containing my ashes next to Butch; Chiro's went next to mine; Peko's is beside Chiro's; and the largest one for Koro is in the middle. So now, there are five urns making up the shrine. Mom regularly places drinking water and pieces of certain treats, the ones each of us used to crave, next to our ashes. It isn't uncommon to see a piece of broccoli, small bones, catnip, or mint candy on the piano top, and we love it!

Mom switched from referring to us as her "furry kids" to her "furry angels." She is quick to make it perfectly clear to anyone who'll listen that her 3 nonfurry kids, 6 nonfurry grandkids, 5 furry kids, and 5 furry grandkids, along with Dad and Tommy, the feral tomcat who made a huge impact on her family, have combined to make her life worth living.

The furry kids were such an integral part of the family that Dad felt the same as Mom with a twist—he thought they should have been able to claim them as dependents on income tax returns along with their nonfurry kids. He might have a good point as certain pet expenses—medical costs in particular—maybe should be tax deductible.

Mom marks her calendar each year with the dates the five of us were born and when each of us passed. On the anniversary of every passing date, she converses with Dad, Barb, Steve, and

Brenda about the fond memories and good times had by all. The theme of the conversations is celebration of our lives. It leaves no room for doubt that they were honored by our presence in their household, and wished we could have stayed a lot longer. Mom also keeps track of the passing dates for other important pets in her life—Toby, PJ, Safari, Picasso, and Bo—because she wants to be rereminded of the fun times she was able to spend with each of them.

Our lives (dogs and cats) are far shorter than most other members of the animal kingdom—12 years on average for pet dogs and about 15 years for housecats. We spend far more time up close and personal with human beings than any other animals, and yet our lifespans are among the shortest. Most other animals are not nearly as friendly, playful, or loyal as us, but they live a lot longer—elephants up to 70 years and swans more than 100 years. So, could it be a large body or the ability to fly may factor into increased life expectancy? Not so since humans also live a lot longer than dogs and cats—overall average of 78.5 years in the United States—and they are neither extra-large nor are they able to fly.

Scientists have tried and failed to explain the variances in animal longevity. My favorite comparison is the *moose* with the *mouse*, not because only one letter differs in their spellings, but because the huge one far outlives the tiny one by a ratio of 20:2 in human years.

Dogs and cats are destined to live short lives, and when they pass, their humans grieve. For many people, the loss of a pet is the very first time they experience true grief. They may wonder if the afterlife is reserved only for them, or if pets might go there too. Many people have heard about the famous bridge connecting Heaven and Earth. Because of its band of colors, it's called the *Rainbow Bridge*. On the Earth side of the bridge, there's a spacious meadow where pets go upon passing. There is always plenty of food, water, and *purr*-fect weather there. The pets are young again with no aches or pains.

This is where Butch, Chiro, Peko, Koro, and I play with each other all day long. We'll continue to do so until the time comes when one of us first catches her scent, and signals the rest of us just before she comes into sight. That is when Mom and her quintet of furry kids will be joyously reunited, and then cross the Bridge together into Heaven never to be separated again.

Mom has no way of knowing for sure, but she does believe we are all waiting for her—a great example of proof that she is never wrong. Like all of us, Mom is without sin, so unrestricted access to Heaven is in order. Dad should be alright and get in too because he has confessed his sins.

***

I have described many events involving the dogs in Mom's life, including a few major and several minor things that actually happened. I didn't hesitate to include a couple of my own life experiences. However, make no mistake about it—these writings are about *Mom* in particular, and the dogs and me in general. I trust I've left no room for anyone to wonder if the truth has been altered or any hogwash was included. I reassure you that a cat of my nobility would not be so irresponsible. I have honestly tried my best to walk the tightrope that *purr*-mits me to toot my own horn, but only to the extent I was able to retain my selflessness. To the best of my knowledge, all *earthly* events described herein occurred precisely as I have documented them —my flair for magic empowered me to add-on the afterlife experiences already described along with the ones to come.

Every single word was carefully selected to construct sentences, build paragraphs, and complete a story that presents a cosmic philosophy to accurately portray Mom as the saintly human being she is. Her biography is replete with incidents and descriptions primarily concerning her furry kids with her as a supporting actor. My creative nature empowered me to insert some phenomena designed to stimulate the storyline, but in no way diminish the facts. I trust I have achieved the lone objective of my craftsmanship—to leave no doubt that Mom is, in fact, all my canine housemates' best friend.

Mom shows dog-like loyalty to everyone in her family and small circle of friends, and, like a dog, her affection for each of them is not subject to any conditions. She thinks she must have been a dog in a previous life. She has told Dad she believes that dogs reincarnate as humans and vice versa. She also told Dad that she wouldn't mind coming back as a dog in her next life, and I don't think she was joking.

I offer one more tribute to this grand lady—should anyone reading this be reincarnated as a dog, I wish them the good fortune of being adopted by either Mom herself or someone exactly like her. Dad considers dogs to be God's gift to mankind, but that can work in reverse, as demonstrated by Mom being God's gift to all of her dogs (and me).

***

Until now, the time has not been right to divulge one significant part of this story. On my second day in the meadow by the Rainbow Bridge, a handsome Tabby tomcat caught my eye. Despite his great looks, he appeared to be a loner. If he had been wearing a hat and boots, he could have passed for the lead character in the *Puss 'n Boots* fairytale. My attraction to him stemmed from the picture in my mind of what Tommy might look like. With no aforethought, I walked up to him. As soon as I told him who I was and explained my connection to Mom, and then told him he looked like a feral that Mom and her children had talked about befriending, his eyes lit up. When he confirmed he was Tommy, my heart sank. It was him!

I couldn't believe it as Tommy related why Mom was the only human he would call master. He said he had been wandering around near the Bridge since his arrival in hopes of reuniting with her someday. Without that hope, he would be masterless and left to wander aimlessly for eternity. I informed him that I too was waiting for Mom. Ever since, Tommy and I have been inseparable. Butch, Chiro, Peko, and Koro have all gotten along well with Tommy after I introduced him to them—to be expected since Mom is the pillar denominator for all 6 of us.

Tommy related he was struck by a car and fatally injured while crossing a road one night to check out the whim-*purr*-ing cries of a rabbit in distress on the other side of the roadway. He died at age 7 when I was 4 years old. Mom was the only human that came close to becoming his human companion, so he had been waiting there by the Bridge for her for 11 years by the time I got there. His old wounds and scars were gone. Even his mangled ear was back to normal. He looks fantastic!

> Petology 101: A pet's physical defects disappear upon his or her arrival at the Rainbow Bridge. Pets appear just the same as they did in their earthly prime.

Since Tommy arrived at the Bridge in 1991, there has been at least one guardian angel watching over Mom from above. That increased to two in 2001 when Butch arrived—three in 2002 when I got here—four after Chiro joined us in 2006— five in 2008 when Peko made it to the Bridge—and maxed-out at six when Koro got here in 2016. This means Mom is destined to become the center of attention at one of the biggest welcoming parties ever in the history of the Bridge.

The dogs and I were Mom's brood, and she wanted to grow old with us. Now that we're gone and she's aging, she dreams of having a reunion with us at the Bridge. She imagines we'll all kiss her face while she caresses our heads and looks into our eyes to pick up where we left off bonding. Our physical forms are no longer by her side, but we're never absent from her heart.

***

The butterfly is a flying flower,

JIM HERRON

> *The flower a tethered butterfly.*
> -Ponce Denis Écouchard Lebrun

Mom is an aficionado of flowers. She gets a thrill upon viewing and smelling the wide assortment of beautiful wildflowers growing in the park year-round in the warm Central Florida sunshine. Of course, the flower fragrances she delights in are a whole lot different than the odors of other things in the park that the dogs got a kick out of smelling—if you know what I mean (*wink wink*).

Mom also enjoys the beauty of butterflies around the flowers. The sight of assorted butterfly species fluttering alongside wildflowers at various times has taken her breath away, especially when a passing breeze causes the flowers and butterflies to move in unison. She is fascinated watching butterflies perched on flower petals to collect pollen on their long, thin legs while searching for nectar to dine on.

Mom carefully relocated scores of flowering plants, including milkweed, goldenrod, and sunflowers, from the park to the woods behind our house where they bloomed and eventually spread, and, in turn, butterflies showed-up and prospered. I mean hordes of butterflies unlike anything Mom had ever seen. They were all colors, but the black, white, and orange ones far outnumbered the others, and some of them flew very close to Mom, occasionally stopping in midair within inches of her face as if to say *hello*.

It didn't take long for Mom to put 2 and 2 together—Butch was coming back and flying among the black butterflies, Chiro and Koro were with the whites, and Peko was returning as an orange one. When Mom mentioned this to Dad, it went in one ear and out the other, which made her reluctant to bring it up to anyone else, so she has kept it to herself. Believing that her dearly departed canines are able to return as beautiful butterflies to be near her is a source of continuing pleasure for her.

It goes without saying that birds and fireflies have something very important in common—*wings*. A large number of people believe that birds and fireflies represent deceased humans who use their wings to fly back to Earth for the purpose of after-death-communication (ADC) with loved ones. Butterflies and moths also have wings like angels, and here's the bombshell—deceased dogs and cats fly back as *butterflies* and *moths*, respectively, to engage in ADC with their beloved humans!

Whether they know it or not—Mom does but Dad's in the dark—they have been seeing Butch, Chiro, Peko, and Koro in butterfly disguises many times during the past few years. Butch flies around as a Spicebush Swallowtail, Peko as a Monarch, and Chiro and Koro both appear as Cabbage Whites (double white spots on the wings for Chiro and single spots for Koro to distinguish between female and male). Tommy and I have been showing near them quite often in our moth forms as identical Cabbage Loopers (the only way to tell us apart is the male's antennae are wider than the female's). We are lined-up below in the above order.

I will try to explain this phenomenon so that just about anyone can mentally grasp what has been transpiring. Butterflies and moths leaving the cocoon are an example of natural change and transformation, a mystery resulting in the ancient philosopher Aristotle using the Greek word *psyche*—meaning *soul*—for butterflies. The metamorphosis of butterflies and moths from caterpillars signifies death and rebirth; symbolically, this process is likened to life after death.

A caterpillar may look like a lowly worm, but its appearance shouldn't fool anyone, as it will turn into one of the most beautiful flying creatures in the world. With very few exceptions, butterflies are diurnal like dogs—out and about in the daytime—while moths are mostly nocturnal like cats—wide awake in the nighttime. Hence the ADC link for dogs as butterflies and cats as moths.

Flowers thrive year-round in the Florida sunshine, so the stage of flowers and butterflies galore is always set for Mom. She gets up close to the flowers to smell their assorted fragrances, and that makes it easy for the dogs in their butterfly disguises to get close to her. Quite often, two or more of the dogs have gone back at the same time and fluttered around in unison trying to get Mom's attention.

On the 4th of July 2008, Mom was out in back of our house near the tree line with Peko when Butch and Chiro flew by. Chiro buzzed Peko's right ear, and then her left side, as if to send the message, *Hey sis, why are you still here long after I passed on?* Butch was more interested in Mom than Peko, and Mom couldn't help but marvel at the black-beauty butterfly hovering above her head. She excitedly yelled out, "Oh my goodness Peko, look at how pretty the butterflies are!" She nearly lost it when the white butterfly (Chiro) left Peko's side, flapped its wings, and took up a position alongside the black butterfly (Butch) directly above her head. It appeared as if they were suspended in midair. "Look up Peko," she blurted out as she abruptly twisted her neck upward in awe of the rare sight, "Butch and Chiro want to play." The two butterflies remained in that position for almost a full minute before flying off together. Peko did look up and stared at the two little flying objects with that infamous question-mark look on her face.

Another occasion occurred at Steve's house during a barbeque on Mom's birthday in 2012. She was sitting outside on the patio talking to Steve while he was cooking steaks on a grill when three butterflies—one black, one white, and one orange—landed on the roof of the screen covering the patio. Mom told Steve to look up at them, after which he jokingly replied, "Oh, it's probably Butch, Chiro, and Peko coming back to eat some barbeque." Little did he know that what he had observed was actually what he facetiously said was happening.

A third example took place at an anniversary party for Mom and Dad on August 11, 2017. It took place outside a restaurant where Brenda and her family hosted dinner. While waiting outside for a table, Mom was admiring red roses displayed in a large flowerpot situated near the main entrance, when two white butterflies landed side by side on the top edge of the pot and lingered there for a full minute before flying off together. She was in awe of them for staying beside her for so long. *Could they be Chiro and Koro,* she thought to herself. There was no way for her to know, but she was spot on, as Chiro and Koro had indeed stopped by to get up close to her.

There are many more examples—far too many to list here—hence, the ones cited above will have to do.

***

"Butterflies are God's confetti, thrown upon the Earth in celebration of His love."
-K. D'Angelo

Ending thoughts:

For those dog persons who *match* Mom's passion for making and abiding by a lifetime commitment to canine kids, the accolade *Dogs' Best Friend* is yours to share with her.

For those cat persons who *fully comprehend* the multitude of messages in this book that only a cat narrator can convey, you know there are many intelligent human beings in the world and they all share their homes with cats.

For those persons whose love for dogs and cats is *equal*, you're the best, and this book was written predominantly with you in mind.

For every dog and cat and other animal that has *suffered* abuse or neglect at the hands of cruel human beings, and also for the healthy pets who were *put down* just because there wasn't enough room for them in a shelter, this book was written with all of you in mind in hopes that you are finally blessed with peace.

ENDNOTES

PROLOGUE

American Veterinary Medical Association (2012). *2012 U.S. Pet Ownership & Demographics Sourcebook*. Retrieved on June 15, 2019 from https://www.avma.org/KB/Resources/Statistics/Pages/Market-research-statistics-US-pet-ownership.aspx

CHAPTER ONE. ME

Chiera, B., Kikillus, K.H., Litchfield, C.A., Quinton, G., Roetman, P., & Tindle, H. (August 23, 2017). *The 'Feline Five': An exploration of personality in pets (Felis Catus)*. Retrieved on September 27, 2018 from https://doi.org/10.1371/journal.pone.0183455

McCready, A. (July 19, 2017). *What Sounds Do Cats Hate?* AnimalWised. Retrieved on October 18, 2018 from https://www.animalwised.com/what-sounds-do-cats-hate-1512.html

National Museum of Natural History (2014). *9 Lives in Ancient Egypt*. Retrieved on September 30, 2018 from https://nmnh.typepad.com/100years/2014/10/9-lives-in-ancient-egypt.html

Raiyan, N.A. (October 20, 2017). *Cat's sense of smell approximately 14 times greater than that of a human*. Nature Study Society of Bangladesh. Retrieved on October 18, 2018 from https://www.naturestudysociety.org/cats-sense-smell-approximately-14-times-greater-human/

Singh, A. (2014). *Cats 'are stressed because we treat them like dogs,'* The Telegraph, September 16, 2014. Retrieved on March 19,

2019 from https://www.telegraph.co.uk/news/newstopics/howaboutthat/11097503/Cats-are-stressed-because-we-treat-them-like-dogs.html

Zax, D. (June 30, 2007). A Brief History of House Cats. The Smithsonian Institute. Retrieved on November 26, 2018 from https://www.smithsonianmag.com/history/a-brief-history-of-house-cats-158390681/

CHAPTER TWO. MOM AND DAD

Alba, B. & Haslam, N. (2015). *Dog People and Cat People Differ on Dominance-Related Traits.* Published in Anthrozoös: A multi-disciplinary journal of the interactions of people and animals, Volume 28, Issue 1.
doi: 10.2752/089279315X14129350721858

Anderson, J.R., Chijiwa, H., Fujita, K., Hori, Y., & Kuroshima, H. (August 2015). *Dogs avoid people who behave negatively to their owner: third-party affective evaluation.* Animal Behaviour, Vol 106, 123-127.

Nakajima, S. (2013). *Dogs and Owners Resemble Each Other in the Eye Region.* Published in Anthrozoös: A multi-disciplinary journal of the interactions of people and animals, Volume 26, Issue 4, pp. 551-556, 2013, doi: 10.2752/175303713X13795775536093

CHAPTER THREE. BUTCH

Clayton, N. (March 17, 2015). *Feathered apes who say thanks with shiny trinkets.* New Scientist. Retrieved on September 4, 2017 from https://www.newscientist.com/article/dn27174-feathered-apes-who-say-thanks-with-shiny-trinkets/

Coren, S. (November 10, 2016). *Do Dogs Grieve Over the Loss of an Animal Companion?* Retrieved on September 11, 2018 from https://www.psychologytoday.com/us/blog/canine-corner/201611/do-dogs-grieve-over-the-loss-animal-companion

Romero, T., Nagasawa, M., Mogi, K., Hasegawa, T., & Kikusui, T. (June 9, 2014). *Oxytocin promotes social bonding in dogs*. Proceedings of the National Academy of Sciences Epub 2014 Jun 9, doi:10.1073/pnas.1322868111

CHAPTER FOUR. CHIRO

MacLean, E.L., Gesquiere, L.R., Gruen, M.E., Sherman, B.L., Martin, W.L., & Carter, C.S. (2017). *Endogenous Oxytocin, Vasopressin, and Aggression in Domestic Dogs*, Frontiers in Psychology. doi: 10:3389/fpsyg.2017.01613

National Institutes of Health/National Human Genome Research Institute. (2005, December 8). *Researchers Publish Dog Genome Sequence; Analysis Sheds Light On Human Disease; Differences Among Canine Breeds*. ScienceDaily. Retrieved April 16, 2019 from https://www.sciencedaily.com/releases/2005/12/051207175814.htm

Tsuruoka, H. (July 1, 2016). *Shoguns and Animals*. Japan Medical Association Journal 59(1), 49-53. Retrieved on September 22, 2018 from https://www.ncbi.nlm.nih.gov/pmc/articles/PMC5059174/

CHAPTER FIVE. PEKO

Bond, A. (August 6, 2009). Dog Collar Claims to "Translate" Dog Barks. Discover Magazine. Retrieved on September 18, 2018 from https://www.discovermagazine.com/technology/dog-collar-claims-to-translate-dog-barks-experts-are-dubious

Lees, K. (2015). *Puppy Love: Oxytocin Plays a Part in Our Role with 'Man's Best Friend.'* Science World Report, First Posted April 16, 2015

Nagasawa, M., Mogi, K., & Kikusui, T. (2009). *Attachment between humans and dogs*. Japanese Psychological Research, 51: 209-221, doi: 10.1111/j.1458-5884.2009.00402.x

CHAPTER SIX. KORO

Herron, M. (October 15, 2010). *Animal Behavior Case of the Month*. Journal of the American Veterinary Medical Association, Volume 237, No. 8., Pages 916-918. Retrieved on September 12, 2018 from https://avmajournals.avma.org/doi/abs/10.2460/javma.237.8.916?journalCode=javma

National Institutes of Health/National Human Genome Research Institute. (2005, December 8). *Researchers Publish Dog Genome Sequence; Analysis Sheds Light On Human Disease; Differences Among Canine Breeds*. ScienceDaily. Retrieved April 16, 2019 from https://www.sciencedaily.com/releases/2005/12/051207175814.htm

Shaw-Becker, K. (November 20, 2017). *New Study Sheds Light on Canine Aggression*. Healthy Pets. Retrieved from https://healthypets.mercola.com/sites/healthypets/archive/2017/11/20/hormonal-influences-dog-aggression.aspx

Volstad, S. (October 23, 2017). *The Role of Hormones in Aggressive Dogs*. Veterinary Medicine News, Center of Veterinary Medicine, North Carolina State University

EPILOGUE

Curry, B.A., Donaldson, B., Vercoe, M., Filippo, M., & Zak, P.J. (2015). *Oxytocin Responses After Dog and Cat Interactions Depend on Pet Ownership and May Affect Interpersonal Trust*. Retrieved on June 14, 2019 from https://www.neuroeconomicstudies.org/images/pdf-files/Oxytocin-Responses-After-Dog-and-Cat-Interactions-Depend-on-Pet-Ownership-and-May-Affect-Interpersonal-Trust-2.pdf

Dahl, M. (2016). *Please Pay No Mind to This Anti-Cat Propaganda*, The Cut, February 5, 2016. Retrieved on March 17, 2019 from

<u>60891456_10157090560545053_5188434765467877376_n[
1].jpg</u>

Keim, B (2019). *Secrets of Animal Communication*, National Geographic Special Publication, 2019.

Rowan, A.N. (January 21, 2009). *Animal Sheltering Trends in the U.S.: A historical lesson from--and for—U.S. animal shelters*. The Human Society of the United States. Retrieved from http://www.humanesociety.org/animal_community/resources/timelines/animal_sheltering_trends.html

ABOUT THE AUTHOR

A career in U.S. government service took Jim Herron and Yoriko, his bride of more than 50 years, on several assignments both domestic and abroad. During their travels, they added five pets to their family, a cat and dog born in the U.S. and three dogs born in Japan. Jim wrote this partial biography of his bride to memorialize the maternalistic interconnection she nourished with each of their pets in particular, and her all-out advocacy of animal welfare in general. He became obsessed with chronicling the myriad of true stories swimming around inside his head that centered on her fairy-tale interaction with their pets. After combating procrastination for years, he won out by finally finishing this memoir of his bride. His vivid imagination enabled him to tell it all through the perspective of their only cat, and also allowed him to spice it up by mixing-in figments of pet activities in the afterlife.

THE DOGS' BEST FRIEND: A CAT'S EYE VIEW

Manufactured by Amazon.ca
Acheson, AB